From

The Women's Press Ltd
34 Great Sutton Street, London EC1V 0DX

Kath Davies is a founder member of the Edinburgh Women in Media Group and the Scottish Convention of Women. From 1981 to 1982 she compiled a report for the Equal Opportunities Commission on images of women in the British media. She is a freelance book editor and has written a number of books for children, including *Women Explorers* (Macmillan, 1985).

Julienne Dickey was born in New Zealand and has lived in Britain since 1976. Since 1985 she has worked for The Campaign for Press and Broadcasting Freedom with special responsibility for the monitoring of sexism, racism, heterosexism and disability issues within the media. She helped to found the Women's Media Action Group in 1980 and was active within the group until 1984.

Teresa Stratford campaigned with the Women's Media Action Group for several years, and is now active in the women's group at the Campaign for Press and Broadcasting Freedom. She has written for a number of publications, including *Spare Rib*, *Sanity* and *Fitness*, and currently works on health issues for *City Limits*. She works as an Educational Therapist in a London hospital.

KATH DAVIES, JULIENNE
DICKEY AND TERESA
STRATFORD, EDITORS

Out of Focus

Writings on Women and the Media

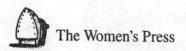

The Women's Press

First published by The Women's Press Limited 1987
A member of the Namara Group
34 Great Sutton Street, London EC1V 0DX

The authors and editors are grateful to the following for
permission to reprint articles: Women's Monitoring Network,
pp. 14, 72, 176; *The Guardian* and Chinyelu Onwurah, p. 39;
Virago and Beverley Bryan, Stella Dadzie and Suzanne Scafe,
p. 45; *City Limits* and Sheila Jeffreys, p. 77; GLC Women's
Committee and Jennifer Simon, p. 131; BMA/Health Education
Council and Amanda Amos and Bobbie Jacobson, p. 164.

British Library Cataloguing in Publication Data
Out of Focus: writings on women and the media.
1. Women in mass media
I. Davies, Kath   II. Dickey, Julienne
III. Stratford, Teresa
305.4   P96.W6
ISBN 0-7043-4059-3

Typeset by Boldface Typesetters, London EC1
Printed and bound in Great Britain by
Hazell Watson & Viney Ltd, Aylesbury, Bucks

Contents

Foreword   viii

Introduction   1

1   AGE   14
Sugar and spice – how the media stereotype
children   *Women's Monitoring Network*   14
Everything a girl could want?   *Jane Apsey*   20
Girls and the media – reporting sexual assault
Cambridge Rape Crisis Centre   25
Older women   *Older Feminists' Network*   27

2   RACE   38
Sexist, racist, and above all capitalist – how
women's magazines create media apartheid
Chinyelu Onwurah   39
Black women in British television drama – a
case of marginal representation
Preethi Manuel   42
Racism and culture   *Beverley Bryan, Stella
Dadzie, Suzanne Scafe*   45

3   CLASS   50
Class and gender in images of women *Jo Spence*   51
Working-class women and the media
Common Thread   54
Page 3 – dream or nightmare?
Teresa Stratford   57

4 PHYSICAL DISABILITY   62
   'The courage of crippled Clara' – the media
   and disability *Micheline Mason*   63
   Blind people and the media *Sue Hancock,*
   Kirsten Hearn   66

5 SEXUALITY   70
   Women as sex objects *Women's Monitoring*
   Network   72
   Women for sale – the construction of
   advertising images *Julienne Dickey*   74
   The body politic – the campaign against
   pornograph *Sheila Jeffreys*   77
   Heterosexism and the lesbian image in the
   press *Julienne Dickey*   81
   Lesbians in film *Caroline Sheldon*   89

6 VIOLENCE   95
   Violence against women *Jennifer Peck*   96
   Pacific Comics – neither pacific nor comic
   Julienne Dickey   104

7 WOMEN IN THE PUBLIC.EYE   108
   Women, media and pop *Sheryl Garratt*   109
   Greenham and the media *Carola Addington*   118
   Women in public life *Veronica Groocock*   126
   Media facts and fiction – a case study
   Jennifer Simon   131
   The media, women and political violence in
   Ireland *Liz Curtis*   136

8 ROMANCE   140
   Brand of possession *Teresa Stratford*   141
   Feminism and soap opera
   Charlotte Brunsdon   147
   Soap: Diana and the Royals *Teresa Stratford*   150

9 HEALTH   153
   Women and fitness *Norma Cohen*   155

The shape of slimming *Gill Cox* 160
Smoke gets in your eyes – women and smoking
Amanda Amos, *Bobbie Jacobson* 164

10 THE DOMESTIC SPHERE 168
Radio Times – private women and public men
Anne Karpf 169
Women and food *Women's Monitoring
Network* 176
Women and food production in the Third
World *Sheila Dillon* 180

11 WORK 188
Images of tradeswomen
Liz Allen, Paddy Stamp 189
Just my type – images of secretaries
Typecaste 192
We're no angels – images of nurses
Jane Salvage 198

12 CONCLUSION: WHAT ARE WE DOING
ABOUT IT? 203
Campaign information 206
How to complain 207
Putting media sexism on the agenda 214
Women's Initiatives (groups and activities) 215

BIOGRAPHICAL NOTES ON
CONTRIBUTORS 223

SELECT BIBLIOGRAPHY 227

Foreword

Although this is a book about media sexism, the oppression of women is inextricably linked with other oppressions. The media are doubly prejudicial to black women and working-class women. For these women in particular, the media's claim merely to reflect reality is simply not true.

In fact, the media project the idealised experience and often inaccurate perceptions of a small but privileged minority of the population as though that were reality. We see how the world ought to be – but for the inconvenient presence of those (the majority) who either have the misfortune to lack the necessary attributes (about whom the media are ignorant, prejudiced and patronising), or who refuse to accept their allotted place (towards whom the media are openly hostile).

The hostility meted out to women, especially doubly disadvantaged women, is in direct proportion to the stridency of their objections to rule by the elite, and their demands for change and empowerment. As long as women know their place, assume the mantle of tragic victims and accept help with due gratitude, the media may be charitable, even tolerant. As long as they know their place. Mostly, of course, they are completely disregarded: if you pay no attention to us we cease to exist.

There are three problems inherent in any book about images of women. The first is the risk of perpetuating the stereotypes of which the media are guilty: that women are *either* black *or* disabled *or* lesbian, or whatever. (In other words, all disabled women are presumed to be white; all black women are heterosexual unless otherwise stated . . .) This results from the focus being on one particular characteristic rather than on women as whole human beings. All chapters have attempted to overcome this possible pitfall by being aware of the diversity within each group.

The second problem lies in isolating the issue of media coverage of a particular group, decontextualised from the history of that oppression. For example, it is impossible fully to understand the implications of the portrayal of deaf women without knowing the extent of the discrimination practised against the deaf community for centuries. Scope for imparting this information is necessarily limited, though some insights are offered, and in some cases further reading is suggested.

Thirdly, oppression of a particular group may be shared by women and men. To focus on women only may be artificial and is not always possible (for example, references to homosexuality will often include both lesbians and gay men). But we believe that there is a dimension worth highlighting in being part of an oppressed group and female; there is no intention to be divisive when women and men are united in particular struggles.

*   *   *

The chapters which follow contain women's writings on many different aspects of media sexism. While a wide variety of issues are raised, the collection is not exhaustive; much still remains to be said. Not all groups of women will have been represented, nor all the ways in which we are portrayed analysed. Nor have all possible viewpoints been presented. Furthermore, we do not attempt here to deal with the very important question of the employment of women in the media. This deserves a book to itself.

We hope other women will write and research further. The more we research our own history and experience, the more we express ourselves, the more we communicate with one another and the world in general, so we give the lie to media distortions about us. There are many women's voices speaking in this book. We do not all have the same voice – some of us shout, some cry, some sing, some laugh – but we are all speaking for ourselves. The greatest antidote to neglect and stereotyping and misrepresentation is an increased wealth and diversity of our *own* images.

JD
TS
KD
London and Edinburgh, 1986–7

Introduction

It is difficult to avoid the media in western industrialised countries. Most people see the television, hear the radio or read a newspaper every day. More people buy a daily paper in Britain than in any other country in Europe, and they each watch an average of three hours of television a night.

The mass media can serve useful purposes. They can be entertaining, lifting people's spirits, providing company, offering an escape from the drudgery of everyday life, articulating human creativity, humour and joyfulness. (The fact that society appears to be unable to provide adequate alternative means or stimuli to achieve these things is more society's fault than the media's.)

The media can also be educational, promoting understanding and breaking down prejudices by exposure to people and cultures that would not otherwise enter our lives. They also inform us about the workings of our own society, and can provide vital checks to the power of established institutions. They may contribute to a sense of identity with a particular group or region, or with all our fellow humans. A whole range of specialist columns, magazines and programmes stimulate and inform people's interests in numerous fields.

There is a continuing and unresolved debate about the extent of media influence on our lives. Some critics on the right argue that its 'excesses' cause violence, crime, sexual perversion and permissiveness, and sap the moral fibre of the nation. Some on the left claim a huge conspiracy that brainwashes people into voting Tory – and drugs the masses into powerlessness and inactivity. Both tend to decry the 'mindlessness' and 'crassness' of the more popular products of the media, such as soap operas and tabloid newspapers.

These arguments tend to overlook the fact that media participation is a two-way event, that people are *active* consumers of the products of the media, bringing to bear attitudes and values formed also by other institutions, as well as their own intelligence and judgement. There is no conclusive evidence of a causal relationship between, say, violence on TV and its enactment in real life – nor is the massive support given to the Tories by mainstream media reflected reliably in election results. Critics always argue that it is 'other people' who are adversely affected, not themselves.

Having said that, people's involvement with the media they choose should not be underestimated: most people stick to the same daily newspaper, regularly watch the same television programmes and listen to one preferred radio station. (Though within monopolistic mainstream media, apparent choice may be something of an illusion.) Furthermore, everything the media offer us, whether news or entertainment, is channelled through people, processes, prejudices, traditions and the pressures of time, resources and competition. What is selected for exposure (and what is not), how it is edited, constructed and presented and by whom – all this is of paramount importance in structuring (and limiting) our perceptions.

With the best will in the world the media must inevitably fail in any attempt at objectivity – and few try. Rather they both reflect and, consciously or unconsciously, perpetuate a set of values which we are encouraged to believe is appropriate for us. Techniques are used to predispose the reader, viewer or listener in a certain way: for example sensationalist headlines, the use of images and their captions, the juxtaposition of material, reliance on 'experts', the angling of stories, the familiarity of signature tunes and format, the setting of the agenda by interviewers and presenters.

Since those who control the media are almost all (rich) men, there is every incentive for them to present the capitalist, patriarchal scheme of things as the most attractive system available – and to convince the less privileged that the oppressions and limitations of their lives are inevitable. If people can be persuaded of this, the imposition of social control becomes unnecessary, for they regulate their own behaviour.

One way in which this is achieved is by the 'depoliticisation' of news, a process which in itself is a highly political act. The use of avuncular but authoritative male, and of young and conventionally attractive female, newscasters, with their 'neutral' (i.e. white, middle-class, southern) accents renders the media's pronouncements unchallengeable – and sanitised. In newspapers, which have no obligation to be politically unbiased, there is considerable pressure on factual reporting to be a form of entertainment in order to attract readers. The tabloid newspapers demonstrate that the distinction between news and entertainment is a permanent – and dangerous – blur.

Another form of 'depoliticisation' convenient for capitalism is the ideology of individualism. News reporting may highlight personalities rather than issues, as with Arthur Scargill during the coal dispute. Chat shows also promote the cult of the personality, discussing issues of the moment with urbanity and frivolity. Game shows shower 'ordinary' people with material goods amid showbiz dazzle. Investigative entertainment, in programmes like *That's Life* (BBC1), or stories highlighted in the popular press and women's magazines, reveal individual human tragedy and inspire individual acts of charity, but mostly stop short of analysing the wider context of poverty and oppression. The personal lives of film and soap opera stars are often given greater prominence than the events of the day which actually shape people's lives. Sports programmes promote individual competition and national chauvinism, devoting a fraction of their attention to sportswomen and monopolising vast tracts of media space for largely male audiences.

A capitalist 'democracy' depends on available and willing wage labour – no elite, however powerful, could continue without the consent of the majority. This consent will only be forthcoming if correct information is withheld, and inaccurate, biased or partial information is circulated – or if information is packaged in such a way as to cause minimum disquiet and rebellion. People are not stupid nor inherently apathetic, and would not otherwise tolerate such a situation; they would use their collective strength to change it.

Yet the system is not foolproof. Witness the support for the miners during the 1984 coal dispute, in spite of almost universal media hostility. Witness the collective voice of disaffected black youth in the burgeoning black arts sector as well as on the streets of Brixton and Handsworth. Witness public anxiety about radiation after Chernobyl despite government use of the media for reassurance. And witness the mid-1986 slump in Tory popularity despite the party's support from almost all sections of the media.

With more specific reference to women, the media provide us with models of behaviour aimed at shaping us into socially acceptable females, and with cautionary tales warn us of the unpleasant results of ignoring their advice. The messages start when we are very young, shaping our expectations. Children acquire traditional concepts of sex-related roles even when those are in conflict with their own experience, the media being among the prime socialising agents. Children living in one-parent families or with relatives, or in institutional care, still grow up with the concept of two-parents-and-children as the norm.

If gender roles are learnt in childhood, they are practised in adolescence: a time of rehearsal for performing adult roles. The large number of magazines and TV and radio programmes aimed at the teenage market indicates an awareness among media makers of how acute, and how profitable, teenagers' sensitivity to cultural stereotypes can be.

It might be hoped that, having learnt and practised the appropriate 'feminine' role in youth, we could then relax a little, safe in the knowledge that we have acquired the correct bearing and behaviour. But there is considerable pressure placed on adult women to maintain this role; to be a perfect mother, lover, wife, homemaker, glamorous accessory, secretary – whatever best suits the needs of the system. It is not that these jobs are not important; just that they are ascribed to women, and then systematically devalued. Often these demands are contradictory, and place great strain on women.

In terms of appearance, the pressure finds expression in the media chiefly as fashion, beauty, and health features and advertisements, particularly in women's magazines. These may give the reader interesting and useful information, but they also place her under considerable pressure, with their constant urge toward self-improvement. Not only is she told what is 'normal' and desirable, she is also admonished for not trying harder. Yet the effort to keep up with demands is self-defeating, because of shifting trends in fashions for clothes, body size, hair colour, facial characteristics, and so on.

This ideal of femininity is impossible to achieve for the majority of women, who are not white, young, able-bodied, hetero-sexual – and affluent. Women who do not achieve or – worse – do not aspire to achieve this ideal are regarded as strange. For these women, when they do appear in the media, they are counterposed negatively to the ideal in terms of their lifestyle and behaviour as well as appearance. These women are 'other'.

Of course in one sense all women are 'other' when male is the norm. The very language most frequently used by the media excludes women: the generic use of 'he', 'man', 'mankind' and so on. Words associated with maleness have positive connotations, while those associated with femaleness often have negative ones. As women we learn to adapt ourselves to this male bias in language – the end result being that, assisted by our exclusion in other ways, we feel alienated from our own world.

For it is not only how we are portrayed, but also how we are *not* portrayed which is significant. Which kinds of images or repre-sentations of women are absent? Images of women being strong and powerful; demanding their rights; forming close, loving rela-tionships with one another; images of women in all our diversity, each as beautiful and important as the next. These are the images most threatening both to individual men and to patriarchy as a whole. In particular, the women's movement is denied its rightful place as one of the major contemporary social, political and econ-omic phenomena.

The tabloid press seems able to deal with feminist activity only by caricature and sneering. The *Guardian* does (selectively) report our activities but ghettoises them to a page where they are separate from the rest of the paper's news and features. (It used to be called 'Guardian Women', but is now known by other names such as 'First Person'.) Magazines such as *Cosmopolitan* sometimes feature feminist issues – in between articles on how to look more alluring for your man!

Women feel increasingly angry about media sexism because it fails to portray accurately the reality of our lives or to articulate our demands and our experience. We find much of the representation of women highly offensive. We have internalised many of the media's messages about ourselves and have therefore been disempowered. We have been divided from one another, forced into competition and kept ignorant of the possibility of united, collective action which transcends class, race and other boundaries.

Women are aware of the way that media myths about us and our capabilities affect the perceptions and actions of men. Researchers may have been unable to prove a direct connection between any particular instance of media sexism and any particular act, but there can be no doubt that media distortion contributes to a general climate of discrimination and abuse of women. 'Porn is the theory, rape is the practice', affirms Andrea Dworkin. In any case, responsible media could be doing much more to end this discrimination and abuse; and this requires positive action, not just omission of offensive and stereotyped material.

In western society we have a particular reason to campaign against the current media stereotyping of women. For the western ideal of femininity has been used as a tool for propagating western cultural imperialism and cultural values. British and North American television serials are sold all over the world; successful women's magazines like *Cosmopolitan* and *Vogue* bring out issues in a number of countries. It is no wonder that Latin American women now shave their legs and Japanese women undergo surgery to have their eyes enlarged, for what is being marketed along with the soap opera or journal is the western capitalist way of life. The wealthier media of North America and western Europe have potential markets and therefore spheres of influence in many third world countries. Viewers and readers there can be seduced into imagining that the way of life which western media brings to them is something to which they should aspire, despite its financial and cultural inappropriateness.

We must remember, however, that no matter how powerful the media are, they are not ultimately all-powerful. The ruling class has always attempted to control the flow of information, yet uprisings, revolutions and social movements have continued to happen. Knowledge of, and therefore participation in, the women's movement *has* increased dramatically – and the movement has also exerted an important influence in many spheres of society. This has occurred through the agency of supposedly 'safe' programmes like *Woman's Hour* (Radio 4), marginalised ones like the lesbian mothers programme on late-night Channel 4, and other items incorporated into mainstream media. And of course there are our own feminist media, the collective and mobilising voice of women in revolt. There is no doubt that patriarchy cannot effectively suppress women activists, nor can it any longer depend on the collusion of those women the media like to label 'ordinary'.

All studies of the media, including the media treatment of women, must be placed in the wider context of how the various branches of the media operate and who owns them. The implications of ownership and structure are crucial to the issues raised in this book. How do the media collude with and perpetuate exploitative rule by an elite, and what is women's position in this process? What follows is a brief description of a selection of the British media; for fuller analysis, a number of books are recommended in the booklist (see page 227).

Newspapers

The ownership of newspapers has become increasingly concentrated in the hands of a very few. Two-thirds of all daily and Sunday papers (national and local) are owned by the three leading corporations: Pergamon (Robert Maxwell), News International (Rupert Murdoch) and United Newspapers. And not only do the corporations which own newspapers have financial interests in other kinds of media (e.g. Maxwell: Central TV, Pergamon Press; Murdoch: Collins, Satellite TV; United: TV-AM, Capital Radio), they also have investments in and are invested in by other non-media, frequently multi-national, industries. The *Observer's* proprietor, Lonrho, has investments in financial companies in Zimbabwe and South Africa; Pearson, which owns the *Financial Times*, controls companies including Lazard Bros merchant bank and the Fairey Holdings engineering group (which makes nuclear and defence equipment). The only national newspaper not part of a larger corporation and without other investments is The *Guardian*.

The financial interests of newspaper corporations explain why ownership of newspapers is so attractive to capitalists. A newspaper may in fact even make a loss, but is being subsidised by the corporation in order to engender the kind of climate that elects the kind of government that best protects their owners' interests. Small wonder we have such a right-wing press.

Advertising is the other main source of revenue for newspapers. Publications which do not pursue a safe capitalist line do not attract advertisers. The 'quality' newspapers, with their far smaller circulations, survive partly because they attract expensive advertising since their readers are in the top socio-economic bracket. (At one point in its history, *The Times* decided to extend its appeal to other socio-economic groups and its circulation rose dramatically – but its advertisers rebelled and it was forced to return to its former style and its smaller elitist circulation.) There are of course specialist radical publications which carry little advertising, but these have high cover prices.

The distribution of newspapers and magazines also ensures the overwhelming domination of the establishment press: the three major companies wholesaling to newsagents (W.H. Smith, John Menzies and Surridge Dawson) are all extremely conservative in their approach. Publications which they consider unlikely to be 'morally unsuitable' or commercially profitable find it extremely difficult to be accepted for distribution at all. *Gay News* was banned by Smith's after the successful Whitehouse prosecution on the grounds of its 'moral unsuitability'. The rows of porn magazines on sale at Smith's own stores give us a clear indication of their criteria for 'moral suitability'.

To what extent are newspapers able to maintain editorial independence? There are many factors which ensure that papers by and large reflect the establishment position. Financial interest and the fact that directors of newspaper companies often have directorships in other companies inhibit newspapers from dealing objectively and penetratingly with certain issues or stories. How can a paper which has investments in nuclear technology report critically about nuclear matters?

Editors of papers usually belong to the same social class (and gender) as their proprietors. Furthermore they are often subject to considerable interference by them: Lord Matthews (former owner of the *Express* newspaper group) said that editors would have complete freedom as long as they agreed with the policy he laid down. Pressure on the editors of *The Times* and the *Sunday Times* by Rupert Murdoch led to their resignation and replacement by more acceptable editors.

Journalists on the whole are paid well to keep within the narrow bounds of accepted news sources and values. Most tend to agree with the politics of their papers. The National Union of Journalists has taken a number of initiatives to eliminate the worst excesses of media bias, for example their code of conduct and guidelines on sexism and racism. However, union leadership tends to be far in advance of the general membership, and guidelines do not yet appear to have had much effect upon the general workforce.

Those who physically produce the newspapers, the print workers, have had little opportunity to influence newspaper policies, though they have occasionally won the right of reply in industrial disputes. During the coal dispute of 1984, workers at the *Sun* refused to print a front page with a photograph of Arthur Scargill appearing to give a Nazi-style salute, with the headline 'Mine Führer'. The paper appeared with a large blank space on the front page and an explanatory note. Printers at the *Sun* and the *News of the World* produced on their own initiative two issues of a newspaper in support of the miners. However, the print unions are notoriously male-dominated, and there would be considerably less inclination to boycott sexism! In any case, new technology and direct input from journalists, in increasing use in the newspaper industry, pose a considerable threat to their livelihoods. Their replacement at Murdoch's Wapping plant by members of the electrician's union is (at time of writing) a current trial of strength.

Finally, newspaper content is determined to a large extent by market forces. Market research shows that human interest, entertainment features and sport command the largest readership, so that is what the popular press concentrate on, at the expense of public affairs coverage. Human interest stories and women's features (mostly domestic in nature) are most popular with women, but media studies seldom actually speculate on why this should be so. The assumption is frequently made that women are too ignorant, apathetic or stupid to want to read anything else – nobody suggests that 'public affairs' generally means 'male-defined public affairs', or that women, to their credit, are actually interested in *people* and that 'politics' and 'economics' are usually presented in such a way as to appear to have nothing to do with people. In fact 'public affairs' are generally presented in such a way as to have little appeal to working-class men either.

A free market is often cited by conservatives as being the best way to cater for diversity. Yet analysis of British newspapers proves the opposite to be the case. To launch a newspaper, or to maintain one without external financial backing, is prohibitively expensive. Free market forces mean that only the rich and powerful are able to command mass readership. There has been no truly left-wing mass circulation daily for decades (despite the pretensions of Maxwell's *Daily Mirror*).

News on Sunday, with financial backing from the labour movement as well as some capitalists, ran its pilot issue in autumn 1985. It certainly did not live up to feminists' expectations: continuing pressure from women, including those involved in the venture, may yet bear fruit.

Television

The two organisations licensed to broadcast are the British Broadcasting Corporation (BBC) and the Independent Broadcasting Authority (IBA). The BBC, which derives almost all its income from licence fees, is governed by twelve 'worthy' people appointed by the Privy Council. In practice decisions are generally made by the Director-General and the Board of Management. The Home Secretary has the power to veto any programme but in fact both he and the Governors prefer to let it be known 'unofficially' that they disapprove of a particular programme. (In August 1985 the Governors did take the unusual step of demanding the banning of a programme on Northern Ireland after such 'unofficial' disapproval by the Home Secretary. This act prompted the first national strike by journalists and other workers in broadcasting which resulted in a complete blackout of news and current affairs on both BBC and IBA channels and radio stations for a whole day.)

The IBA is governed by twelve people appointed by the Home Secretary. There are fifteen regional companies franchised to provide programmes for ITV; these companies pay for Channel 4, which commissions programmes from small independent companies as well as from the regional companies themselves. The IBA has a strict set of guidelines which the ITV companies rarely challenge. The independent companies commissioned by Channel 4 are less likely to 'toe the party line', but Channel 4's commissioning editors involve themselves at all stages of production, which may well limit controversial content. Despite Channel 4's brief and their original commitment to provide programming for under-represented groups, their record on women and black people has been fairly dismal, and their record on lesbians and gay men even worse.

Both the BBC and the IBA operate a 'public service' broadcasting policy. They are required by law to be 'impartial'; and provide 'balanced' programming. A minimum requirement of local and national news, current affairs and other 'serious' programmes is laid down, and there is a commitment to providing programmes for minorities.

All the indications are that a Conservative government would like to deregulate broadcasting and see instead the operation of free market forces, as in the press. The commissioning of the Peacock Report, which was published in July 1986, was an attempt by the government to see if the introduction of advertisements into the BBC was politically feasible, as the first stage to privatisation and deregulation. The report in fact did not recommend this, and the idea seems likely to be shelved. Should a Tory government be elected again, some deregulation and the commercialisation of Channel 4 (a Peacock suggestion) seem highly possible. Some kind of pay-as-you-view system, favoured by Peacock over a licence fee in the long term, may also be introduced.

Although regulation of TV continues for the moment, the situation is far from ideal. 'Public service broadcasting' is a very fine notion, but which public is currently being served? Broadcasting certainly does not serve the relatively powerless or disadvantaged groups in society well at all, and their means of access or redress are minimal. The notions of 'impartiality' and 'balance' are also highly suspect. TV is controlled by, and programmes largely made by, white middle- or upper-class men. Impartiality is impossible. Programmes are bound to reflect the establishment viewpoint. This is called 'objectivity', or 'neutrality'. Anything else is, by definition, subjective, biased, 'other'.

Similarly, what is 'balance'? If there is a continuum of opinion, where is the central point, the 'neutral' ground, held to be? In fact, it is generally to be found at the conservative end of the spectrum. Furthermore, whatever point one occupies on the spectrum is in itself a political position. And where is the 'balance' in counterposing a programme with a right-wing male viewpoint with one with a liberal male viewpoint?

With regard to commercial television, the five largest ITV companies are in the five richest regions in the UK. All other regions are neglected. These companies are all part of larger media and leisure conglomerates; their directors are often also directors of banking and industrial organisations; and they are supported by a powerful lobby of MPs and newspaper corporations.

Advertisers may not sponsor programmes in this country as they do elsewhere, and the amount of advertising time is limited – this curtails the direct influence of advertisers over programme content. However, advertising does have a great effect on programme scheduling, which ensures, for example, the marginalisation of 'minority' programmes. And the need for Channel 4 to attract more advertising has seriously undermined its originally stated good intentions and commitment to more 'radical' content in programmes and programming.

Radio

The same principles of broadcasting apply to radio as to TV. The BBC has four national stations, three 'national regional' stations (Wales, Scotland and Ulster), many local stations and the World Service. Each area has an Advisory Council, but membership of these is as 'establishment' as the management of the BBC itself. Certainly there is no more accountability or democracy in operation in radio broadcasting than there is in television.

One of the recommendations of the Peacock Report was the privatisation of Radios 1 and 2, but with the probable shelving of the report this seems unlikely to happen.

The IBA at present leases out franchises for local commercial stations. The franchises are almost all held by business conglomerates, many interlinking, and most programming consists of safe, cheap and unchallenging pop music, phone-ins and so on. None of them appears to make a serious attempt to fulfil their charter obligations with regard to minority and local community programming, and most are notoriously sexist. The IBA does have local radio Advisory Committees – but like the BBC's regional Councils they are a sop to local public participation. They may actually serve to prevent other, more active participation. Once the machinery for consultation is set up it is very difficult to change even when it is seen to be inadequate.

Partly as a means of countering the growing number of pirate radio stations, the Home Office announced in July 1985 a community radio experiment. Twenty-three pilot stations would be authorised. They would not be subject to existing broadcasting regulations, and would be dependent on advertising and programme sponsorship for revenue. Although some of these stations would have been purely commercial, some of them represented local neighbourhood and special interest groups (including black communities). For the first time women would have gained a significant voice on the airwaves. However, a change of Home Secretary, new thinking about finance and increasing government fears about possible radical programme content on some of the stations meant that one year later the plan was dropped, leading to disappointment and financial losses for the applicants. The government instead promised a Green Paper on radio, but as with television, major changes are unlikely until after a general election.

1
Age

Introduction

When we look at the ways in which the media distort reality, it seems as though the old, 'gentlemanly' adage 'Women and children first' applies here too. Our lives are rearranged for us – here is reality, this is how it will be.

Children are most vulnerable to media manipulation because they are least able to understand what is happening, but none of us is immune. In the several Ages of Woman, the first and the last seem particularly ill served by the media. Children are being given role stereotypes which will limit their life choices and their personal development. Older women are being told that they no longer matter – that they have ceased to exist. They are of no further interest as they have outlived their usefulness. Their absence from most media productions tells us that 'after a certain age' women should not be seen.

We must claim for our children the right to grow up as whole individuals, and for ourselves we must reclaim our own identities. The articles in this chapter help us to understand how the media's stereotyped imagery – thoughtlessly delivered day after day – prevents us from seeing who we really are, and who our children can be.

Sugar and spice – how the media stereotype children

Introduction

Any discussion about sex stereotyping of children has to be placed not only in the context of the sexism which permeates every aspect of society, but also of 'ageism'. 'Ageism' works like any other form of oppression: one group systematically mistreats another group, by imposing its own attitudes and behaviour patterns, invalidating the thinking and experiences of the oppressed group, and not respecting them as full human beings.

Children are in an especially vulnerable position in that they are receiving from people whom they trust and depend on for their survival much misinformation and mistreatment which they are less able than adults either to evaluate or to fight against. Further, they have information withheld from them, deliberately or otherwise, which would enable them to perceive the world more accurately.

In common with women and other oppressed groups children have little or no access to, or control of, the media and the image-making process. Adults decide which images of children will appear in the media and also what is fitting material for children's consumption. As part of this process certain characteristics are emphasised at the expense of others, and children are channelled into an adult model of perceived correct behaviour.

One of the ways this happens is through sex stereotyping. The following report summarises our findings of how the media present an inaccurate and incomplete picture of boys and girls and their potential, and also pressurise them into adopting 'appropriate' gender roles. We monitored a selection of printed media, looking both at the representation of young people and at magazines aimed at them. We also noted the invisibility of black children.

Birthday cards

A girl and a boy born on the same day have the same potential for social and intellectual development. However, right from the beginning they are systematically presented with images which shape their attitudes towards their respective roles in society. Many manufacturers produce matching cards for each year of age, one for a boy and one for a girl. In these, girls are portrayed as passive, decorative and domestic, boys as active and adventurous.

This contrast is often reinforced by the bold typeface used on the boys' cards as compared with the more 'dainty' typeface for girls.

Birthday cards for boys aged about eight years and onwards often depict adult men engaged in 'manly' pastimes. By contrast the cards for girls of the same age depict them as 'sweet little things'. On one card for a twelve-year-old, the girl is wearing adult-style clothes and make-up but is still presented as a 'cute little girl' – reflecting the contradictory expectations of female as seductress and innocent child.

Black children are noticeably absent from these cards.

Images for parents: catalogues

Catalogues aimed at parents present and reflect society's stereotypical notions about children. Some examples: 'The Duplo Farm has a farm house, farmer, tractor and animals. There's even a farmer's wife and furniture for inside the Playbox farm house' (*Duplo* catalogue). 'Little Girls' Cleaning Trolley complete with cleaning materials. Including vacuum cleaner that actually works . . . broom, apron and cap, mop, carpet sweeper, carpet beater, dustpan and brush, bucket and sponge and feather duster' (*Heinz* catalogue). The *Early Learning* catalogue has a section for Pretend Play depicting girls engaged in domestic activities, and a section for Manipulative Play showing boys constructing things, operating pedal cars, etc. The *Mothercare* catalogue begins: 'Your baby has a whole world to discover. When he is tiny he will find . . . '

The clothing section of the *Mothercare* catalogue does show both black and white children. But the girls are passive, coy and decorative, and the boys active and confident. The first section of the *Pollyanna* catalogue makes an attempt to portray boys and girls as equally active. However, the second section has 'party' clothes for girls and young women who are presented in the same coy, decorative way.

Children in newspapers

The way children are generally treated in newspapers (particularly local newspapers) illustrates the desire of adults to mould children into appropriate roles. Children are seen as 'cute', especially when mimicking adult 'ideal' behaviour. Girls are encouraged to see appearance as all-important. Junior beauty queens are great favourites of the media. One piece from a Croydon newspaper featured a young boy and girl posing as bride and groom (actually they were advertising clothes for a bridesmaid and 'elegant escort').

All this reflects the contradiction held out to females all their lives: to exhibit alluring availability and attractiveness while maintaining their immaturity, dependency and vulnerability. The same papers that portray girls in this way bristle with outrage at sexual attacks on girls (while revelling in the sensationalist reporting of every titillating detail).

No images of black children were sent in during this monitoring exercise, but general surveys suggest that they are most commonly found portrayed as 'problem' children, the victims of deprivation or neglect, or as candidates for adoption.

Advertisements

Advertisements provide yet another illustration of stereotyped male and female behaviour. Two headlines make the point: 'She doesn't know it's the cleverest, safest shower available. It just feels nice.' 'His grip on life is as strong as MK's grip on safety.' The stereotyping is also shown through the relationships between girls and their mothers (for example, shopping together in one Boots advertisement) and boys and their fathers ('Just like Dad: new junior zip suit . . . Mum, this play overall is useful too – his clothes will stay clean even helping Dad paint, dig and tidy-up').

All this takes place within the institution of the heterosexual family. Adults are encouraged to perceive and condition their children according to these stereotypes. Children are taught to imitate appropriate role behaviour, and, from the point of view of the advertiser, are channelled into their respective consumer roles.

Comics

In *Buttons*, a playschool magazine, there are ten picture stories. In these, male characters outnumber female by 3 to 1, and only 2 have women as lead characters. One of these is a story about two female characters, Mavis the incompetent fairy and Evil Edna, the malevolent walking television set. The other story presents a grandmother winning a boat race.

In the comics analysed below female characters are again greatly outnumbered by male. There are no female lead characters at all in *Dandy* and very few in the others:

Comics: numbers of male and female characters

	Whizzer & Chips		Dandy		Whoopee		Nutty		Total	
	m	f	m	f	m	f	m	f	m	f
Main characters	17	2	16	0	12	2	13	4	58	8
All characters	97	38	102	8	137	39	52	21	388	106

Analysis of occupations/roles of female characters

	Whizzer & Chips	Dandy	Whoopee	Nutty	Total
Housewife/mum/ shopper	16	3	5	10	34
'Scaredy-cat'/ victim	11	–	–	–	11
Aggressive gang member	1	1	4	4	10
Shopkeeper/ nurse/teacher	2	1	2	1	6
Fusspot/simperer	1	–	–	1	2
Princess/bride	–	–	2	–	2
Witch	1	–	1	–	2
Neutral (background/ crowd, passive gang member, sister, daughter)	6	3	25	5	39

On the whole boys are presented as rough, aggressive, stupid, greedy, and so on. Girls are portrayed as 'goody-goody', timid, simpering and fussy. Adult females are shown in domestic roles, often as drudges and nags. Black families and children do not feature at all.

Tracy and *Judy* are comics aimed at ten- to twelve-year-old girls. Nearly all the stories in these two magazines conform to two plot lines or a mixture of the two. First, there is a personal tragedy, for example the parents dying or the girl becoming disabled. Note the use of the words such as 'dumb' or 'cripple' in these stories. Sometimes she unwittingly brings misfortune or disrupts family life, and, although not usually to blame, she is tormented by feelings of guilt. Then there is the plot which depends on 'living a lie'. The girl has secret knowledge or must pretend to be nasty. In one story her intelligence made her unpopular and she had to pretend to be stupid.

Most of the stories play on girls' fears and insecurity. They are obsessed with the need to conform, haunted by guilt and the burden of secret knowledge. Their aspirations are conventional (e.g. ballet dancing) and they constantly compete against each other. In general we found that the girls were passive victims of circumstance, reacting to outside forces and having no power of their own.

Girl, for slightly older girls, continues with the same themes and unlikely plots, although with a more modern presentation. The girls are overwhelmingly insipid despite the pseudo-reality generated by the photo-pic technique; perhaps this technique is more insidious than the old-fashioned drawings of *Judy* and *Tracy*. The boy/girl theme makes its appearance here, continuing the theme of competition between girls. The introduction of the pin-up and the somewhat glamorous front page reinforce this theme. This is the beginning of a trend which continues and becomes dominant in the magazines aimed at older girls and young women.

Editorial spacefillers between the stories are frivolous and trivial, with mindless puzzles and fillers; nothing challenging, outward-looking or thought-provoking.

In contrast, number one of a new magazine for boys, *Look Alive*, has informative articles about the real adult world, albeit a preoccupation with militarism, cars and technology. There is a complete absence of any discussion of emotions or personal matters, with the exception of a fashion page, which is an obvious consumer hype.

The orientation of boys to an adult male world continues the theme illustrated in the birthday cards. Also, in contrast with the girls' magazines, advertisements here are for very expensive items (are parents prepared to spend more on boys than on girls?).

There are only three images of women in *Look Alive*. They fall into the familiar stereotypes, including the seductive, sword-bearing evil women on the SF strip, and the cartoon woman reversing her car into a lamp-post.

from: *Women's Monitoring Network
Report No.4, 'Sugar and Spice'*

Everything a girl could want?

The 1960s cult of youth was reflected in the publishing business by the launching of several new magazines for teenage girls. Some lasted only a few issues; the most durable ones were *Jackie*, *Mirabelle*, *Petticoat* and *Fab 208*. *Petticoat* (no longer in circulation) was like a women's magazine for teenagers, with its mixture of fashion, beauty advice and features. The other three depended on picture stories (either cartoons or photographs), with pop gossip, a little advice and a couple of pages of fashion and beauty in each issue. While it comes as no surprise to learn that their emphasis was on looking pretty to catch a boyfriend, it is ironic and sad that, in the decade of almost full employment, there was so little space devoted to work opportunities for girls. A further irony is that, in an era of supposed sexual liberation, these magazines refrained from challenging the established double standard that boys could be 'lads' but the girls in the *Jackie* cartoons said goodnight after the doorstep kisses.

The magazines available in the mid-1980s fall into three categories aimed at different age groups: the romantic, photo-story style of *My Guy*, *Patches*, *Blue Jeans* and *Jackie* for thirteen-year-olds and under; the pop music orientated *Smash Hits* and *No. 1* for the mid-teens and the newest trend of the more stylish, glossy 'younger sister of *Cosmopolitan*' in *Just Seventeen* and *Mizz*, aimed at older teenagers. These magazines form part of a continuum from *Bunty* and *Judy*, for girls, through younger women's magazines like *Over 21*, to those aimed at older women like *Woman, Woman's Own, Woman's Realm*, and *Good Housekeeping*. There are no equivalent general interest magazines for boys. Boys buy science fiction magazines or those which focus on particular activities such as fishing, football or computers.[1] This poses lots of questions about the value systems behind magazines aimed at young women. By emphasising the centrality of relationships in women's lives they espouse romance as the insurance against loneliness, failure and isolation. They invade the areas of our lives where we are most vulnerable, especially in our adolescence. This is particularly prevalent in the romantic photo-story magazines. Although their circulation figures are declining, they are still a powerful influence, and the age group they are directed at is becoming younger. *Jackie* has been produced for twenty-two years and has steady weekly figures of some 330,000, *Patches* sells 126,805, *Blue Jeans* 175,766 and *My Guy* approximately 118,000.

The format of these magazines is similar: two or three photo-stories, fashion and beauty features, posters and gossip about pop stars and a problem page (which often belies the material in the rest of the magazine). In the photo-stories particularly, the girls are characterised by the lack of control they have over their lives – 'I'd never been interested in darts before, but if it meant getting to know Rick, I was willing to try anything' (*My Guy*, 15 December 1984). Since self-worth and confidence are dependent on (male-defined) physical beauty it is no surprise to the system to learn that Princess Diana and Page 3's Samantha Fox are more popular role models for girls than less conventional women like Helen Terry, Alison Moyet or Annie Lennox. (Madonna may have traditional sex appeal but she is still the 'dodgiest dresser' of 1985, according to *No.1* readers.) The photo-stories are almost without exception based in a white lower-middle-class setting with no acknowledgement that we live in a multi-racial, predominantly working-class society.

It is argued that this material is instantly readable, immediately forgettable and has no lasting influence. But it could be said that because it is packaged as 'mindless and innocent' – to be read by schoolgirls at lunchtime or during lessons – its effect is even more powerful. The stories touch a chord in girls; feelings are generated in response to something already there. Girls in love are usually portrayed as being insecure, frightened, jealous, possessive and racked with self-doubt and the message is that this is to be expected in the pursuit of true happiness. Girls' friendships are often devalued and second to the pinnacle of achievement – getting the boyfriend. And if you're not in love, every trip to the local shopping centre or even going to school presents the possibility of meeting Him. It is this constant fantasy that is so limiting. The only other possibilities presented with much verve and excitement are opportunities to improve your appearance: 'Next week we've got an illustrated page showing how to reshape your face with blushers, shaders and highlighters' (*Jackie*, 3 November 1984); 'Free eye-catching pencil, only in *Blue Jeans*'; 'These feet are made for . . . kissing' (*Jackie*, 16 March 1985). Mawkish sentimentality and melodrama also characterise the stories. Their titles need little explanation: 'Kiss me Constable – Carol was looking for a lifetime's sentence . . . in the loving arms of the law'; 'I became the office bitch'; 'Tragedy made him mine'; and 'I tortured my teacher'.

Much of the magazines' appeal lies in the sense of liberation from parents which they hold out to girls. 'Here's something that's all for you', they say, 'which cannot be shared by the folks at home.' The problem pages and advice columns talk about personal and sexual subjects that never get discussed at home. In fact the magazines do have restrictions about what to print although they are often accused by the right-wing press and other organisations of encouraging under-age sexual activity. This makes advice and features about sex, contraception and abortion particularly problematic.

It is interesting that while the sales figures for photo-story magazines are gradually decreasing the pop music format of *Smash Hits* and *No. 1* has met with colossal success. *Smash Hits* sells 520,619 weekly, 60 per cent of its sales to girls in their mid-teens. *No. 1* sells 238,000 weekly. They repeat the formula of the early '70s magazines with music lyrics and gossip but are more sophisticated. They are wittily presented in a lively colourful layout.

Ridicule is often poured on girls' obsessive behaviour towards groups like the Osmonds, Duran Duran or the Bay City Rollers and only recently has a positive perspective been given to these young girls' experiences by Sheryl Garratt in *Signed Sealed and Delivered*.[2] Here their energy and camaraderie is re-evaluated and given the credence it deserves. Although obviously capitalist engineering of idols from Elvis Presley to Wham! is exploitative of young girls' enthusiasms, dismissal of those enthusiasms by journalists, parents and the stars whose careers are made from the girls is a denial of very real experiences. In this patriarchal society girls are supposed to wait for boys to approach them. Expectations of boys and romance are great and worshipping pop stars gives an outlet for the fantasies and feelings which as a sexually passive female, a teenage girl is not expected to have. The image of idyllic love with Simon Le Bon or Gary Glitter fosters romantic fantasies about the ease and bliss of the real thing. Any sexual appetite is suppressed or diverted. The old contradiction of 'doing it and being a slag or not doing it and being a drag' still exists. To complicate things, many of the popular stars cultivate an ambiguous gender identity: Marc Bolan, early David Bowie and Boy George have all attracted a great deal of attention from teenage magazines and teenage girls. Additionally the openly gay Frankie goes to Hollywood, Bronski Beat and Jimmy Somerville have large teen followings. It will be interesting to see what the next fashion will be.

The third and newest trend in young women's magazines is toward a more sophisticated and glossy style aimed at the sixteen-plus market. *Just Seventeen* has an expanding market of 269,000 weekly. *Mizz* sells approximately 162,000 fortnightly. However, *Etcetera* has folded after less than a year in circulation, suggesting the market was not as ripe for exploitation as was first anticipated. *Mizz* and *Just Seventeen* pave the way for the readership to progress to *19* and *Over 21*, whose content is more of the same – fashion and beauty advice, pop stars and gossip, astrology, problem page, short stories and articles on one-size tights, wrapping paper and how to throw parties. Very little space is devoted to work opportunities for girls or about successful women in any walk of life. This either reflects the genuine lack of them or is a glaring omission!

The insistence on male-defined beauty fosters feelings of inadequacy in those who are boyfriendless and do not weigh 7½ stone: 'The Big Makeover – We Transform 6 Readers and Their

Boyfriends' (*Mizz*, 20 December 1985); 'Is your Boyfriend the Face of 86?' (*Just Seventeen*, 18 December 1985); 'I hope we'll still be friends; how to end it all' (*Etcetera*, January 1986). It sounds churlish to comment that surely not everyone is having fun and into fashion and heterosexuality. Despite this though, there is an excitement, vitality and independence which comes across from these magazines. The advice columns are responsible, assertive and honest-readers' worries are answered from a positive feminist perspective. It is unfortunate that the responsible attitude found in these columns is not shown in other features. The title *Mizz* is probably indicative – hinting at the feminist Ms, but not quite delivering the goods!

From a feminist viewpoint there may seem little to cheer about in young women's magazines, but there *are* signs of change. The cover of *My Guy* for example used to have a young woman literally draped around the neck of a fashionable young man. These days the young women are looking directly at the camera, with the boys staring away into the distance. The magazines are now being produced with more integrity and care, often by women who have grown up with the women's liberation movement. As yet there is no clear woman-defined philosophy which celebrates young women in their own right, but magazines are beginning to articulate and maybe even fulfil some of the needs and feelings of young women today.

Jane Apsey

Notes

1 For further discussion of boys' culture see: S. Cohen, *Folk Devils and Moral Panics*, MacGibbon & Kee, 1980; D. Robins and P. Cohen, *Knuckle Sandwich*, Penguin, 1978; Paul Corrigan, *Schooling the Smash Street Kids*, Macmillan, 1979; and Dick Hebdige, *Subculture, the Meaning of Style*, Methuen, 1979.
2 Sue Steward and Sheryl Garratt, *Signed Sealed and Delivered*, Pluto Press, 1984.

Further Reading: A. McRobbie and A. McCabe (eds), *Feminism for Girls*, Routledge & Kegan Paul, 1981.

Girls and the media – reporting sexual assault

More than one in five women have been raped or sexually assaulted as children. This crime is far more common than was previously believed . . .

Eighty per cent of rape and sexual assault is committed by a man or boy in a position of power and trust over a girl. This means that the rapist could be the girl's father, brother, uncle, teacher, priest. The abuse can carry on for years . . .

The other twenty per cent of rapes and assaults are committed by a stranger. It is these cases that seem to draw the attention of the media, and most often hit the headlines.

Journalistic sensationalism perpetuates many myths about sexual assault. It also offers up 'excuses' for a type of behaviour which is in fact criminal. Our image of a child abuser may well be that of an extraordinary person – a real pervert in a dirty raincoat who creeps around children's playgrounds offering sweets. Such a person is obviously peculiar and any adult will be able to spot him a mile away. This image is largely false. It does not allow us to believe that we might know a child abuser. That he might appear quite unexceptional. Words such as 'beast', 'brute', 'monster' and 'sex fiend' are commonly used to describe the rapist. Yet we rarely see the simple word 'man', which the rapist invariably is.

Such media imagery is totally irresponsible. It means that we receive a distorted view of the attacker, as someone unknown, 'other', a stranger. Most sexual abuse of girls happens in the home, when the mother is out.

A superficial glance at any selection of media reporting on child abuse shows some of the common 'excuses' for criminal behaviour: 'uncontrollable urges'; 'I was only teaching her about sex'; 'rapists are perverts'; 'she asked for it'; 'he had sex with his wife rarely and wanted to keep it in the family'; 'he was illiterate and ignorant'; 'it only happens in poor families'; 'it only happens in black families'; 'it only happens where there is a family dysfunction'; 'I did it because . . . '

This perpetuation of myths disguises the reality – that child abusers come from any background or culture. They are not necessarily 'perverts' or 'sex fiends', they are 'normal' heterosexual men. The decisions of the courts declare this to be so. Only 2 per cent of convicted rapists are sent for psychotherapy.

Most rapes and sexual assaults are planned; they do not 'just happen'. We often see words like 'pretty girl', 'seduced' and 'relationship' used in cases that are reported. The fact that the girl is pretty is irrelevant, for that is not why a sexual crime happened. Rape is violation, not seduction. Sexual abuse is not a relationship, no matter how long it carries on. No girl wants to be raped or abused – that is a male fantasy.

If an article contains the excuses that rapists use in court, using words like 'relationship', we might well feel sorry for the rapist and put the blame on the child or mother. This shifting of blame is unfair and is very common in the media. Not only is it unfair; it perpetuates the present situation where it is estimated that only 8 per cent of child sex abuse is reported to the police. It denies the fact that an adult has abused his position of power and responsibility to the girl.

In many newspapers and magazines we see soft porn photographs of young women. Many of the young women are under sixteen years old and are portrayed as 'sensuous, sizzling' sex objects. Some advertise clothing, jewellery or cosmetics suitable for (and intended for purchase by) adults. What is really 'on offer' in these advertisements is the youthful sexuality of the women.

Cases of child abuse and rape are frequently printed next to soft porn photographs. It would seem that the print media condone the sexual abuse/rape/assault of girls, young women and women.

Advertising and television are not innocent of this either.

If the printed media are 'concerned to stop child abuse' as they often state, why continue to print these myths, excuses and soft porn photographs? If the television channels are 'concerned about the issue of child abuse' why do they continue to show films that portray violence against women and girls?

The media have the power to change attitudes and inform people. Instead, they reinforce the myths and stereotypes which condone the sexual abuse of girls and women. Is this all accidental? Are the media really so unaware of what they are doing?

Cambridge Rape Crisis Centre

General background
Home Office Statistics
Newspaper examples from *Sunday Mirror, Daily Star, Daily Mirror*

Older Women

Introduction

As women grow older it seems we fade away – at least as far as the media are concerned. If we were to believe the images of older women which we see in the UK media, we might view the prospect of growing older with utter gloom. If we appear at all, we are more often portrayed negatively, as the ailing dependant; the economic liability; the social outcast (no place for a single woman, widowed, divorced or single by choice); the medical problem; the safety hazard (most advertisements for safety appliances feature women, not men); the victim of violence. And if we are black, non-middle-class, disabled in any way or lesbian – or all of these – we are invisible.

When do we become an 'older woman'? Should we believe the birthday cards which tell us not to mind being over forty – to put on a brave face because 'life begins at forty'? This tells us of course that forty is the beginning of the downward slope. What nonsense!

Women are judged by society according to age and appearance, and we have learned to judge ourselves in these terms. If we are continually ridiculed, admonished to take care of our (rapidly) failing looks and health, or ignored altogether as we get older, we will continue to devalue ourselves and our contribution to society. Whether we are thirty-five, fifty-two, seventy-six or one hundred and ten, we need positive images which more truly reflect our varied lives. We should be seen not to dwindle as we age, but to flourish!

In this section a group of women analyse and describe some of the images of older women they found – or failed to find – in the UK media.

Images of older women in the media

This section is a result of a monitoring study conducted in the early 1980s by members of the Older Feminists' Network. The first thing that needs to be said is that the older women portrayed in the general media, and thus described here, are without exception white – older black women are doubly invisible. When we looked at the black papers and magazines, we found that older women did not feature any more prominently than in mainstream media; in the glossy magazines like *Ebony* and *Roots*, although there were some articles about older and middle-aged women, they did not appear in any of the fashion, hair or make-up articles, nor in any of the advertisements.

Turning to the mainstream media, we found that features about any women, but especially older women, who were doing something entirely outside their 'normal' stereotyped roles were rarer than those about women whose lives are special in some way but who still conform to the traditional family/couple situation. (Older lesbian women appear not to enter the collective media consciousness at all.) For example, women like Elinor Bennett, who helped her husband become a Plaid Cymru MP while at the same time herself a concert musician and mother of two severely disabled sons and two younger children, are held up as models to imitate – superwomen (*Woman*, November 1984). Perhaps 'ordinary' women are made to feel inferior by these exceptional women, who are generally supported (as are most men) by other women, who are largely invisible.

Media images of older women seem to reflect closely the values of our patriarchal, commercialised, capitalistic society. Older women suffer from a complex combination of sexism and ageism. We are considered inferior to younger women because we are seen as less attractive and less desirable (to men). Older women are both subtly and overtly made to internalise the sense of outliving our 'usefulness'. As sex-objects, as wives (supporters of husbands), as mothers (supporters of children) or as general carers (perhaps for aged parents or ailing husbands) as well as wage-earners, once these areas, of 'usefulness' diminish or disappear, we are apparently of little or no further interest to readers, listeners or viewers. We can attain visibility only by becoming very eccentric or by doing something exceptional, or by becoming the subject of violent attack.

News coverage of older women as compared with older men is very limited. Most newspapers are concerned with politics, business, finance, sport – all areas which are dominated by men. Older women are likely to appear in the more sensationalist tabloids, often as victims of male violence. Even in those women's magazines (e.g. *Woman's Weekly* and *Woman's Realm*) which aim at the 'not-so-young' woman, the message is still that older women, once past the child-bearing, child-rearing age, are no longer as useful or alluring as they once were. The media's discrimination against older women seems to be successfully effected by ignoring them completely or, when represented, devaluing them – at best patronising, at worst mocking them. It also creates and reinforces many wrongful assumptions about their real interests and capabilities, that is, that they are 'past it'. 'Most of them are younger than me, so they're much more energetic', said a woman journalist in a television interview about her work ('A will to win', BBC2, 27 January 1985).

Men are depicted as gaining distinction, even glamour, as they grow older. They are not constantly and blatantly urged to delay physical signs of advancing age in the way that women are expected to do. A woman who does not diet, disguise her grey hair and hide her wrinkles is regarded as drab and uninteresting, whereas balding, often paunchy men are considered still macho and interesting to women. (We only have to think of the Telly Savalas advertisement or features like *Cosmopolitan*'s (November 1984) on Paul McCartney: 'Still cute after all these years'.)

Where are we? The table below is the result of a survey of six different national daily newspapers, carried out on 29 November 1984. It shows that older men were featured approximately 3.5 times as often as older women, younger men a similar amount, and younger women about 2.5 times as often. In pictures, younger women featured nearly 3.5 times as often as older women, younger men 3 times as often, and older men 2.5 times as often. In advertisements, nor surprisingly, young women had the highest representation, followed by older women and older men. (Advertising is looked at in more detail later on.)

Survey of national daily newspapers (29 November 1984)

	Older women			Younger women			Younger men			Older men		
	N	P	A	N	P	A	N	P	A	N	P	A
Daily Star	1	1	1	4	8	–	6	6	–	2	7	–
Daily Telegraph	1	–	2	4	8	–	15	8	–	15	7	4
Sun	2	2	1	4	9	2	12	1	–	4	2	1
Daily Mirror	4	2	2	7	10	5	10	12	–	9	6	–
Daily Mail	6	–	2	10	7	2	10	12	–	9	5	–
Guardian	2	2	–	9	11	2	3	10	–	17	15	–
Total	16	7	8	38	53	11	54	49	–	56	42	5
Overall Total	31			119			103			103		

N = News
P = Pictures
A = Advertisements

Middle-aged and older women are newsworthy, it seems, only when in roles determined by the family unit – wife, housewife, mother, mother-in-law, widow, divorcee/ex-wife. Married women are almost always referred to as 'wives' and rarely appear in the news in their own right. An example in many popular newspapers in September 1984 was that of murdered 'Mrs Laitner', featured as wife and mother, only secondarily as 'Dr Laitner'. Women also feature as wives of famous men, and only rarely is the wife as famous as the husband. Women in mining communities – 'miners' wives' – have received a fairly good press, on the whole, probably because they were seen as bolstering up their men and still performing their roles as wives and mothers with courage and initiative. But the Greenham Common women, *many* of whom are older women, have received much less sympathetic treatment in the press and on television (except in the *Guardian* and the *Morning Star*). They are made to look ridiculous, weird or aggressive – partly for political reasons, but also because they are acting independently of men. They have been specially chastised in the media for 'leaving' their homes, men, children and grandchildren.

Women, cast as they are by society in the role of carers for that society, particularly of children, are seen to be more involved in their children's education and problems than are men. Many articles and programmes feature middle-aged women worrying about their wayward teenage sons and daughters. Single women, especially older single women, are represented scarcely at all in the media (though they too may be shown as carers) reflecting their invisibility and insignificance in our society as a whole. The *Guardian*'s Woman's Page (19 December 1984) has rightly publicised the Association of Carers, founded in 1981 by a (younger) middle-aged woman, and of the six cases mentioned, five concerned women carers (of husbands and elderly parents) and one a man, (caring for his wife who had multiple sclerosis).

The elderly woman features even less often than the middle-aged woman. The media find it difficult to fit her into a role and therefore seem to consider her less interesting still. Older women are considered unhealthy, uninterested in sex, incapable of having fun or of letting the young enjoy themselves. Whereas the middle-aged woman's contribution to the world of work is rarely acknowledged in the media (unless she is professionally famous), the older woman, often no longer in paid work, is of even less interest. There does seem to be a move towards providing more information to older women about their housing, employment, health and pension rights (see *Cosmopolitan*, October and November 1984), for example, but is this a move towards a recognition of older women as separate individuals with independent lives, or does it reinforce the stereotype of women as dependants – this time of a patriarchal state?

Home Office statistics in 1981 showed that women over sixty are the *least* likely group to be the victims of violent attack, yet elderly women (more than men) feature frequently as victims of attack. This may create a bond of sympathy between the newspaper and its readers, but it does so at the risk of unnecessarily frightening those elderly women about whom the publications purport to care. The *Wimbledon and Morden Guardian* (22 November 1984) carried two items about elderly women being attacked: 'A 77 year old woman broke three ribs as she was dragged along the pavement by a teenage thug', and ' . . . battered Bridget after brutal attack: 1984 and no one's safe in their own home . . . '. This latter article showed the badly bruised face of '70 year old widow, Mrs. Bridget Flahive'.

Similarly, there is strong evidence (*Which?*, December 1984) that shoplifters, far from being mostly middle-aged menopausal women (as we are generally led to believe) are mainly young men; another example of the media distorting reality at the expense of women.

The independent older woman who is leading a full but 'ordinary' life is not newsworthy. To be interesting she must have the stamina of a woman like Gertrude Leather, who, in her eighties, recently retraced the steps of a 1,400 mile journey from London to John O'Groats and back that she had made by local bus services thirty years earlier (*Woman*, 15 December 1984). Or she must be the first to win a million pounds in the *Daily Mirror* bingo, as did 'Grandmother Maudie Barrett' (3 October 1984). 'Gran in a hurry' was a story we noticed in the *Daily Star* about an 80-year-old woman in the USA who won a running race (two miles in seventeen minutes); then there was 'Racing granny Vera Hedges who has slimmed [(!)] to fit behind the wheel of her speedster' (Bristol *Evening Post*, 3 September 1984). These are the sort of stories that astonish, but most of the coverage of older women seems to stress equally exceptional circumstances. Notice, too, how the labels 'granny' or 'widow', often irrelevant to the news item, are nearly always affixed to elderly women.

Women in late middle age feature frequently in cartoons in the popular press and magazines and on television's 'comedy' shows and sitcoms, where they are stereotyped as nagging or stupid wives or mothers-in-law. They gossip all day and are occupied only with washing and shopping. Society's assumptions that older women are usually incompetent (especially at driving) or silly are reinforced by news items which are meant to be humorous, but entertain at the expense of women, for example, 'Ethel runs into trouble – at 5mph' ('pensioner Ethel Kolk', 'Mrs Kolk, 78', 'the widow . . . ') (*Daily Mail*, 4 September 1984) and 'Catastrophic shopping day: a 56-year-old West German woman faces a bill for DM 100,000 (£26,000) in damages after her cat, left in the car, bit her when she returned from shopping and began to drive off. She lost control, rammed a parked car and demolished a sausage stand, which dragged a fish-frying stand down with it, burning an assistant with boiling fat. A passer-by fainted and the woman's car was a write-off. A policeman drove her, and the cat, home' (*The Times*, 4 September 1984).

The advertising industry does not, as it so often claims, simply reflect reality. It shapes reality, making suggestions to people, not only about the products but also more significantly about themselves. It constructs society. Older women are represented in advertising in much the same way as they are in news items, features and other coverage – *virtually not at all*. In a survey in *Woman* (3 November 1984) younger women appear in 14 advertisements, men in 6, children in 4, and older women in none. This kind of ratio is not atypical. In many publications the only image of an older woman in advertisements is the 'Adopt-a-Granny' scheme! Out of 151 advertisements monitored on television during two weeks in September 1984 only 6 featured older women (40+), and out of 118 'voice-overs' only 9 were female!

There are several issues worth noting here. Advertising aims to sell products, but most older women on state pensions are no longer affluent buyers. They are therefore no longer worthy of the per-suaders' attention. *Working Woman*, the 'career woman's' magaz-ine, has carried advertisements for Porsches driven by a woman and for a video watched by a woman – but not an older woman. Many consumer products are intended to show women how to make themselves glamorous and attractive (to men) and assume little or no significance for older women. Alix Palmer voiced the blatantly sexist–ageist opinion that 'There comes a point in a lady's life when sexual compliments from men of almost an ilk are pleasing. And at 59, Mrs. T. passed that point some time ago'! (*Daily Star*, 30 January 1985). Even when the advertised products – clothes, knitwear, shoes – are as likely to be bought by older women, young, usually glamorous women model them.

In fact in publications like *Woman's Weekly*, *People's Friend*, *The Lady*, much of whose content is supposed to appeal to the older woman, their visual representation is minimal. We did find one or two exceptions – a greyhaired older woman appears in a full-page coloured advertisement for Selenium-Ace, holding aloft the vitamin tablet (*Woman's Weekly*, 2 February 1985) and older women, hardly ever older men, are pictured in advertisements for therapeutic chairs or stairlifts, etc. Both *Yours* and *Choice* (for older women and men) carry advertisements of older women and men in about equal proportions. Holiday advertisements (apart from Saga holidays which are only for the over-sixties) hardly ever show older people enjoying themselves. The young nuclear family advertises holidays; indeed, some holidays are explicitly recommended for their lack of 'disapproving old grannies'.

Generally, older men are much more visible than older women, even in women's magazines. *SHE* (November 1984) carried a double-spread photo of men modelling tartan clothes ('Plaid all over'); of the eight men, at least four look 'older' and one has white hair. Contrast the women modelling similar clothes on the following two pages. Two of them could be thirty-five-ish, the rest are all younger, and not a grey or white hair in sight! Are older women not capable of looking smart? A significant proportion of advertisements for cosmetics, skincare and haircare denegrate the (women's) ageing process as something to be at best concealed, at worst postponed. Youthful allure, we are told, must be retained (to remain attractive for as long as possible): 'The need . . . is urgent' (*Clarins*). These advertisements construct a negative image of older women's bodies (note: '*Equalia* helps prevent premature ageing . . . keeping your skin looking *younger* for longer'; '*Oil of Ulay* will help keep your skin *young* looking'; and (Innoxa) 'How can you match her *youthful* glow?'). Strategies such as these manipulate older women into 'passing', i.e. passing for younger, at the expense of confronting the reality of ageing in all its aspects. Cynthia Rich has this to say about it: 'Passing . . . is one of the most serious threats to selfhood . . . our true identity, never acted out, can lose its substance, its meaning, even for ourselves. Denial to the outside world and relief at its success . . . blurs into denial of self'.[1]

In these ways women's ageing process is invalidated; our identity denied. The stigma of age is a powerful one.

Advertisements which feature older women often depict them in stereotyped roles, for example as knitting grannies ('If your grannie doesn't knit, borrow someone else's') or irritable housewives. There are a few positive images in television commercials, such as the capable, cheerful older woman, but generally we are shown young women (for sexual objectification) plus a few babies and children. At the same time, the voices we hear urging, cajoling, instructing or authorising us to buy are overwhelmingly male. TV gives us pretty young women to look at and smooth men to listen to!

Most features in the media dealing with health and sex are directed at younger women but there are now appearing more articles and programmes on television and radio which are of interest to the older woman. For example, in some articles women are no longer told just to put up with the menopause, but given details of symptoms and professional advice on where to get help individually. One article encouraged women to find a sympathetic GP who would not automatically hand out tranquillisers, but who would listen attentively and answer questions properly (*Woman*, 3 November 1984). Jay Howard in her article, 'Desirable older women' (*SHE*, December 1984) took a positive approach, 'Well, I'm over the hill having just hit 49, and I'm having as much and more love and fun than I ever had when young', urging women to enjoy an active sex life during and after the menopause. There is also a growing awareness of how important it is to question treatment and take responsibility for one's own body, particularly as regards the need for hysterectomies. The media, notably the sensational tabloids, are still preoccupied with older women marrying or having affairs with younger men. The opposite situation is not nearly so newsworthy, men's attractiveness supposedly being eternal!

When positive images of older women occur in the media we are often pleasantly surprised, but women may be lulled into a sort of complacency that the position is improving satisfactorily. If these positive images are examined, however, and the background of the story looked into, the images often have some negative connotations, and even fall into the 'granny', 'witch' or 'victim' category.

Many positive images are confined to women who have had the benefits of good health care, money and education – Joy Kinsley, governor of Brixton (all-male) prison (*Guardian*, 7 December 1984), Edna Healey, traveller and writer (*Guardian*, 21 November 1984), Setsuko Thurlow, Hiroshima survivor and peace worker (*Guardian*, 18 April 1984) and Dr Ana Aslan, geriatrician (*Guardian*, 4 September 1984). On the whole it was felt that the *Guardian* no longer focuses on *women's* matters, and hardly at all on older women. There are plenty of examples of positive images of women in the alternative press and peace journals, but the readership is limited. Generally women with low incomes get the worst media coverage and are therefore most patronised or manipulated: 'Granny Vi wins £40,000' (*Sun*, 3 September 1984) or the customary 'first name only' title (like Baby David, Little Anne) is given to the older woman. Even in the best written and sympathetic journalism, older women fall into stereotyped categories. However careful the journalists, they just do not seem to be aware of when they are being ageist or ageist/sexist.

On television, ITV does rather better at providing informative programmes for older people. Women are well represented in the Sunday afternoon series, *Getting on* (and also in *Coping* for disabled people). *The Afternoon Show* (BBC) and *Woman's Hour* (Radio 4, daily) do not devote much space to the older woman's interests and needs.

Probably the most constructive and sensitive characterisation of older women in the media for a long time was *Tenko* (BBC1/2), especially the last series when the women were shown trying to readjust to life outside the prisoner of war camp. Many of them developed a much stronger sense of self as a result of their individual and collective experiences – Beatrice the doctor, Joss the aristocratic rebel, Sister Ulrike the nun – these are all powerful women, superbly compelling images, notable, sadly, for their absence in the media in general.

I had lived my life without novels, movies, radio or television telling me that lesbians existed or that it was possible to be flad to be a lesbian. Now nothing told me that old women existed, or that it was possible to be glad to be an old woman. Again the silence held powerful and repressive messages. Again I had to chart my own course, this time into growing old.[2]

Tina Davidson, Molly McConville,
Joan Hammond, Jinnie Tew, Pat Hayslip and
Marj Fleming – Older Feminists Network

Notes
1 Barbara Macdonald and Cynthia Rich, *Look Me in the Eye: Old Women, Ageing and Ageism*, The Women's Press, 1984.
2 Barbara Macdonald and Cynthia Rich, op. cit.

2
Race

Introduction

The continuing process of political and economic colonialism has resulted in Britain's containing a vast array of cultures, races and nationalities. Such diversity is a source of strength and richness, and humanity's best thinking and greatest concern is called for in overcoming the problems associated with such a huge legacy of oppression.

Yet this is a viewpoint rarely adopted by the media. Diversity tends to be seen as inherently problematic – 'conflict' is after all more newsworthy. Any challenge to the white political, economic, social or cultural hegemony of which the media is a part is also seen as a threat. Furthermore, by pandering to the racism of their predominantly white audience the media can use black people as scapegoats to disguise the inherent weaknesses of the capitalist system which they support.

Even well-intentioned attempts by the media to describe black experience are suspect, since virtually all such coverage is mediated by white perceptions. The number of black workers employed in the media industry is still minimal, particularly in any decision-making capacity, and is especially so for black women. Those who do work in the media must conform to acceptable (white middle-class) standards of accent, style and behaviour – and must curb any critical impulses in order to safeguard their jobs.

Most image-makers are men, and their treatment of black men and black women differs. In the reporting of riots, street crime, job competition or drugs offences black men tend to be shown as a threat. Black women on the other hand tend to be represented as victims – of parental or marital abuse, arranged marriages, even famine – and therefore in need of paternalistic intervention. Alternatively they are seen as exotic sex objects, for example airline stewardesses, 'geisha girls', nightclub singers. When black women led the rioting in Brixton in October 1985 this was reported with amazement. The women were denounced as much for being 'unwomanly' as anything else.

Racist stereotyping and racist reporting are all the more damaging because of the virtual lack of media access for black people. There is little opportunity to communicate experiences and viewpoints (which are not themselves homogeneous). Material of interest to black people or which shows black people and their contribution to society in a positive way is neglected, dismissed or trivialised. For black women this is doubly true, even within the 'alternative' media.

All this has the desired effect (from the establishment point of view) of denying all people their right to correct and unbiased information. Media racism perpetuates society's racist attitudes and inhibits the growth of a politically active black movement.

Sexist, racist, and above all capitalist – how women's magazines create media apartheid

'Isn't it nice to be brown when everyone else is white?' So runs the copy for an advertisement which appeared in most of the glossy, monthly women's magazines. My answer would be no, not always, and in any case 'nice' hardly conveys the emotion such a situation arouses. But in this context my experience is immaterial as the advertisement is aimed solely at white women, and the advertisers expect that it will be read solely by white women, because of the attitude of the magazines themselves. Their attitude helps to provoke and perpetuate the women-equals-white-female myth by ignoring the existence of black women to an extent far surpassing the innocent and reaching the deliberate.

For a time I accepted the lack of black women in glossies because, after all, they were white women's magazines and I was black. When I realised that some of them had multiracial pretensions my amusement bordered on hysteria. I will credit them with multiracial ideals, for they are blatant in their determination that

their 'liberalism' and 'social awareness' should be common knowledge, but their acceptance of the theory in no way excuses their
disregard in practice.

In reality, they employ a most stringent form of apartheid in
which blacks are consigned to specific areas – entertainment, art,
perhaps travel – and kept in their place. If they are mentioned
outside these areas it is always in the context of them and us; they
(blacks) deserve equal status and we (nice, liberal whites) are
going to make sure they get it but not in this magazine, not yet
anyway. One of the few articles I can remember on the subject of
racism was written by a woman whose sole experience of racism
consisted in having received one racial insult when she returned
from a holiday heavily tanned. This may constitute wide
experience to white readers but any black woman would have
more familiarity with the subject.

Yet the coverage of black female concerns (such as it is) is
extensive in comparison to that accorded lesbians. Gay men are
occasionally featured in 'let's see what the freaks are up to now'
type articles, generally more insulting than illuminating, like this
quote from an article in *Cosmo Man*; 'To be gay is to be totally
selfish if not blatantly narcissistic.' But they do not even bother to
generalise or insult lesbians, who are simply ignored. How can a
women's magazine justify disregarding the sexual preferences of a
large proportion of women?

The limitations and imperfections of the glossies gradually
dawned on me after many years of reading, but like many women,
I considered them unimportant. Then I obtained an issue of South
African *Cosmopolitan*. It was all so familiar; there were the same
glamorous white women, the same handsome white men, the same
startling revelations of new lipsticks and coming hairstyles, the
same avowed liberalism tempered only by absolute silence on all
important matters. All this in a society I knew to be evil and, at the
time, writhing in its own corruption. It made me look at British
magazines again. If the South African *Cosmopolitan* woman
(white by definition) is fiddling with her hair as Soweto burns then
how is her British counterpart occupied? Counting her orgasms
perhaps, or restructuring her man or her wardrobe.

The imperfections of women's magazines are important because
their repercussions are important. They are read by thousands of

women every day. Gradually the multitude of exaggerations and biases builds up to become an aggressive pressure on women to conform.

For all their superficial radicalism, glossy magazines perform a considerable service for the established sexist, racist, but above all capitalist, order of things. They typify a specific caricature of modern woman, for women en masse to emulate and assimilate into their values; the New Ideal Woman. She is white, hetero, confident and partnered. She has a Dulux glossy-but-hard-as-nails coating to hide any possible irregularities or realities. She may be feministic, but as the glossies are about as feminist as playschool and not half so innovative, she poses no threat to the status quo. Brighter than bright, whiter than white, the New Ideal Woman strides purposefully forwards. Her mission? To consume. For she is the super-consumer. Manufacturers may have been afraid that feminism was creating a new breed of woman but they soon realised it was only a new breed of consumer. They found she was nothing to be afraid of, indeed she was something to cultivate. Women's Lib truly liberated her, for she is now perceived as a consumer in her own right, and not merely on behalf of her parents /husband/children.

The effective, even if unintentional, result of this idealisation of white womanhood is to aid manufacturers in their exploitation of all women, for this image of the perfect white woman is all that black readers have to emulate. Black women must therefore spend twice as much in order to achieve a double impossibility – to be perfect, and to be white. And this is probably why, on average, black women spend more than white women on cosmetics, in spite of the predictable differences in average income.

It is unfortunately true that to a certain extent at least, all media which rely on advertising for a large proportion of their income must promote the interests of the principal patrons, but the glossy women's magazines make an idol out of an expediency. By extending the impact of transitory fashions to every dimension of our lifestyles the glossies make us super-consumers – by default, for in order to keep up with fashion we must change our lifestyles, and to do that we must consume.

To be fair, some magazines admit that they are little more than promotional sheets, and their honesty is something. The real harm is done by the 'radicals', those glossies which coat their manipulation in the soothing honey of pseudo-enlightenment. They placate our guilt about our indulgence by allowing us to place it under the heading of 'self-improvement' and at the same time leave us more open to attack.

Most women recognise that they are being exploited, not merely by the manufacturers who seek their patronage but also by the magazine itself which claims their loyalty on the basis of advancing their interests while using the relationship to further their manipulation. However, the alternatives are few. That yawning chasm between *Cosmopolitan* and *Spare Rib* is effectively empty, and *Spare Rib* itself, though a fine liberation magazine, is not aimed at the majority of women who are still, in spite of everything, interested in their physical rather than ideological appearance.

What is needed is a magazine which caters for all women instead of for a privileged majority or politicised minority. This might go some way towards overcoming the lack of unity between women as a whole. At the moment we are moving towards 'apartheid media', wherein black and white, hetero and lesbian women all have their own different magazines. Without some kind of bridge, separate development may succeed in Britain where it has failed in South Africa.

Chinyelu Onwurah

Reprinted with permission from the *Guardian*, 2 September 1985

Black women in British television drama – a case of marginal representation

During 1984 I researched the 'Representation of Blacks in British Television Drama' and part of the research looked particularly at the portrayal of black women. Here I aim to present the main findings and raise questions that need to be answered regarding black women and television drama.

For the purposes of the research, the term 'blacks' is used to refer to people of African, Indian, Pakistani and West Indian origin.

This has merely provided a working definition for analysis though I am aware of its limitations.

During the year, over 650 programmes were recorded with approximately 8,700 male and female actors in total on cast. Of these, only 73 were black female actors, less than one per cent of the total. Not only were the roles available to black women very few in number, they were also limited in scope. They were cast as models, striptease artistes, seamstresses, accomplices in crime, nurses, secretaries, checkout assistants, shopkeepers, reception-ists, students and hotel maids. There were some exceptions to this 'narrow casting' with the brief appearances of black women as privileged ladies – as a princess, a daughter of an African presi-dent, and as society ladies. There was a marked absence of black girls in other than school-related situations even when a parallel story might have shown the white girl in a family situation. In a children's pantomime, the 'genie of the ring', a role with positive connotations, was played by a black woman. Another positive role was that of a peace campaigner (American). However, both were supporting roles. Leading roles and especially archetypal heroine roles such as Detective Forbes in *The Gentle Touch* and Nurse Megan in *The District Nurse* (both BBC1) were preserved for white actresses (Jill Gascoigne and Nerys Hughes). In *The Far Pavilions*, the role of Princess Anjuli, a significant role in the series, was taken by a white actress, Amy Irving, while the smaller part of the petulant Princess Shushila was played by a black actress, Sneh Gupta. Black women nearly always play 'black roles' and there is very little evidence of integrated casting as can be seen from this extract from *Tripper's Day*, a comedy series where the store manager escorting another officer approaches a black checkout assistant:

TRIPPER: Ah, now you see . . . this young lady here on no. 2 Miss . . . Miss . . . Pinter . . . the darkish non-pink person (*crowd laughter*). Head office are very very keen on that sort of thing . . . you know . . . non . . . non-pink people . . . peo . . . people who are . . .

MISS PINTER: (*cheerfully*) Black.

TRIPPER: Who are . . . black . . . , that's it . . . that's it . . . black

... that's the colour, yes, yes, yes ... we're not even aware
that she is ... carry on Miss Pinter.

Significantly, the research found that not a single 'traditional'
black family appeared in full shot during the year's monitoring.
When resemblances to a family were seen, either one or both
parents were missing. When one parent was missing, it was more
likely to be the mother – in *King* the mother was dead and in *Return
of the Saint* it was again the mother who was absent.

In relegating black women to the fringe, to minor and marginal
roles, in excluding black women from the greater part of drama
output, it is clear that television is making a political statement
that this group belongs to the fringe and has little of importance
to say. Even if one were to argue that the roles in which black
women appeared were fictitious, this necessarily raises questions of selection and responsibility. In television drama, every
image is constructed. A deliberate process of selection is carried
out by those involved in the production process. The audience
is asked to accept the viewpoint presented and 'the provision of
a consistent picture of the social world may lead the audience
to adopt this version of reality. The media are often held
as a source of information about the world outside direct
experience'.

The effect of the limited and stereotypical portrayal of black
women on the audience must be cause for concern. For although
one may not be able to provide empirical evidence to prove that
particular programmes produce particular effects, demonstrating
the potential for harm is as good as empirical data in the area of
human values. In terms of role models, black children are growing
up without significant and positive role models of black women in
the media, and the effect on white children is potentially as
damaging.

To conclude, black women appear as victims of a double
oppression: of racism because producers deny significant and
positive roles to black women, and of sexism because television
writers, the majority of whom are male, continue to neglect the
spectrum of the black woman's experience.

Preethi Manuel

Racism and culture

The mainstay of British culture has been the assertion of its superiority over others, its total negation of non-European cultures in
general and Black people's cultures in particular. The message
that European culture and whiteness itself represented 'civilisa-
tion', while African culture and blackness represented the primitive and the barbaric, was transmitted around the world through
the white man's religion, literature, music and art. The myth
served to distract attention from the decadence of his own culture,
an extension of which was the savage and barbaric way he asserted
his superiority over the 'inferior' races. White men have always
known the value and richness of the peoples and cultures they have
sought to dominate. This is clear from the way in which the
material forms of those cultures have been stolen, sometimes to be
recreated and passed off as part of the British heritage, sometimes
to be hoarded in their national museums. Continuous attempts to
negate and undermine Black culture are, in themselves, a
recognition of the threat we pose as a people to the legitimacy of
the system.

But Black women have always had to contend with more than
racist definitions. As slaves, we were confronted daily with an
image of womanhood which sought to negate our very existence
outside the role of breeders of human livestock. For colonial societies in the nineteenth century, the 'ideal' woman was European
and white. Black women had to resist negation by a culture which
valued only a woman's physical appearance, a culture which
debased in women those very attributes which we found it necessary to cultivate, such as self-reliance, courage, strength and physical endurance. In a culture which was obsessed with creating and
recreating the ideal through fashion, art, poetry and other forms of
European self-expression, there was no room for any appreciation
of African beauty. The very term implied a contradiction. The
only images of women we were exposed to, outside our immediate
communities, were those depicting white, female perfection, from
the Virgin Mary to the slavemaster's wife. Self-denigration and
self-denial would have been unavoidable, had it not been for the
strength we were able to draw as women from within ourselves,
our culture and our communities.

Entrenching the stereotypes

As the dominant culture developed a more advanced technology, and mass media with which to conform and perpetuate itself, cinema assumed the role formerly played by books, sermons and the lectures of eminent speakers. The religious, scientific and philosophical arrogance of European racism transported itself on to the big screen. The negative images and insulting stereotypes which had been developed as a justification of slavery were thus carried forward, unchallenged, into the twentieth century. So it was that the same cultural tools which had become, for us, a means of self-assertion and self-defence became a source of ridicule and vulgar exaggeration for the entertainment of white audiences in Europe and America.

Although, to begin with, few Black women were ever shown on the screen, those who were invariably portrayed characters who were obese, ugly, clumsy, stupid and above all, servile. According to American cinema's romantic depiction of slavery in the South, Black women had no other role than to loyally serve their white masters and mistresses. To care for a white family was the only valid aspiration for us, and the screen mammys treated it as such, appearing to love their white charges more than their own 'piccaninnies' (for children, too, came only in one colour). Such sentiments were seen as inevitable, of course, particularly by the white audiences which flocked to see films such as *Gone With The Wind* and *Birth of a Nation*. In the absence of any of the popularly cherished physical characteristics in oneself, one's children or one's race, what could be more gratifying than to serve perfection in others? For the isolated Black women who appeared on the screen in roles other than the devoted mammy or the invisible maid, the only other options were to play the tragic mulatto, caught between two cultures yet belonging to neither, or the Black whore and seductress, exotic, amoral and invariably fair-skinned. In both roles, our 'rampant' sexuality became our dominant 'attribute', the factor which explained why men were driven to desperation and women to jealous distraction. By labelling Black women as sexually promiscuous in this way, white men were thus exonerated for their sexual excesses under slavery. The function of this stereotype, even today, is neither to flatter nor to bestow on us an identity as sexual beings. It is simply a justification for the centuries of sexual abuse of Black womanhood.

Even the first, and for a long time only all-Black cinema production, *Carmen Jones*, tells the story of a clean, conventional, noble Black hero, driven to distraction and eventual death by the wild, faithless, emasculating (and fair-skinned) Black woman. The power of such media stereotypes is constantly being challenged by Black women who reject them as irrelevant and sterile. Yet even without this historical perspective, a casual glance at the porn magazines and sex shows in London's Soho reveals the extent to which white men have debased our sexual identity for their own self-gratification. Our sexuality is neither uncontrollable nor indiscriminate, yet the myth survives.

British television and the new 'ethnic' awareness

Many of the stereotypes which continue to pass for real Black women have survived because of, rather than in spite of, the new ethnic awareness which we have witnessed recently on British television. Mirroring the American experience of a decade or so ago, the token presence of a few Black faces is gradually beginning to make way in the eighties for an entire Black media ghetto, characterised by a general lack of resources and technical expertise. Its success depends on how closely it can emulate the ethics and values of the existing media industry, and its control remains firmly in the hands of middle-class white men who also determine when, in what form and how often programmes are broadcast. Nevertheless, this apparent liberalisation has meant that we no longer have to make do with a limited number of standard stereotypes. Instead, we are confronted with a full range of them, which may well appear on first sight to be less obviously objectionable, but are frequently more insidious.

For Black women, this has meant an increasing repertoire of roles which are mere variations on the original themes – the domestic, the night-club singer, the hooker, the prolific breeder and the state scrounger. Recently, Black women singers, dancers and athletes have appeared in growing numbers, too. Yet the absence of 'successful' Black women in any other roles has tended to confirm the notion that sport and entertainment are the only areas in which we can excel. To succeed in any other profession, a Black woman must dress, think, talk and act white. In other words, she must first lose all sense of her Black cultural identity if she wishes to find acceptance from the mainly white audiences which determine TV ratings in this country. Where attempts have been made on either of the channels to portray Black women outside the usual stereotypes, we have invariably been treated as a 'social problem', whose lifestyle and culture are responsible for any disadvantages we encounter.

The advent of Channel 4 in 1982 held the promise of a real alternative, one which would stop regarding us voyeuristically and cease treating our lives as a 'sub-culture' based on crime, weed and reggae. However, in an apparent attempt to look beyond the stereotypes, liberal/left television productions have, for the most part, only succeeded in projecting Black women in the role of 'oppressed victims', dependent on state benefits, council housing and the intervention of social workers. Thus Channel 4 has failed so far to meet the expectations of the Black community as a whole and in particular those of Black women. And this is despite the appointment of a Black woman, Sue Woodford, as commissioning editor at Channel 4 from 1982-84, crucial of course for Channel 4's image as the 'alternative' channel. This in itself has not given Black women a voice, and the few Black women who work in the television industry are still concentrated in the jobs which offer the lowest pay and the least decision-making power.

Arguments about TV ratings have been used to divert the public's attention from the real causes behind the suppression and distortion of our culture by the media – namely, the longstanding recognition that Black people represent a subversive and potentially radical influence on the indigenous population. Every effort has been made to ensure that programmes which are for or about Black people have kept well within the limits of what is 'acceptable', despite the newly awakened 'ethnic' consciousness of television producers and playwrights. How much easier it is to concentrate on multi-culturalism, feeding viewers with a diet of *Reggae Sunsplash*, *No Problem* and *Frontline* than seriously to attempt to challenge racism by debunking the stereotypes and historical distortions which perpetuate it. Perhaps the clearest example of this failure can be seen in the ethnic current affairs programmes such as *Black on Black** (Ch4) and *Ebony* (BBC2). The brief of all such programmes has been to stay 'balanced' and uncritical at all costs within a light-hearted, chat-show formula. The result has been a general trivialisation of the real issues which face the Black community, and an untimely easing of the pressure from the Black and anti-racist lobby for better representation of Black people on TV.

But our community has sought out ways of challenging these media distortions. We have looked for alternative ways of communicating the realities of our lives and our history, and because we have no power within the white-controlled media, we have had to find ways of turning the technology of mass communication into a weapon which we can use for ourselves.

As our lives here have taken shape and form, we have had many rich sources to draw on, a long tradition of creativity and inventiveness. It is these solid foundations, laid by our African foremothers, which have aided, inspired and sustained us in this process. It is therefore to them that we owe our militant heritage.

Any expression by a Black woman of her cultural and political identity must be seen to represent centuries of struggle. Whatever we present and however we define ourselves comes directly from that history. Our sense of self cannot be divorced from our collective consciousness because every statement underscores the reality of a poor and oppressed people struggling to be free. Whether our statement is conscious or instinctive, whether it is expressed superficially, through outward appearance, or through fundamental changes in outlook and lifestyle, it will serve to reaffirm our rejection of the dominant culture and its attempted negation of our way of life. So any act of cultural defiance or ideological independence – whether it be through song, dance, our use of language, the way we style our hair, our dress, our view of the world, a painting or a poem – testifies to our existence *outside* the roles in which British society has cast us.

> *Beverley Bryan, Stella Dadzie, Suzanne Scafe*
> Reprinted with permission from *The Heart of the Race:*
> *Black Women's Lives in Britain*, Virago 1985

---

* *Black on Black* has been replaced by *The Bandung File*, which is still a male-dominated programme.

3
Class

Introduction

In order to maintain itself, any establishment must have control over the communications network through which the population receives information. Material which is favourable to the establishment must be disseminated; that which is not must either be neglected or rendered 'safe' in some way.

We do not live in a totalitarian society; there is no 'official' censorship or manipulation of news. But the ownership, structure and employment patterns of the media ensure that they operate as a major force for the ruling class, as agents of patriarchal capitalism. Britain still has no major newspaper which articulates the views of the working class, nor are their interests served by broadcasting. Even potentially subversive programmes like Spitting Image *(Central) and some investigative documentaries all too often become absorbed within the system, and are presented with the same middle-class smoothness that characterises the rest of broadcasting. Furthermore they are almost never subversive to patriarchy.*

Those who suffer most from this state of affairs are working-class women – black, white, able-bodied, disabled, lesbian, heterosexual, young and old. Contemptuous treatment of working-class women inhibits their consciousness of themselves, both individually and collectively, as a potentially powerful force within society. The nation's prosperity rests on the shoulders of working-class women, and their rebellion would lead to its collapse.

The sexism with which working-class women are treated by the media necessarily affects the perceptions of working-class men.

This has direct consequences for those women who are most dependent on men, and have the least power to change the circumstances of their lives. Such sexism, along with racism and the other oppressions, inhibits the emergence of a united working-class movement.

Class and gender in images of women

Much of the work on decoding images of women has underestimated the ways in which the meaning of an image is determined by the historical and institutional contexts in which it is constructed and received. They also concentrate on the male/female opposition at the expense of other oppositions, notably that of labour/capital.

Everything revolves around individual personal relationships and women's 'natural drives' to seek feminine perfection – which leads to love, family life and (dependent) financial security.

The visual presentation of women as not needing to work, as the glamorous property of men, effectively displaces the idea that women do work, and so inhibits their sense of themselves as workers. Also, images of 'wife' and 'mother' – usually decoded as 'natural' roles – mediate the crucial work of women in unpaid domestic labour and in reproducing the labour force.

The contradiction between this work and maintaining 'femininity' can be seen in the 'negative' part of the women's narrative. This imagery depicts social, physical and mental breakdown. Processes and products are offered to revive women's flagging, flabby bodies and faces, so that they may sustain the 'love' of the men in their lives (and presumably their financial security).

The constant theme running through both the positive and the negative sides of the narrative is that women – truly feminine women, that is, 'natural' women – are 'naturally' dependent in all areas of life, especially financially.

Since the mid-1970s the distinction between the positive and the negative has become less clear. It is acknowledged that not everything in the female garden is lovely: family problems, lack of childcare facilities, low pay, price rises, isolation, racism, violence. Furthermore, women can now be seen as financially independent (or at least as major contributors to the family budget). Women can make their own decisions about their leisure time, they can instigate relationships and need not be passive sexually.

But although there are more representations of women at work, they are seldom shown actually working – and often it is still beauty, glamour and sexuality that are emphasised in women's magazines and the tabloid press. Women continue to display themselves and to be displayed. To picture women only as consumers in spite of representing their (potential) labour creates an ambivalence in decoding these images. Are we dealing with the 'point of production' (the sale of labour) or the 'point of consumption' (the purchase of commodities)? This is important in trying to understand the connection between the ways that women's labour power is exploited in the labour process, and the visual representation of women.

As an illustration we can look at one contemporary stereotype – the secretary. This stereotype is probably the most common of the more recent images of 'women at work'. By analysing it as a visual construct we can see to what extent these images are part of a gender narrative of sexual oppression and exploitation, and to what extent they are part of a class narrative of economic exploitation.

Images of secretaries do not show the woman working. Instead, they show her as a consumer at work. The common interests of secretaries as women and as workers are systematically negated. Why has this particular emphasis been placed upon the construction of the image? During the Second World War the media responded to government demands to bring more women into paid employment by positive images of women working in factories and elsewhere. Nowadays, rather than needing more labour from women, capitalism is in a crisis which needs less labour and more consumption as a short-term remedy. At the same time many women now assume that it is their right to enter and stay in the labour-force – even if working-class women are also condemned to the double shift of running a home as well. They are also discriminated against within the education system and the labour market, and are working in badly paid, dead-end jobs.

In this context the idea of being a secretary can be important. It can represent one of the few attainable dream jobs for working-class young women. Thus, the secretary stereotype can be a ploy in advertisers' attempts to reach their target audience. What is never revealed, however, is the women's economic exploitation. In publications aimed at women, the advertising industry seems happy to add the image of woman as worker to its repertoire of images of wife and mother, and women's objectified sexiness. What these changes emphasise, though, is individual earning and consumption, not the collective practices inherent in the struggles within the women's movement and the labour movement.

Different stereotypes of secretaries are found in magazines aimed at a male-dominated managerial and professional audience. Here it is not the individual spending power of women that is emphasised but more 'universal' aspects – in particular their sexual objectification, often in the form of jokes. But they are also represented 'realistically', in a way that does not seem to stress their sexuality. According to some of the advertisements, they need the best equipment, good pay, better ventilated offices, modern surroundings and facilities. They also, claim the medical journals, need drugs to keep them on their feet and carry on in their servicing capacity, producing surplus value.

In other words, the secretary presented to women office workers as a consumer and the secretary presented to employers as source of surplus value for capital are totally different and are kept apart. This contributes to an inhibition of the development of a class conciousness and of political organisation amongst white-collar workers.

An important concern in decoding images should be that of under-mining the ways in which dominant forms of visual representation reduce complex issues and relationships to a few 'recognisable' aspects which appear to constitute an acceptable totality. This work is already being done widely in terms of gender, but it also needs to be done in relation to class. We need to take apart and break down the apparent unity of ideology which leads to the construction of such images, and to understand the structures that lie beneath the surface images.

Jo Spence

Working-class women and the media

Working-class women are rarely asked to share their experience in any serious way by the mainstream media or even by the feminist press. We cannot in this article hope to convey all the many aspects of working-class women's lives in relation to the media. The issue of class does not exist in a vacuum: it is linked to race, disability, sexuality, and so on. We are concerned that this complexity is reflected in our own writing, as well as that of others. You do not have to be working class to write about the treatment of working-class women; to avoid writing anything beyond our own immediate experience cannot be excused.

According to the media, working-class women do not exist or exist only as stereotypes. The most common stereotypes used and recycled by all areas of the media, but especially television, are the cleaner, the cook, the tart, the housewife and the victim. We live in a television age. It is the most popular, widely used and therefore influential medium for generating ideas, information, propaganda and entertainment to the mass of people. The newspaper industry struggles to stay financially afloat, the cinema is attracting smaller than ever audiences, many people only occasionally buy a magazine – but few people are without a TV.

Since the formation of the Common Thread (a collective committed to publishing working-class women's writing) one name has cropped up time and time again as a symbol of what is insulting about the media image of working-class women. And yet she is one of the most beloved characters on TV: Hilda Ogden, *Coronation Street*'s cleaning lady. She is permanently rigged out in curlers and pinny, she's a gossip, her mind full of trivia, and she speaks in malapropisms, understanding nothing of the world beyond her street. Recently the hard-edged, malicious side to her personality has softened in widowhood; but there she is, twice a week, representing the 'typical' working-class woman to millions of viewers.

Coronation Street in particular, and TV programmes dealing with working-class life in general, often pass up the opportunity to explore the richness of working-class dialects and languages. It is far simpler for scriptwriters to record working-class speech as an amusing deviation from the norm. Newspapers and magazines are also guilty of this, phonetically reporting working-class speech, quoting dropped aitches and so forth, while middle-class speech is presented in standard dictionary spelling.

Working-class women are usually seen as losers: the spinsters, the tarts, the housewives, always being knocked down, but unfailingly picking themselves up, dusting themselves off and getting back into the ring for more of the same. This victim stereotype is common throughout the mainstream media.

Contrast the coverage given in the media to working-class women waving off sons and lovers possibly to their deaths during the Falklands fiasco – how brave we were then! Noble, wonderful women, women who wait and worry. Look at working-class women essentially playing the same supportive role (note supportive!) during the 1984-5 coal dispute. Then we were screeching banshees, foul-mouthed trouble-makers. Yet these women showed great courage, not to mention political development and strengths as women. How many Fleet Street boys sought the women's opinions as the political strength of the women grew and the fight became theirs as well?

Television writers tend to make working class and 'realism' synonymous – anything which needs a 'real-life' feel is set in a working-class environment. The more arty, intellectual or abstract drama is invariably given a middle-class setting. Even though the majority of the media's consumers are working class, television, newspapers and magazines seem content to pander to mainly white, heterosexual, able-bodied, middle-class tastes. Thus the media perpetuates the myth that the middle class is the norm, rather than the minority. This is reflected both in programmes and, equally significantly, in advertisements.

Programmes which attempt to portray working-class life – the soap operas – include few black women in their casts. In Channel 4's Brookside the token black woman, Kate, was written out of the series. In the BBC's *EastEnders*, the black characters are seen only in relation to white people. Saeed, whose wife left him, appears to have no black friends or relations, nor has Sheena, the 'hard-nosed stripper'. None of the black characters is developed or has a life that is placed within their own community. The same applies to Shirley Armitage in *Coronation Street* who has been a minor character for years – she has remained the token black woman.

Lesbians and women with disabilities barely exist as far as soaps are concerned. Working-class women, and more particularly those working-class women who are black, lesbian or have some form of disability, do not appear in their own right, only as 'token' representatives – that is if they appear at all. The only time they do appear (and then with appalling regularity) is when cast as 'social victims' in documentaries.

The mainstream magazines tend to push the notion that 'there is no such thing as a class sytem'. Those which are selling on the back of the women's movement – peddling feminism as it is lived by up-and-coming, heterosexual, white, able-bodied, and stereotypically beautiful middle-class career women – have a definite ideal women to whom they are selling. Their fashion pages assume high wages, white skin (how many more times are we going to get the 'white, pale and interesting is in this year' rubbish?), stock size 12; their features are variations on the theme of getting ahead at work (how many of us have the education/contacts/jobs or nannies to be able to compete?) They give us the 'Superwoman' image – that of pleasing men sexually as we struggle up the rungs of the social ladder.

When working-class women are not earning their keep as stooges and victims, television especially has a tendency to roman-ticise our lives. This no doubt eases the conscience of middle-class viewers who can reassure themselves that, although times are tough for the lower orders, at least they enjoy endless support in the bosom of the caring working-class community.

The authors of this article have never lived in such a community – they probably do exist, but are nowhere near as prevalent as the television writers would have us believe. Extreme poverty as experienced by people fighting to survive during the Depression of the thirties, or as servants in an Edwardian upper-crust home, are dramatised with sentimental affection, much like the black slave in the white middle-class home. This kind of treat-ment makes poverty and slavery seem both a thing of the past and, worse, not without its compensations.

Working-class women's lives are too diverse to allow us to catalogue within this paper the psychological and emotional effects of the damaging caricatures hurled at us by the media. These distorted images are internalised and affect the perception of our true selves. They restrict our development and so often become a self-fulfilling prophecy.

We are in a 'Catch-22' situation: either we are reduced to a stereotype or we aspire to be middle class and so 'better' ourselves. As working-class women in all our rich variety *we* have to define who and what we are – define our hopes and aspirations on our terms.

We need the support of middle-class women to challenge the way we are pigeon-holed in the media, and their commitment to changing their own prejudices about us. Middle-class women must explore the class issue – this means not only recognising that a class system exists but also considering their position in it and the part they play in perpetuating it.

April, Linda Bean, Julie Cotterill:
members of the Common Thread

Page 3 – dream or nightmare?

Photographs of topless young women are a fairly recent newspaper feature. The *Sun* started this practice, to be followed, in the bid for increased readership, by the *Daily Star* and the *Daily Mirror*. (The *Mirror* later changed its policy to featuring scantily clothed young women – hardly any better.) Originally sold to the public as a daring and risqué venture, 'Page 3 girls' have become a tabloid institution.

When Samantha Fox (the most successful Page 3 girl so far because she has managed to branch out into other areas and make money) announced that she was quitting Page 3 work in favour of a singing career, the *Sun* (6 June 1986) printed a mock obituary next to her picture, and invited readers to write in and 'save Sam's charms for the nation'. This kind of phrasing is to be expected from a paper which poses as an upholder of British traditions, and which professes a patriotism so dogmatic that it can be offensively racist. But the *Sun* still tries to maintain the risqué image of Page 3: readers are told, in the same write-up, that a 'saucy photo' of Ms Fox 'landed her in trouble with her teachers' when she was sixteen.

Liberated, rebellious Page 3 girls, and, by commercial association, daring and modern *Sun* editorial: why should their uninhibited, money-making fun be spoilt by boring feminist prudes – like

MP Clare Short, for example? When Clare Short introduced her Bill to ban nudity in daily papers, under the House of Commons 10-minute rule, she was received by jeering abuse from (mainly Conservative) male MPs. The tabloid press called her 'Crazy Clare', a spoilsport, a killjoy, even, with predictable denigration, 'the buxom Ms Short'. Yet she had put Conservative MPs on the spot, for if they supported Winston Churchill's Bill against degrading and offensive material on television, radio and film, why should they not also support a Bill which extended concern over such matters to newspapers?

The MPs' hostility to Clare Short's Bill made them look a little ridiculous: do they really believe that immobile nudity is all right but if it moves, it becomes dangerous? Their difficulty is reflected in the *Daily Telegraph* (13 March 1986) report of the debate. Unable to take a convincing serious position on it, the paper was reduced to reporting it as a comedy episode: 'It was really very funny', it weakly told us, reporting on her reintroduction of the Bill. But Clare Short received over 3,000 letters of support for her Bill, and many of them came from young women aged sixteen to twenty: the age range from which most Page 3 girls come. The Bill was welcomed by women of widely varying occupations, ages and political beliefs (as some stated in their letters: 'I don't usually agree with you, but . . . ').

There has been little concerted feminist action specifically against Page 3.[1] When asked to support an anti-Page 3 demonstration in Liverpool in 1984, I can recall feeling slightly surprised that Page 3 was to be the focus of the protest. For weren't we fighting pornography and sex-stereotyping already, and with partial success? Page 3, maintained by the sharp fear of circulation losses, seemed impossible to shift: it seemed an institution, just as the tabloid press directors had intended it to be. Moreover, there was the fear of exposing class differences, already painfully divisive in the women's movement. For what right did women who never bought the *Sun* or the *Star* have to interfere with their contents? Shouldn't intervention come from the women who did buy and read them?

In fact, Clare Short's letters show that there is support for her Bill from women who read these papers, and a survey carried out by *Woman* magazine during June and July 1986 reinforced this: the respondents were overwhelmingly in favour of banning nudity in daily papers, even when they bought the papers concerned themselves. But this is still a point on which feminists need to take care. For class is central to the Page 3 issue. Middle-class people tend not to read the *Sun* or the *Star*. Middle-class young women tend not to dream of appearing on Page 3. They don't need to: most of them have job prospects which promise more interest, more respect and a longer career, elsewhere. It is no accident that most Page 3 girls come from working-class homes. As photographer Harry Ormesher has said: 'Unemployment is the biggest factor. A young girl with a nice body can be led to believe her charms can get her off the dole queue'.[2] What would the alternative be for these girls?

It is evidently a question asked by their parents too: far from hiding her topless modelling activities from Mum, a Page 3 girl today is likely to have been groomed, dressed and accompanied to the photo session by her mother – even persuaded into it very often, according to model agency director Yvonne Paul.[3] This is a far cry from the 1970s when, as model Jilly Johnson has said, to pose topless was an act of rebellion from traditional family standards. Nowadays, it is a bid for more conventional aims: a good income, travel, fame, and perhaps the chance to break into something more interesting: fashion modelling, acting, dancing, singing.

Whatever they hope to do, these young women and their families should certainly make sure there is life beyond Page 3. For they are unlikely to get 'glamour' work after the age of twenty-five (Joan Collins is an exception, not an example), and, despite Samantha Fox, their chances of branching out into other forms of entertainment are slim. Samantha Fox is more fortunate than most, because she is managed by her father, Pat Fox, rather than by an agency. They are both evidently aware that Samantha's success as the most popular topless model will last only as long as it takes for another Page 3 girl to emerge; hence the part-ownership of a wine bar, and her recent promotion as a pop singer. Linda Lusardi, who is now in her mid-20s, presumably has the same anxiety, since she too is diversifying and is also releasing a pop record.

Although supported by their parents in the initial attempt to get started, most hopeful topless models sign on with an agency, like Panache, in Clapham, South London, or Spice, in Edinburgh. When she accepts work, a model is required to forfeit all rights to her photographs by signing a Model Release Form. Ownership of the photographs is the publication's, or the photographer's if he or she works freelance. The model is paid a set fee, irrespective of how many times the photos are sold. £75–150 for a day's work is typical. This may follow considerable investment from the model's family: one mother sold her motor-bike for £500 and spent the money, plus a bank loan, on her daughter's wardrobe of sexy underwear.[4] A model has no control over the caption to her picture; this is written by someone on the publication's staff ('whoever fails to get out of the room fast enough' according to one senior journalist I asked). It has little to do with the girl herself, but this doesn't matter: biographical details are irrelevant. For the caption, the pose, the scene, the situation are all contrived by others; the girl is merely a vehicle for female sexuality – in the way that men find most comfortable (and white men at that – seldom does a black woman appear topless in the daily press). Friendly, approachable, smiling (always), she has a child's fresh, open face, but a mother's large, nurturing breasts. 'She is waiting for you – and she wants it too, really.'[5]

Women's bodies have become coded as sexually available.[6] They are extensively used in the business of capitalism: women's bodies sell products, and women's bodies can themselves be bought. It is no accident that Page 3 girls are commonly described like food: 'luscious Linda Lusardi', 'dishy Helen Steed', 'scrumptious Sandra Jane', 'tasty Tracey Elvik' – they are available for consumption.

The models' poses of smiling topless compliance, and the corny sexual puns of the copy create an air of carefree gaiety which reflects on women's sexuality in general: 'Don't take us seriously, we don't really mean it.' This reflects on to whatever else is printed near the Page 3 picture. The column next to the topless photograph is often used for stories of a personal, even disturbing nature, yet they are inevitably trivialised by being placed next to the jolly Page 3 girl, and the language used to describe them often continues in the same relentlessly saucy vein.[7] Despite protests, there is as yet no Press Council ruling on what is appropriate material to be placed on the same page as the topless girl.

Samantha Fox has defended her topless modelling by comparing herself, and other Page 3 girls, to the pin-up stars of old films: Garbo, Dietrich, Monroe. The comparison is inappropriate: stars like those were remote, unreachable figures while the Page 3 girl is presented as compliant and accessible. Still, it is natural for her to defend her means of gaining fame and fortune, for there are few ways for an unqualified working-class girl to earn a lot of money and become well-known nowadays. The sixties, when to be young and working-class (like Cilla Black, Lulu or Twiggy) seemed more of an advantage than a deterrent, were twenty years ago: another decade, under a different government. Nowadays, it is more likely to be the rich who get discovered: Helena Bonham-Carter (Lord Asquith's great-grand-daughter) a film star, Catherine Oxenberg (related to the Queen) in *Dynasty*, Princess Stephanie of Monaco reaching the European charts with a pop record. The best that most Page 3 girls can hope for is some advertising modelling: better paid and more prestigious than topless work. However, since models are in demand for looking decorative at clubs and presentations, there is the possibility of meeting and marrying a famous man. So the Page 3 girl may achieve the rise in status and class that she and her family have sacrificed so much to achieve. This is the way that women have traditionally climbed the social ladder: through marriage to a man who defines his wife's social position for her. Meanwhile, there is the temporary triumph of having escaped from the threat of a tedious job or the dole queue. As 'lovely Julia Morse', 'the Welsh Wonder' is quoted as saying in the *Star* (5 June 1986): 'All my friends in Cardiff read the *Star* and they will know I've made the big time when they see my picture'.

Teresa Stratford

Notes

1 See p.216 for groups campaigning in this area.

2 *Sunday Mirror*, 8 June 1986.

3 *ibid*.

4 *ibid*.

5 Sally Vincent and Marcelle D'Argy Smith, 'Page 3 Passions', *Cosmopolitan*, June 1986.

6 Rosalind Coward, 'What's in it for Women?', *New Statesman*, 13 June 1986.

7 'Page 3 Passions'.

4
Physical Disability

Introduction

Disability is not an issue which affects only those who currently have disabilities. It is an issue for all of us.

There are two concepts beloved by the media: 'normality' and 'beauty'. Despite the fact that these are no more than abstractions, the media persists in pretending that there are certain concrete and objective standards against which to measure us all.

'Normality' and 'beauty', as they are defined by the media, mean able-bodied. Disability (and by extension the person with the disability) is seen as abnormal and undesirable. This profoundly affects the self-estimation and expectations of people with disabilities. It affects how those of us who will become disabled in the future deal with that change of circumstance. And it affects the attitudes of those currently without a disability: on the basis of their ignorance, fear and misinformation they construct a disabling environment, both physical and psychological, which creates a far greater handicap than any disability in itself.

The concepts of 'normality' and 'beauty' towards which we are all conditioned to strive – despite the fact that, being abstractions, they are unattainable – are deeply divisive for women. They separate us on the basis of standards which accord with patriarchal and capitalist values. It is not in the interests of women to be divided in this way. We all need to work together to eliminate the artificial barriers separating able-bodied women from women with disabilities. For able-bodied women that means reassessing the values they have absorbed relating to 'normality' and 'beauty' and seeking out correct information from their disabled sisters.

'The courage of crippled Clara' – the media and disability

The most noticeable thing about women with disabilities in the media is our absence. I mean *real* women with disabilities. Those of us who live and breathe and argue and laugh and get cross and lose our keys and cannot decide what to wear to the office or what to give the kids for tea. Those of us who are happy some days and depressed some days, and some days wonder what life is all about. Those of us who get together and giggle, sometimes cry, abut the strange problems so-called able-bodied people have in their relationships with each other and with us. Those of us who get tired trying to explain that we are just ordinary, abnormal humans, like everyone else.

The media, of course, are almost exclusively vehicles for expressing the conceptions of people who believe themselves to be able-bodied. Therefore it is not surprising that nearly everything written, said or shown about us is a fantasy created by lack of information, by stereotyping, and by fear in the minds of people who do not have disabilities.

Today's journalists and programme-makers were yesterday's children reading how Heidi's friend Clara got up and walked and lived happily ever after, or how the little boy in *The Secret Garden* got up and walked and lived happily ever after. Young women today still grow up reading stories like 'The Courage of Crippled Clara' (*Bunty*, October 1985), a picture story dripping with sad images of a thin embittered girl in a wheelchair: 'I'm not pleased to meet you. I hate people who pity me and stay just out of sympathy'; she is lonely: 'I like animals better than people . . . they love you no matter what you look like'; manipulative: 'Please don't say no, then I'll know you really are my friend'; longing to be 'normal': 'Oh this [horseride] is super! . . . I don't feel like a cripple at all!'; and longing to be saved by able-bodied friends: '*Please, please* don't desert me. Only once in my life have I been happy – that was yesterday when I met you . . . '

Or there's the story of the able-bodied children helping out at a children's hospital on bonfire night (*Judy*, October 1985). Tracey, in her incredibly old-fashioned wheelchair, says 'Don't let me spoil your fun, Jill. I shan't enjoy it. Just leave me in the hospital tomorrow night . . . It won't be any fun for me, knowing that I'll never walk again.' But in the end Tracey rescues a small boy from the bonfire and discovers she really can walk after all. 'I can do it. I can walk! But how?' 'You could walk all along! You just didn't try hard enough! . . . All it took was a little inner strength!' The conclusion of this story encourages one of the most dangerous misconceptions of all about disability: that it is the fault of the victim, caused by some character weakness. Not a far step at all from the idea that disability is a punishment from God!

Almost all images of disability suggest that not being able-bodied is something terrible and tragic. For example, 'Former cabinet maker Audley McDowell suffered months of helpless misery after a crippling stroke left him totally blind' (*Hackney Gazette*, September 1985). Of course disability is something most of us would rather do without, but describing the experience as 'months of helpless misery' denies the power and initiative and learning and growth which nearly always accompany the rage and grief at losing capacities which one once enjoyed. Able-bodied people seem to need to believe that they *make* us better by *doing* things to us – medical treatment, rehabilitation, special holidays – and so take away what we know to be our real achievements.

At the same time, events which are perfectly ordinary to us are exaggerated and romanticised in the endless stories about 'brave and cheerful' people with disabilities such as: 'Plucky Kathy Webb, who was struck dumb in an 80-foot horror fall, will signal "I do" at an amazing hospital wedding tomorrow . . . ' (*Sun*, August 1985) or 'These are the smiles of brave brother and sister Simon Pashley, twelve, and Emma aged eight. Two years ago blonde Emma had an operation to rebuild her defective heart. Simon also had heart trouble and had to have a pacemaker fitted . . . like his sister he has kept cheerful' (*Daily Mail*, August 1985). In fact you only have to look at the headlines 'The bravest bride', 'The smiles of courage', 'Brave foursome' to guess who the story will be about. Most of these stories reflect the low expectations able-bodied people have of our lives, and their invariable surprise that we carry on living the way we do.

Then there are all the stories about disabled people being cured or becoming at least more 'normal', and therefore of course happier (and more acceptable). 'Blind cure wife will see all the sights'

(*Daily Mail*, June 1985); 'Miracle cure for blind man' (*Hackney Gazette*, September 1985); and so on and so on. Our issues are always seen as individual misfortunes which we must accept bravely, or which we must overcome cheerfully, otherwise we are not news. Never are there stories of people with disabilities being angry or out-raged at our treatment, nor of us getting together, powerful and united and articulate about the real problems we face. The tiny media coverage of our political triumphs nearly always insinuates that we ourselves have not really done it at all. For example, in reporting the banning of disabled South African athletes from the Stoke Mandeville paraplegic games the *Daily Express* said in 1984, 'It's absolutely despicable that handicapped people should be used as part of a political campaign.'

At the heart of the oppression of people with disabilities is finance. Life is more expensive if you have a disability. Because our lives, rights and needs are paid no more than lip service by the statutory authorities, we have to rely a great deal on charities. Charities have to sell their causes in order to raise their funds. It is necessary therefore to retain the image of disability which will encourage people to dig their hands into their pockets: pathetic, suffering, poor, helpless, etc. There are posters, leaflets, collecting boxes and even 'please help spastics' stuck like stamps all over Christmas card envelopes. It is very hard for spastics – like the rest of us with disabilities – to feel proud and dignified, full human beings under this onslaught.

It is only when we represent ourselves that our reality will begin to be recognised as very different from all of this. Writing in *SHE* magazine in August 1985, Donna Taylor said: 'I get so angry about the bureaucracy and lack of co-ordination in Social Services. You have to fight, beg, scream and lose your temper to get things moving, and when you do get angry they say " . . . the disabled are so touchy".' And Sue describes how, 'Going out became a nightmare. I was public property, people either staring intently into my face, or quickly looking away . . . places I had taken for granted became inaccessible to me, cinemas, restaurants, many shops, people's houses . . . '[1] Carole Steele points out that, 'The charity case stigma must be eradicated to enable more people to enrich our lives without our being humbled and degraded any more by having to ask for help.'[2]

Access to the media has not yet been achieved for people with disabilities. We need to become journalists ourselves. We need to become photographers ourselves. We need to write our own books, magazines, poems, plays and film scripts. We need to have editorial power over articles and programmes about us (which now are often done without our request or permission). We need to be considered as a large percentage of the readership or audience of all media available to the general public, so that, for example, all events mentioned or advertised include access details. Finally we need to be able to read, watch or listen to all information accessible to the general public.

Micheline Mason

Notes

1 Jo Campling, ed., *Images of Ourselves*, Routledge & Kegan Paul, 1981.
2 Carole Steele, *In from the Cold*, Autumn 1982. *In from the Cold* is the magazine of the Liberation Network for People with Disabilities.

Blind people and the media – a conversation between Kirsten Hearn and Sue Hancock.

K: When first asked to write about images of blindness for this book, I didn't think that I could do it because most of the media is not accessible to me. I felt that with the exception of radio and sound tracks of films I was largely ignorant of how we are portrayed, except when friends take pains to read to me from a newspaper or describe visual images.

S: When I was little I always studied the appearance of blind people in the media. I never wanted to listen, although I always did – standing at the doorway if a blind person was on the telly, ready to make a quick getaway if it got too awful!

K: Picture this! A typical Hitchcock heroine being pursued through a dark strange house by a sinister villain. She flings open doors, gasps, screams as she nearly plummets down the flight of stairs she didn't know were there! She almost faints with terror as something nasty brushes against her face! And the special twist – she is blind! Thus she is a helpless victim, deserving to be persecuted.

S: Yes I remember those films; and of course she's always rescued by the gallant and inevitably sighted hero. When I watched them I felt guilty for not wanting to have anything to do with the heroine. I felt embarrassed too, because I knew that the actress, sighted of course, would be portraying the blind woman with stereotyped mannerisms – groping hands, eyes either tightly closed or vacantly staring! But my paramount feeling was always that I too might end up a victim, helpless and pathetic like her.

K: Or how about this – the helpless little waif, dishevelled and pathetic, warbling away in an orphanage: 'I'm nobody's child, nobody wants me because my eyes are blind' – a popular song a few years ago: guaranteed to have everybody reaching for their Kleenex. Or how about the malevolent old blind Pugh from Treasure Island, the impression of his nastiness heightened by the tapping of his stick as he creeps along within the shadow of the wall.

S: And let's not forget about the other stereotypes – the saintly blind such as you find in Dickens; the bitter and twisted blind; the heroic and martyred blind of the war novels 'beavering away at the old Braille!' Stiff upper lip very much to the fore. In newspapers it was always people writing *about* us. We didn't write about ourselves. We were always passing our A-levels and going off to university saying things like 'What I really want to do is make a life of my own, get married and have children.' Or we were doing wonderful things like climbing Mount Everest and people were saying, 'Aren't they brave, aren't they wonderful!' The articles always infuriated and embarrassed me: they were never about the sort of person I thought I was. I wanted to write something wicked and rebellious for newspapers, to say outrageous things about sighted people. But of course that wasn't what a sighted readership wanted to read.

K: Some time ago I was featured in a number of tear-jerking articles when I took part in an exhibition of drawings by the blind. Marge Proops featured one of my drawings, 'a touching little sketch of a robin'. Obviously the idea of a blind person drawing touched her heart – 'aren't they wonderful!' Yuck!

S: The articles were so melodramatic and sentimental – they used phrases like 'darkness fell upon her when she was only 16 years old' or 'in her world of darkness'. What wouldn't I have given for a chance to write an article to prove the stereotypes wrong, to dispel some of the myths. But as I hardly ever read the papers I felt I wouldn't be able to say things properly in their language. And so I felt my article would just be dismissed.

K: The trouble is, the media are controlled by white able-bodied men, on the whole, who know little about our lives and care less. They're not really interested in what we feel because we don't exist for them. All they want is sensationalism, a melodramatic story, something to tug the heart strings. Something that sells papers, that's got nothing to do with our lives. I want to have access to all the media, not just the bits that people choose to read to me occasionally. I want to be able to monitor what is said about me and other people with disabilities in the media. They get away with accounts of our lives that are basically lies. If the media were accessible to me I would have the right to reply, which I don't now.

S: When I was asked to take part in writing this piece my first and rather inconsequential thought was 'I wish there could be a blind woman in *The Archers*.' I still think it's a good idea. However, it would have to be a woman who just happened to be blind – not someone who appeared suddenly and dramatically with a problem about blindness, then disappeared two weeks later having had her problem solved by a sighted do-gooder, having come to terms with her blindness, or, best of all, having been cured by some miracle! No, it would have to be someone who appeared at the pub or the post office, and we hear about their whole life – not just about their blindness. We would do the same thing with *Coronation Street* and *Brookside*. It would be such a powerful thing to do – and of course the actress would be blind herself.

K: Some hope! Seriously though, we have to write the scripts ourselves, we have to have control. We'd want the character to be a positive force in the programme, giving as well as taking. Her presence could bring out other people's needs too.

S: Yes but I can't imagine this happening while the only problem the media want to recognise is that we can't see.

K: It's also that their problem with us is that we exist. I think if they could recognise that *everybody* has needs which have a right to be met, they wouldn't find *us* so threatening, and then we'd be portrayed more accurately.

S: Yes that's true. But I'd like to see us doing a lot more portraying of ourselves in the media, and those in control acknowledging that we're the best ones to do this.

Sue Hancock and Kirsten Hearn

5
Sexuality

Introduction

It is perhaps in this area of women's lives that the most pernicious distortions of reality are delivered by the media. By reducing women's sexuality to a very few, limiting stereotypes, determined by their own fantasies, the men who control the media attempt to control womankind.

The message is that we do not – must not – exist in ways which do not fit these stereotypes, for that is beyond male fantasy, beyond male control and therefore threatening. It would challenge the structure of our society, because our capitalist patriarchy depends on our acquiescence for its continued existence. The men whose illusions of female sexuality never apply to their own partners and even less to their daughters, are the same men whose sense of self-respect appears to depend on disrespect for, and degradation of, women. Degrade and control – a variation on divide and rule?

We are more than half the population. Why should we go on supporting a system which offers us only oppression?

Here the personal truly becomes political. If we understand the ways in which our sexuality has been denied, distorted and devalued, we will see that we do have the power to make change. If we rediscover and reclaim our sexuality in all its forms for ourselves – become the subjects of our own lives not the objects of others' – we shall be free from the tyranny of always existing in someone else's unreality, not our own reality.

These articles look at the ways in which the media look at women. They examine the images of female sexuality constructed by men to maintain social control. They show how powerfully our sexuality is exploited. They raise important questions about our views of our own sexuality (is there more to life than virgin/ whore, goddess/earth mother choices?) and how we have been manipulated into colluding in our own powerlessness.

The last two sections in this chapter deal specifically with society's assumptions of heterosexuality.

The media generally take people's sexual orientation for granted. If a woman or a man is lesbian or gay, it is a special feature – otherwise the writer or broadcaster assumes a heterosexual subject. She or he also assumes a heterosexual reader, viewer or listener. These assumptions ensure that homosexuality is either completely ignored, or subject to the shocked and horrified tones which promote prejudice and alarm. The most glaring example of this in recent times has been the AIDS scare. In Africa AIDS is a predominantly heterosexual disease, but who would know that, informed only by the populist British media? Here, AIDS has been described in terms of just retribution for the sins of sexual non-conformity – that is non-conformity to heterosexual roles. Yet lesbians are in the lowest risk category for AIDS.

In this way (as in many others) lesbians and gay men are used as scapegoats for a society which does not assume responsibility for its own shortcomings. When blame is to be allocated, a minority becomes the victim of majority prejudice, disguised as an anxious morality. The resurgence of the extreme right in the early 1980s provides a fertile ground for moral backlash against lesbians and gay men.

Making moral assertions about people's sexuality is doubly effective. It devalues their identity and it effectively prevents political analysis of society's lack of responsibility in dealing with prejudice. Lesbians have been subject to this kind of treatment even more than gay men. (Gay men sometimes win an individual affection from the media, but where are the female equivalents of Quentin Crisp or the late Christopher Isherwood? We do not know because they are ignored.) Lesbians are generally invisible in the media and where a woman's lesbianism is mentioned it is usually in tones of ridicule or disapproval. Lesbians are deeply disturbing to the men who control our society. The western patriarchal system in which we live depends on women's submission to men for its survival. Whether actively involved in politics or not, lesbians challenge the sexual rules which we are supposed to apply to our lives. In doing so, they show up the limitations of these rules, and point the need for change. With few exceptions, the media, who could be paving the way for change, are preventing it.

Women as sex objects

The Women's Monitoring Network held its first nationwide monitoring day in 1981. It focused on the use of women as sex objects in the printed media. Pornographic magazines were specifically excluded, though of course pornography and the use of women as sex objects in mainstream media spring from the same view of women, and share common conventions. Over a thousand cuttings were sent in.

The portrayal of women as sex objects trivialises, degrades and dehumanises us. This affects the way we are viewed by men and the way we view ourselves. The male-controlled media industry uses women's bodies or parts of them for titillation and to sell products and publications. The way they do this is to present women constantly as glamorous, alluring and available. This results in women being viewed as objects, to be used for the pleasure and profit of men. Inevitably, men's attitudes towards women are influenced by this voyeuristic approach.

For women the result of such stereotyped portrayal is doubly oppressive. Not only do we suffer from the effects of men perceiving us in this light, but we also absorb and internalise the images presented. We are led to view ourselves as being at the service of men, and to conform to their ideals of women: young, slim, 'beautiful'. Failure to achieve this idealised image results in feelings of inadequacy and inferiority. We constantly devalue ourselves and our sex, and in addition we are encouraged to compete with one another. This is highly profitable for both the media and the manufacturers. Women are the pawns of our consumer society – we are used to sell the products we are urged to buy.

In some cases the woman is depicted naked or semi-naked, in a seductive pose suggestive of her availability. The image may be used to sell a particular product or certain publications (for example 'Page 3' in the tabloids). The use of such images in advertising may be wholly gratuitous and irrelevant to the product. At other times the woman is shown using the product; but she is still posed in a seductive manner, and her relationship is with the viewer (potential purchaser) rather than with the product. In fact she is more likely to be caressing it, rather than engaging with it (or any part of her environment) in a realistic or purposeful way.

Sometimes only a part of a female body is used to suggest allure and availability: a caressing hand, a beckoning eye, a seductive leg. Disembodied, and therefore doubly dehumanised and disempowered.

The language employed by advertisements further contributes to the portrayal of women as sexually available and there to be 'bought'. Typical slogans for jewellery are: 'Put a little magic into her life before someone else does'; 'Gold on her finger will touch her heart'. Sexual innuendo is frequently used: an advertisement for a pocket memo is captioned, 'Talk to your secretary in bed'. A tights advertisement depicts a pair of legs and pelvic area with the caption (strategically placed) 'A cut above your average tights'.

Pornographic films, videos, strip shows, sex aids, etc, are frequently advertised in mainstream media, often with explicit pictures and descriptions. Bondage poses and attire proliferate, as do descriptions of violence: 'Burning Passions. Innocent young women fall prey to a gang of sex-starved escaped convicts . . . Virgin of the Beaches. Nudism, rape, carnage and insanity in a fast-moving sex thriller . . . ' References to and images of young women and schoolgirls are commonplace.

Even images of women which are not blatantly sexual proclaim an ideal of slimness, hairlessness, odourlessness, 'beauty', youth and smooth (white) skin, that supposedly makes women more attractive – to whom? These advertisements exploit women's anxieties ('Do you look older?') and promote competitiveness ('Isn't it time to shape up to the competition?').

Though black women rarely feature in advertisements, there is an arena in which the stereotype of their 'exotic and extra-sensual sexuality' is commonly exploited: travel advertisements. For example, airline advertisements with their 'hint of Eastern promise'.

Of course it is not only pin-ups and advertisements which portray women as sex objects. News stories, particularly in the tabloids, frequently emphasise women's sexuality rather than their

achievements. 'Shapely C_____ K_____ is sending temperatures
soaring at a port's fish dock. For blonde C_____, 19, . . . has taken
over the family fish firm – and proved a real catch for Hull Docks'
(*Daily Express*). Cartoons often employ blatantly sexual portrayal
of women, sometimes in a gross and offensive way; for example
one strip in *Custom Car* is a deliberate attempt to humiliate and
denigrate women. Art photography sometimes differs little from
pornography – indeed, it is merely an excuse for it.

Women's Monitoring Network Report no. 1

Women for sale – the construction of advertising images

> Dürer believed that the ideal nude ought to be constructed by
> taking the face of one body, the breasts of another, the legs of a
> third, the shoulders of a fourth, the hands of a fifth – and so on.
> The result would glorify Man. But the exercise presumed a
> remarkable indifference to who any one person really was.
> (John Berger, *Ways of Seeing*, 1972)

The relationship of male image-makers to the female body has a
long and inglorious tradition. By convention, male artists painted
female nudes (or semi-nudes) in passive poses facing the spectator, with a look suggestive of intimacy and the promise of gratifi-
cation. These paintings were not available to the public. They
were privately commissioned and privately enjoyed. The spectator
was invariably male, as was the owner. By owning the painting, he
also 'owned' the woman.

By convention the female body was portrayed without body
hair; hair was after all associated with sexual power. 'Her body is
arranged the way it is, to display it to the man looking at the picture. The picture is made to appeal to *his* sexuality. It has nothing
to do with her sexuality . . . Women are there to feed an appetite,
not to have any of their own . . . ' (*Ways of Seeing*). Image-maker
and consumer have thus colluded in an act of male imperialism
over women's sexuality.

The conventionalisation and stylisation of the nude – the removal of any characteristics that *particularise* the subject of the

painting – is the tradition that informs both advertising and pornographic photography today. Although the models chosen are no doubt conventionally beautiful, the images produced are in fact distortions of reality. They are distorted for precisely the same reasons as in art: to create a vision that accords with a male-defined ideal.

For a start, the model is either decontextualised completely or placed in a fantasy setting (whose fantasy?), or else she is posed in an idealised context that 'puts her in her place' – decorating a car bonnet, caressing a cooker in a crumb-free kitchen, beaming at her (male) boss from her brand-new typewriter, and so on.

Secondly, photographic technique further strips away anything that makes the model a unique woman. Any 'blemishes' like grey hairs, spots or wrinkles are removed. Her legs may artificially be made to look thinner. A thousand shots are taken and only one is chosen. Harsh lighting, soft focus – many different techniques to produce a 'look'. The model herself is depersonalised, dehumanised by the process.

Her function after all is to sell a product. Her *humanness* is irrelevant – only the look is important, her idealised form to hang things on or drape over objects. She is herself objectified. She becomes part of the packaging of the product – or even the product itself, as in pornography. She is woman made 'perfect' in the eyes of Man.

This ideal is of course not only sexist. It is also supremely racist, ageist and heterosexist.

Every day we are bombarded by a plethora of these larger-than-life 'perfect' images: glossy magazines, pin-ups, roadside hoardings. We cannot escape this fetishised ideal, which is by the very nature of its construction and its philosophy impossible to attain. It is the representation of a male-defined ideal; we might argue that men find it easier to 'consume' depersonalised images than to relate to 'real' women, and that this consumption enhances their perceptions of their own power. That is their very great loss. But what of the effects on women?

For we also learn to view ourselves in this way – we internalise this depersonalised ideal and judge ourselves and each other by it. After all, where are the alternative images of real women with which we might identify? Analysis of any glossy women's magazine reveals an overwhelming abundance of glamourised models, and *a very few* small photos of real women. Assaulted by this greater abundance of idealised images, it is they that become 'real' in people's minds – next to them we are the imperfect imitations. We have been displaced, our sense of our own status, beauty and power as women is diminished – we feel as insignificant as those small photos.

Furthermore a massive act of public voyeurism is perpetrated. Male image-makers (or nowadays maybe even a female image-maker but still following a male tradition) portray women as objects to be viewed and consumed. We grow up with this voyeurism and it has deep psychological effects on us. It means we learn to see ourselves as men see us. We see with their eyes, not with our own. As Berger again puts it: '*Men act* and *women appear*. Men look at women. Women watch themselves being looked at. This determines not only most relations between men and women but also the relation of women to themselves. The surveyor of woman in herself is male, the surveyed female. Thus she turns herself into an object and most particularly an object of vision: a sight. (*Ways of Seeing*)

Although these images are often produced to gratify male ego and desire, they are also of course frequently designed specifically for a female audience. The extent to which they *work* (as they indeed do) is an indication of the extent to which our minds and bodies have been colonised. We may know logically that we will never attain a particular look or the nirvana promised if we purchase a particular product. But to such a degree have we internalised the fetishised ideal that we *still* strive, more or less consciously, to come up to scratch. We may eventually give up the attempt either in despair or as an act of political choice – or we may not even enter the contest in the first place (because we feel we cannot compete?) – but still at some level we all feel that since we do not 'measure up', we are not 'real' women.

Advertising images are as cynically motivated as planned obsolescence. You create an image which few can attain and you are ensured of a market forever. (And just to make sure, you change the 'look' regularly.) For though some women will not enter the contest and others will give up, there are always sufficient women addicted to the attempt to be 'perfect' by buying the products to make it highly lucrative. Glossy magazines aimed at younger women – increasingly common – ensure the 'hooking' of new generations as older women get 'past it' and are therefore no longer profitable. The anxieties and insecurities of these young women – the result of growing up in a sexist society – are exploited, and an attitude of consumerism that promises an easy solution is cultivated.

The images are also calculated to play on our racism, if we are white; or on any internalisation of the message that white equals beautiful, if we are black. They make us glad that we are young – and terrified of growing older. They reassure our heterosexuality – or fill us with guilt and a sense of inadequacy if we are, or fear we might be, lesbian. They lead those of us who are able-bodied to believe that to become disabled or disfigured would be a fate worse than death. (And what are women with disabilities to believe?) And they confirm for us all that without money we are nobody.

And the sub-text running beneath it all – the covert function of the depersonalised idealised female image – is to teach us to know our place, to make us feel disempowered, inadequate, second-rate. Capitalism and patriarchy, after all, go hand in hand.

But we need to remember that powerful as the propaganda is, it doesn't entirely work. We do not become robots manipulated at the whim of the image-makers. We retain enough of our own power and our own individuality to construct our lives in a way that is more or less good for *us*. We may not look like the models, but people fall in love with us anyway! The more conscious we become of how the images are created and what their purpose is, the more we can choose to reject their message. We can raise the subliminal to the light of inspection so that it no longer enslaves us. And the more we ourselves produce positive images of real women in all our diversity, particularity, and human magnificence, the greater pleased we shall all be with ourselves as we are.

Julienne Dickey

The body politic – the campaign against pornography

Andrea Dworkin, the American feminist, writes: 'Pornography is the graveyard where the left has gone to die. The left cannot have its whores and its politics too.' The antagonism of the left against the campaign is usually expressed in one of three ways: feminists are accused of interfering with sexual freedom, with threatening freedom of speech and with being a reactionary force in alliance with the 'new right'.

Yet the campaign against pornography arises quite logically from the traditional concerns of mainstream feminism. Feminists have always been concerned with challenging the restriction of women to the roles of sexual object, wife and mother and have campaigned against such stereotyping of women in school textbooks, in advertising etc. This has become fairly respectable and acceptable to those who see themselves as pro-feminist.

The multi-billion-pound pornography industry and the sex industry of which it is a part, promotes an image of woman simply as a sex aid for men. In pornography woman is represented over and over again as simply a hole or part of a body. Women are shown as loving rape and abuse. In 'snuff' movies women are actually murdered for entertainment.

Feminists are asked to prove our assertion that there is a connection between the view of women in pornography and sexually violent films and the harassment and violence against women which happens in the home, in childhood, at work and on the street. Such a degree of proof is not required to show a connection between sex-stereotyping in school textbooks and television advertisements and men's expectation that women should perform all household tasks. Moreover such a demand for proof shows a remarkable blindness to the abuse and exploitation of millions of women in the actual production of pornography.

The campaign against pornography has been quite a late development for feminism. The reasons why we have found it so difficult to recognise the significance of pornography and fight it may help us to understand the resistance of the liberal left.

Those of us who grew up in the 'sexual revolution' of the 1960s or its aftermath were allowed to take only two positions on pornography. If you were pro-sex you said pornography was all right. If you objected you were anti-sex. Research for the US president's commission on pornography in 1970 divided subjects into two groups according to their reactions. In one piece of research those who objected to pornography were labelled 'sexual conservatives' and those who did not were 'sexual liberals'. In another the objectors were labelled 'anti-intellectuals' and the others 'intellectuals'. Not surprisingly, most of the objectors were women. In such a climate a campaign against pornography was difficult. None of us wanted to be called 'prudes' or 'puritans'. The situation is not much different today.

Porn does have something to do with sex. Women are presented as objects to service men's sexuality. In rejecting porn we are not rejecting sex but the prevailing male view of women and sex. But when feminists dare to criticise the way in which sex is currently constructed or suggest their hopes for the future they are accused of 'moralism'. Only 'prudes', it seems, may suggest that sex could take undesirable forms. Sex is judged by standards quite different from those applied to other kinds of human behaviour. Sex is seen as private and beyond politics except in so far as prejudice and the law restrict the right of individuals to act sexually in any way they wish. The campaign against porn is seen as an attack on 'sexual freedom'. Sex is assumed to be exempt from normal debate as if it is a 'natural' form of human behaviour subject to no social influence.

Economics, on the other hand, is seen as a valid issue for debate on which we may express our hopes for the future. A critique of current forms of economic organisation is not dismissed as moralism. The existence side by side of different forms of economic organisation is not seen as a situation of glorious polymorphous perversity. Those who defend 'sexual freedom' against the feminist critique are defending the privileges of the ruling class of men to exploit and abuse women, just as those who proclaim the necessity of an unrestricted free enterprise economy are upholding the rights of the ruling economic class.

Sex is constructed as any other forms of human behaviour are. The pornographers are involved in the construction of sexuality. Feminists want a voice in the construction of sex too. The anti-porn campaign is part of a wider movement by feminists to challenge men's linking of sex with objectification and aggression in the sex industry and outside it. We have no choice but to oppose the view that sex is about male dominance and female submission, sadism and masochism and fetishised femininity and masculinity.

There is not much that is 'personal' and 'private' about sex for women. Sexual harassment restricts our rights to work or walk on the street. The fetishising of women controls the ways in which we may move with restrictive clothing and shoes. The promotion of compulsory heterosexuality and within that, sexual intercourse as 'the' practice of heterosexuality, channels us into dependence upon men, into unwanted pregnancies or the difficult struggle to avoid them. Images of women as vulnerable, passive and abused undermine our confidence and separate us from our bodies. There is no innately 'pure' sexuality. We must fight for what we see to be in the interests of women.

We are sometimes told that lesbians and gay men will suffer from any restriction on 'sexual freedom'. Those of us in the anti-porn movement who are lesbians know that our 'freedom' as women and as lesbians to define our own lives is restricted by the promotion of woman-hatred and the use of lesbianism in porn as simply a turn-on for men. The right of all women to sexual self-determination, on which lesbianism depends, is totally negated by the propaganda of pornography that all women are the willing sexual slaves of men.

Feminists are accused of wanting censorship and endangering the right to freedom of speech. Again 'sex' is being judged by very different standards. Those who make such arguments would never see the fight against racist propaganda outside pornography (pornography contains much racism, too) as endangering 'freedom of speech'. Why is the right of pornographers to promote woman-hatred seen as an inalienable human right?

Feminists have not asked for laws to ban porn and are in no position of power where they could outlaw porn. The law is made and administered by men in their own interests. Feminists have demanded the right to object and to demonstrate their anger. Why is our critique such a threat to the liberal left who would not oppose other feminist campaigns? It could be that the sexual oppression of women is at the root and basis of our oppression, the final bastion, and that those who want only superficial changes to the structure of male dominance have no choice but to oppose a fundamental challenge.

One source of alarm for those on the liberal left purports to be a reputed (but imaginary) alliance between the feminist campaigners and the anti-obscenity brigade like the National Viewers and

Listeners Association. The women in the NVLA who object to porn very likely have the same gut reaction to porn as do feminists. We *all* see the degradation of women. They choose to retreat into the false securities of monogamous, reproductive heterosexuality. We see the only solution as an end to assumed heterosexuality, and to the sexual colonisation of women's bodies by men in the marriage bed, in porn and all its forms.

Sheila Jeffreys

Heterosexism and the lesbian image in the press

The oppression of lesbians and gay men affects the whole population. People are taught early on in life that they must stop being close to others of the same gender – indeed, they are pressured to compete with them for the attentions of the opposite gender. The mere threat of being labelled lesbian or gay is a powerful way of keeping people within their 'gender-appropriate' roles. In spite of all this, however, same-sex friendships *do* remain centrally important to women and men, even though they are hedged about with taboos and restraints.

Two terms are generally employed to describe the attitudes that perpetuate lesbian and gay oppression: homophobia and heterosexism. Both phenomena are commonly found in the media as elsewhere. Homophobia is the fear of homosexuality and of being close to people of one's own gender. Heterosexism is the assumption either that everyone is heterosexual, or that that is the only normal, natural and moral way to be. It is also the assumption that everyone is categorically either homosexual or heterosexual, and that the sex act itself and what gender you choose to relate to sexually – even if you spend practically no time at all engaged in sexual activity! – are the most important and overriding characteristics that define you as a person.

Heterosexism is most strikingly perpetuated by the media in the general invisibility or marginalisation of lesbians and gay men, and of issues relating to homosexuality. The assumption that all readers are heterosexual appears in comments like 'Hey girls! How about this handsome fella!' or 'the wedding dress all you girls will be clamouring for' or 'a quiz to help you find the perfect

[male] mate' or 'women generally like their men to be . . . ' The 1985 Gay Pride March attracted 10,000 people to the streets of central London, yet merited scarcely a word in the media. Gay politics are studiously ignored; as with women's liberation and black liberation, gay liberation is denied its rightful place as a vital force in society and in history.

This invisibility is doubly profound for lesbians. Often, coverage of 'homosexuality' actually refers to gay men – as with much of the reporting of AIDS (although lesbians are also affected by the media hysteria which has greeted AIDS). Television programmes about homosexuality have most often fallen into the trap of providing a platform largely for gay men. Sometimes lesbians appear to be seen as a sub-category of gay men. Although lesbians and gay men must be united against a common oppression, it cannot be assumed that the issues are the same for both groups, or that both share the same viewpoint. However, since the media regard them as one and the same, much of this article necessarily includes both.

When lesbianism or homosexuality *is* mentioned by the media, the assumption is made that all of their audience is heterosexual, and, generally, that all will share the view that gay people are 'sexual deviants' (though this is sometimes expressed in more 'liberal' terms). Whether or not 10 per cent of the population – at the very least – will be offended appears to be of little concern to them.

The most passionate denunciations of homosexuality, needless to say, come from right-wing religious people who feel that this is a disease threatening the moral fabric of society and that AIDS is a divine punishment. Their opinions often come in the form of readers' letters – most commonly in the right-wing press – always a convenient way of propagating ideas without compromising editorial 'fairness'. Sometimes, however, Christians are prepared to take a more 'liberal' view:

I long for the day when, in Christian fellowship groups, a person with a homosexual orientation will be able to share this with the entire group and be certain that the confession will be met, not with condemnation, disapproval or a judgmental attitude, but with the assurance of help and the prayer which heals:

'We're on your side. Thank you for being so open. We'll pray you through to the next stage of maturity.' (*Christian Record*, 12 April 1985)

Do 'confession' and 'next stage of maturity' not imply a judgemental attitude?

Such phrases as 'self-confessed lesbian', 'engaged in homosexual activity' and 'homosexual tendencies' evoke images of lesbians and gay men doing shameful things in dark corners, seedy and guilt-ridden. They completely detract from any attempt to portray lesbian and gay pride.

If one thing is likely to whip up a tide of homophobic hysteria, it is the association of gays and children. The assumption is routinely made that gay people are inevitably attracted to children and can scarcely forbear from molesting them. Sexual assaults by men on boys are given greater prominence and sensationalism than the far, far more common occurrence of the molestation of girls by heterosexual men. Debate about the employment or parental status of gay people with regard to children is frequently reported by giving a platform to a homophobic voice (usually a Tory), for example 'Homosexuals and lesbians are to be banned by Bexley Council from applying to adopt homeless children . . . Cllr Ken McAndrews said "these people – lesbians, homosexuals, transvestites and paedophiles – have unusual sex practices and should not be accepted as suitable." ' (*Kentish Times*, 20 June 1985). Do they enquire into the 'sex practices' of heterosexual couples?

Associating paedophilia (and often incest) with homosexuality causes an inevitable linking of the two in people's minds. The media are not to be swayed by the facts; the confusion of homosexuality and paedophilia is one of the most deliberately scurrilous aspects of media treatment. Gay people are also accused of 'disseminating propaganda' to young people (as though young people weren't subjected to a constant barrage of heterosexual and heterosexist propaganda every day!). The row that erupted in 1986 over sex education hinged mainly on whether lessons would portray homosexuality favourably (or even neutrally); this was translated in tabloidese as 'teaching homosexuality'. Haringey and other councils were branded as perverted for adopting equal opportunities policies in education, and important people were wheeled in for the attack. 'Primate: ban these gay lessons. The Archbishop of York made an outspoken attack yesterday on the teaching of positive attitudes to homosexuality – "gay studies" – to children in Britain's schools.' (*Daily Mail*, 21 November 1986).

Using Tory spokespeople to attack homosexuality is very common in the 'gays-on-the-rates' stories. These stories are nearly always slanted to create maximum outrage amongst the 'decent respectable rate-payers'. The assumption is made that all readers are rate-payers, and that all rate-payers are heterosexual. (In fact, of course, gay people pay rates, from which they benefit far less than heterosexual people.) The most objectionable thing about the 'gays-on-the-rates' scandals is that gay people are being used as scapegoats for what is in fact an attack on the left – if you want to discredit the left and prove how 'loony' it is, you show that it supports sexual deviants. Some quotes from Tory spokespersons: a penfriend service for lesbians 'is "a rotten use of taxpayers' money," Cllr Eric Sunderland said. "It is totally wrong to encourage abnormalities . . . it's bloody nuts" ' (Bradford *Telegraph & Argus*, 10 April 1985). 'The lesbian/gay mob carry on a continual campaign of harassment to force people out of a job with the housing department. They ensure lesbians and gays get the top jobs' (*Daily Mail*, 15 June 1985). 'Conservative leader Bill Bradbury: "This is going barmy in a big way – it is beyond belief " ' (over an Equal Opportunities post on Nottinghamshire council) (*Star*, 26 April 1985). 'County Hall seems to have a bottomless purse for every fringe group that wants money, whether it is to help lesbians and gays or buy dominoes for West Indians' (Birmingham *Evening Mail*, 19 March 1985).

The racism of the last comment is commonly found in conjunction with homophobia. Another example from Alexander Chancellor of the *Sunday Telegraph* (17 May 1985): 'Criticisms of its [Islington Council's] misuse of rate-payers' money seems only to spur it into wilder acts of lunacy. The latest one . . . is a grant of £3,000 to the Borough's Irish lesbians. Irish lesbians are described as "a particularly disadvantaged group" who came to Britain to "escape conservative attitudes and repressive legislation". If this is so, I cannot imagine how money is going to help, unless it is to drown their sorrows in Guinness.'

Lesbianism is also used as an excuse to attack the peace movement.

The deeply offensive treatment meted out to Greenham women, for instance, is frequently based on the notion that all such women are lesbians. As such, they do not need to be taken seriously, since they are beyond the pale of decent society anyway, and have such 'extremist' views. Focusing on this aspect of Greenham is a way of ignoring and detracting from the real issues of nuclear disarmament.

Feminism itself of course is deliberately associated with lesbianism by the media, to enable them to dismiss it more effectively. It is an attempt to dissuade women from identifying with feminism; divisiveness is fostered between 'real' women and those who supposedly are not.

Attacks on lesbians and gay men often take the form of mockery and dismissiveness. A typical cartoon by Jak in the London *Evening Standard* (29 April 1985) shows a row of stereotypically 'butch' women with ties and pipes on guard outside a football ground. A passing football official says to an inspector 'It's a compromise . . . I only switch on the electricity if the GLC lesbian bouncers can't stop them.'

Glenys Roberts wrote a snide report on the London Lesbian and Gay Centre in the London *Evening Standard* (4 April 1985) which showed staggering ignorance of the situation and concluded 'everyone I met in the Centre was delightful if naive – being exploited by politically motivated cynics and their own guilty version of the working classes [meaning?]. All the indulgences of the looney left were on display in Smithfield but not much else to stimulate a grown-up.' So if we're not a dangerous threat we're naive and manipulated!

One of the reasons lesbians don't have to be taken seriously is that, after all, we're not really women – we really want to be men. We like to 'chat up' pretty, feminine women. When Julie Goodyear (Bet Lynch of *Coronation Street*, was 'exposed' as a lesbian in September 1986, much was made of this. 'She [Julie] loves to dress up as a man in collar, tie and three-piece suit – sometimes with leather boots – whenever she visits gay nightclubs . . . Usually she liked ultra-feminine girls . . . But by the time Janet Ross came on the scene five years ago, she was into more butch, very masculine women . . . Julie and Janet were like man and wife – in that order' (*Star*, 29 September 1986).

According to the *Evening Standard* (3 May 1985) a group of lesbians were banned from a pub for kissing, cuddling and petting each other, daubing the toilet with lesbian and anti-male graffiti and attacking some of the regulars. Several of the women even refused to use the ladies' toilet and insisted on using the gents'. (It seems you can be man-hating and wanting to be a man at the same time!) There was a disclaimer to this story by one of the women involved – this, typically, occupied a small paragraph at the end of the article. Nearly always when attacks are made, if a right of reply is granted at all, it occupies considerably less space than the attack, which is presented in a sensationalist form, headline and all. It is the attack which commands the attention – and the gay person or people are put on the defensive, and are thus at a considerable disadvantage.

It is interesting to compare images constructed in fashion photography with the treatment of lesbians by other media: In fashion shots, models are frequently posed in ways suggestive of lesbianism – in fact such pictures are almost the only time you see women being close physically. As with the portrayal of lesbianism in pornography designed for men, it has a titillating value, but is ultimately unthreatening because the women involved are stereotypically 'feminine' and 'beautiful' – and therefore reassuringly heterosexual. The lesbianism is merely the fore-play, the ensuing heterosexual act the real thing. The women in the fashion advertisements get away with being close because they are so patently 'real' women that they don't need to fear being labelled 'lesbian'. They are furthermore unmistakably posing for an audience, not in fact really engaging with one another.

Lesbianism is also used for titillation in press 'scandals'. One case in 1986 which achieved enormous notoriety was the 'lesbian love triangle case' in which a woman severely wounded another with a claw hammer in a jealous rage. This case merited days of coverage in all the papers as the trial progressed, and had the tabloids salivating with salacious detail. A cuddle on the couch, a kiss in the garden, became 'torrid love scenes'. The fact that the attacker was a gym mistress and the victim the deputy head completed their orgiastic pleasure.

Another area where lesbianism features from time to time is in the coverage of women's sport which in general receives very little attention from the media. Frequently it is the details of the women's appearance and personal lives that are given prominence rather than their accomplishments. Sportswomen who are not at the same time 'feminine' are liable to be accused of being lesbian; often this is an attempt to discredit Eastern bloc competitors (anti-gay prejudice again being used as a political scapegoating technique). During previous years' coverage of Wimbledon, Martina Navratilova has been compared unfavourably with the more 'feminine' Chris Evert Lloyd. To her credit Evert Lloyd has always refused to play along with these attempts at divisiveness based on concepts of 'femininity'. The publication of Martina's autobiography took some of the point out of the press slurs about her sexuality, and in fact the coverage of Wimbledon 1985 and 1986 contained remarkably little of earlier excesses. Her autobiography was even serialised by the *Daily Express* (16 April 1986), rather hypocritically in view of their former treatment of her. The *Sun* (25 June 1985) featured a centre-spread headlined 'Martina the Heartbreaker. She's just like a father to the kids!' The next day they ran a story about her relationship with Rita Mae Brown, quoted as saying 'I guess I'm popular because most lesbians are thought to be ugly, neurotic and self-destructive. I just am not.' As a follow-up (28 June 1985) they revealed 'My Martina! Why I'm sending her flowers, by actress Martha. Exclusive!' (The actress ended the article by denying that she had a 'crush' on Martina, but then the *Sun* is not renowned for an interest in the truth.)

But not all coverage of lesbianism is in the form of such blatant attack. More insidious, but just as damaging to an accurate and unbiased perception of homosexuality, is the suggestion that tragedy besets the lives of all gay people. Lesbian characters in television dramas and in films are nearly always sad, pathetic, unattractive creatures who inhabit dingy corners and hanker after heterosexual women; or else they are bitter, twisted and sometimes sadistic 'bitches' who, being unfulfilled themselves, don't want anyone else to be happy.

One might expect The *Guardian* women's page to be reasonably sympathetic and provide a platform for lesbians – but in fact this is rare. One article that *was* published (14 May 1985) was entitled 'How the daily lie gave way to a lonely life of truth'. A housewife and mother who had recently come out revealed 'I am very unsatisfied with the terrible loneliness lesbians suffer and with the difficulties women have living together . . . Relationships don't last because being a lesbian is so insecure, so difficult. With other lesbians there is always the danger of game-playing, of trying out someone else for the night.' Although some recognition in the article is given to the fact that the oppression faced by lesbians is the cause of the problems they encounter, rather than the lesbianism itself, it is very far from presenting lesbianism as a positive alternative to heterosexuality (where, incidentally, people have also been known to play games and try out partners for the night). Not only is there no indication given in the article that many lesbians live happy and fulfilled lives and have long-lasting successful relationships, but also there was no alternative view given in a later article. The distorted view of what it's like to be a lesbian was thus further perpetuated, despite protests from readers in the following week's letters column.

In our newly 'liberated' times, it is sometimes assumed conversely, that we no longer have anything to complain about, and that we are our own worst enemies. The *Birmingham Post* (9 May 1985) tells us that: 'While a handful of gays are assertive, imbued with a new-found confidence, their suspicions of the non-gay world are so deep that they themselves are guilty of discrimination – against the rest of us. So they live in an unaired little sub-culture that contains its own vocabulary and meeting-places.'

So we are back where we came in – it's our fault after all! In fact most lesbians and gay men live most of their lives in the mainstream; the demand for lesbian and gay spaces is a reflection of how unacceptable it still is to be lesbian or gay in that mainstream. If the gay 'sub-culture' is 'unaired', that is due entirely to the refusal of the media to concern itself in any serious or positive way with homosexuality and what it has to offer. And pieces of journalism like this do nothing to alleviate the suspicions about the 'straight' media!

It is difficult to believe, when considering the media of the 1980s, that anything much has changed for lesbians and gay men. However, as lesbians and gay men, we know that things *have* changed for us; we have managed in good measure to resist the homophobic conditioning of the 'straight' media, and without its assistance we have managed to create a movement where we can take pride in ourselves, our achievements and our worth. We already have a public platform, albeit limited, for our ideas and news in various 'alternative' publications. Although the media may increasingly be used to vilify us and to set the forces of reaction against us, our movement will historically prove to be of great significance in the future liberation of the world.

Julienne Dickey

Lesbians in film

The issue of the representation of lesbians in film is inseparable from that of women in film. Lesbianism is about love and sex – but it is also about women making alliances with one another, being independent from men. Clearly this subverts the myth that women need men, physically or emotionally, which is fundamental to men's power in patriarchal societies. In terms of the politics of the media the treatment of lesbians in film is of central importance to women in general.

First it is important to note that the number of films, excluding pornography, in which lesbians appear is relatively small. Until 1961 the US Production Code specifically forbade representations of lesbianism or homosexuality. This meant that Hollywood rewrote original scripts and even history to ensure the exclusion of lesbian material: for example, the 1950 *We Three* heterosexual version of Lillian Hellman's play *The Children's Hour* (made with its original storyline in1961 as *The Loudest Whisper*); or Garbo's portrayal of a heterosexual romance to explain her abdication as queen of Sweden in *Queen Christina*. The British Censorship Board still considered lesbianism and homosexuality (along with exploitative sex and 'unusual sex positions') as taboo images until the early 1960s.

The dropping of the US Production Code and the publication of the Kinsey Report resulted, within a decade, in a rash of lesbian films between 1967 and 1970. Sometimes this had the effect of making a covert lesbian theme explicit (for example, *The Fox*, based on a D.H. Lawrence novella). In general these films came straight out of a limited and limiting view of lesbians – with a few notable exceptions (*Mädchen in Uniform*, *Olivia*). The images contained in them are such that they defuse the threat of lesbianism to men and make it unattractive to women.

Sometimes the woman portrayed is not 'really' a lesbian, but a poor misguided soul, the victim of a 'real' lesbian. The 'real' lesbian stereotypes are: 'butch' women who cross-dress or who are unfeminine in behaviour and appearance (invariably they are domineering, short-haired and often working-class); sophisticated older women who are rich, successful and predatory; or 'neurotic' women who are often femme or closet lesbians.

The Killing of Sister George, written by one man and directed by another in 1968, has all three stereotypes as separate characters, but often various aspects are combined. Butch and sophisticated lesbians have been extensively used as 'castrating bitches' whose threat is defused by the hero. They are often associated with hated politics (fascism in *Rome Open City* and communism in *From Russia with Love*) and are seen as grasping for male power and as being in power relationships with one another.

Another way in which the threat of lesbianism is defused is through pornographic representation (where most film lesbians are to be found). This is not just because women's role in films is to provide sex interest and lesbianism is by definition about sex – but because only by watching can men have any access to lesbianism and feel some control over something that excludes them. Lesbianism may be just a phase, another option on the sexual market (e.g. *Emmanuelle*). Most commonly the hero takes away one (or both) of the women, who was 'not really a lesbian, all she needed . . . ' This theme is also used in commercial feature films, for example, *The Fox*, and *The Bitter Tears of Petra von Kant*. Sometimes hints of lesbianism have been used to charge the sexual charisma of the heroine; this happened in many forties films, notably with Dietrich in *Morocco*.

Getting involved with a man may seem like a bad end, but it is only one among many. Lesbians are also likely to kill themselves (*The Loudest Whisper*); be murdered – often by their lovers (*Les Biches*, *The Hunger*); go mad (*Symptoms*); or find themselves alone with their life in ruins (*The Killing of Sister George*). None of this is particularly encouraging except to the men who would rather see lesbians come to a sticky end.

Until the increasing feminist demands of the seventies, women's friendships fared little better than lesbianism in films. The general rule was that women were rivals for men, and natural enemies, even when they were mother and daughter. A good relationship between women was kept peripheral to the plot. There were only a few notable exceptions to this, for example *Adam's Rib* and *Stella Dallas*.

In the seventies a dozen or so feature-length mainstream films about women's friendships appeared (*Julia*, *The Turning Point*, *The Girlfriends*). This period also saw the beginning of low-budget experimental and documentary films being made by lesbians, aimed at changing conventional received ignorance and exploring film for their own ends. Like all films in the independent sector they get relatively limited distribution and audiences, but more are being made every year. Some, such as Jan Oxenburg's brilliant skits on stereotyping (*Home Movie* and *Comedy in Six Unnatural Acts*), provide entertainment and insight which has not been approached in mainstream cinema.

With the eighties there has been another mini-rash of lesbian films (*Personal Best*, *Another Way*, *Lianna*, *Coup de Foudre/At First Sight*). Women distributors have also reissued uncut versions of the classic lesbian films *Mädchen in Uniform* (1931, Leontine Sagan) and *Olivia* (1951, Jacqueline Audrey) – both set in girls' boarding-schools and exploring the issues of love and power between adolescents and teachers in a strikingly warm and unexploitative way.

In the new commercial films, many of the stereotypes still apply. Although there are some very striking signs of change in image and narrative, the only truly unstereotyped couple is in *At First Sight*, which also manages to be deeply erotic without a single sex scene – to a degree comparable only to *Mädchen in Uniform*. This appears to be a quality that only women film-makers can achieve: all the other recent films were made by men and include the obligatory sex scenes which to a greater or lesser extent have a soft porn content. By far the worst offender is *Personal Best* with its heaving breast and thigh sequences, a film in which the heroine ends up in a safe heterosexual relationship.

By contrast *Lianna* maintains her new sexual identity despite the break-up of her first lesbian affair. But there are similarities to *Personal Best* in the stereotyped more 'feminine' heroine with an older experienced lover successful in a male field (and with short hair – a sure sign!). As with Lianna, Livia in *Another Way* is represented as the object of desire and would more conveniently fit into the 'not-really-a-lesbian' category – but she rejects her husband for her lover in the face of total illegality. This radical disturbing of the conventional narrative delights those of us who wish for change.

Unstereotyped lesbians are sneaking into other feature films too. The main theme of *Silkwood* is a woman's fight with the nuclear industry, but it neither ignores nor glosses over the lesbian issue. Karen's flatmate and her beautician friend both tacitly and openly question the audience's assumptions through confrontations with Karen's boyfriend who is disturbed by their presence – which Karen is not. Because such specific meanings have been assigned to a lesbian presence in a film regarding the proper place and sexuality of women, other meanings and incidental inclusion become radical. In *Born in Flames*, Adele's lesbianism is relevant only because the CIA is looking for something to pin on her. It shows their cynical prurience.

In *The Second Awakening of Krista Klages* lesbianism is the excuse to move Krista and her friend on from the Portuguese communal farm where she had found refuge. To an audience unaware that their relationship was sexual this comes as a complete surprise. In all of Margarethe von Trotta's films, this is the only reference to a specifically lesbian relationship. She has stated that her interest is in the range of emotions between women, so to represent sexual relations would be distracting. Her tremendous contribution to a new women's cinema is to reverse the accepted order so that deep, complex and loving relationships between her heroines are central, while the men in their lives, loved or not, remain peripheral even when they attempt to intervene and control. This critical point of view is at its sharpest in *Friends and Lovers* where Franz's attempts to 'help' his wife through a longstanding mental crisis are revealed as self-gratification in maintaining her as dependent with no place of her own in the world.

All this reflects a dramatic change: men's attitudes and behaviour are finally under fire. Women's friendships, lesbian and straight, are affirmed. *Lianna*'s happy ending is the reopening of communication with her best friend who had been frightened away by her coming out. *Personal Best*'s only real claim to progress is the friendship that the ex-lovers, running competitors, achieve in the end.

Along with the changes brought about by women choosing each other in the face of opposition, has come a change in men's heroic position. Moral disapproval and judgements about mental health are shown up for the oppressive and ignorant attitudes they are (note, for example, Eva being questioned by a police officer who really only wants to know 'how they do it' in *Another Way*). Men are generally no longer shown as powerful; they range from somewhat ridiculous and uncomprehending to destructive and violent. On learning about their wives' lesbianism the husbands' reactions are of a piece: Livia's shoots her at point-blank range in the neck (*Another Way*); Lianna's hits her, throws her out and tries to poison her children's feelings about her; and Lena's destroys her clothes shop (*At First Sight*). Though there may be marginal sympathy for Lena's husband, it is made clear that the other two men would have accepted a heterosexual affair and that their violence is as much punitive as jealous – and justified as such.

However this violence is presented as both unacceptable and survivable – unlike that in previous lesbian films. These developments in plot and characterisation make clear the forces which keep women 'in their place': the threat of individual violence together with the social pressures of heterosexism, moral and medical judgements, ignorance and prurience. These films are giving aspects of lesbian oppression an airing they have not previously had in the mass media, criticising rather than reinforcing them. It is a new kind of coming out, one which clearly shows how women, lesbian and heterosexual, are connected and separated. Friendship and love are possible, but the greater the love the bigger the fight.

Caroline Sheldon

Note

Many 'alternative' lesbian films, including those mentioned, are distributed by Circles (113 Roman Rd, London E2) and Cinema of Women (27 Clerkenwell Close, London EC1).

Editors' note:

Since this article was written two other mainstream films have appeared based on books by lesbians. The first, *Desert Hearts*, was made by lesbian film-maker Donna Dietch from the book *Desert of the Heart* by Jane Rule. The film received a certain amount of critical acclaim but disappointed those familiar with the book. Dietch opted for transforming the relationship between the two women into a conventional romance, consummated by a stereotypical seduction scene where one of the women refuses to take no for an answer: a scene which would be totally unacceptable to feminists had it occurred in a heterosexual relationship. The film, by being set in the largely pre-women's-movement 1950s, was able to ignore lesbian feminist ethics.

Alice Walker's *The Color Purple* achieved international renown through being turned into a film by Stephen Spielberg. Alice Walker herself approved the script, despite the down-playing of the central lesbian relationship between Shug and Celie, on the grounds that it would alienate large sections of the potential audience. One can only speculate whether, given the enormous popularity of the film, greater recognition of the lesbian element would have damaged it, and it is a great pity that we should have been denied one of the most beautiful portrayals of a lesbian relationship in literature. However, the relationship between Shug and Celie *was* portrayed in a strongly positive way, and the film has done much to affirm the value of women's friendships.

In addition, in 1986 British television's Channel 4 broadcast a series of lesbian and gay films, which achieved very good viewing figures for the 'Eleventh Hour' slot. One of them, *November Moon*, a lesbian romance set in German-occupied France, was watched by one and a half million viewers, one of the programme's best figures ever. (This film will be on general release in 1987.) However, Caroline Sheldon's film *17 Rooms: what lesbians do in bed* – a light-hearted satire on voyeurism and prurience – was twice withdrawn from the series 'on technical grounds'.

6
Violence

Introduction

Those people who benefit from violence in the media are the few who make money from it; the rest of us are the losers. Men lose out because media violence reinforces the way in which our society brutalises boys and men in order to make them conform to the acceptable image of maleness. And women lose out because we are repeatedly the victims of media violence. The process of victimisation reduces women to the status of objects: to acknowledge our human strengths and qualities would disrupt the stereotype of female weakness and vulnerability on which the 'victim' image is built. The exception to this is the stereotyped woman who becomes a victim because 'she asks for it'. These images are explored in the following pages.

It has become commonplace to see a woman mistreated in a magazine, TV programme or film. Readers and viewers have become so accustomed to seeing violence against women that magazines imagery can now feature women looking injured and bruised under the guise of fashion, record sleeves can include bound or gagged women as part of their designs, and advertising imagery can play on innuendoes of pain to sell more products.

Selling products, be they books, albums or household items, by attacking and insulting women is exploitative and also dangerous, because it condones violent behaviour against women. This is linked to what is done to condition boys. Women are allowed access to, and expression of, the feelings of vulnerability and dependence from which men are debarred. It is the inability of the male in western society to cope with this dependent, vulnerable side of his character which gives rise to the violent attitude towards women, all too visible in the media. Women are punished for being the gender of motherhood, but we are also penalised for our independence. The 1980s have seen a media backlash against feminism. Crueller, more punitive images are now being used – to teach us a lesson?

The restriction of violence in the media has been taken up by several right-wing personalities, among them Mary Whitehouse, and Winston Churchill, MP, who has brought the issue into Parliament. It has yet to be taken really seriously by the left; this despite continuing lobbying by feminists, notably WAVAW (Women Against Violence Against Women), to get it adopted as a campaigning issue. But so far, the right has claimed it as their own political initiative, and the left has done little but leave the door wide open.

Violence against women

The portrayal of violence against women in any of the media – advertising, films, newspaper reporting of sexual offences – is one of the most insidious as well as one of the most effective ways of showing where power lies in our society. It lies in the hands of the image-makers: men. To accept the media-makers' excuse that 'we are not creating reality, we are only reflecting it' is to accept that violence against women is a fundamental part of the relationship between the sexes (thus deserving accurate 'reflection'), rather than a symptom of the way men and women are taught to view each other.

Little boys are still being taught 'polite' behaviour towards little girls – not to hit them, kick them, punch them (behaviour which is condoned as 'a real boy's' way of dealing with his male friends or foes). At the same time they are learning through comics, cartoons and television programmes that kicking the stuffing out of the 'weaker' members of society is the way to get on, the way to win. In our competitive, male-defined society, where men make the films, write the dictionaries, run the newspapers, this is seen as the acceptable way to behave. While there is such a direct contradiction in early male upbringing, no little boys will last long if they persist in being gentle, non-aggressive, friendly and generally 'unmanly' in the way they relate to other boys and, more importantly, to girls.

There is still no greater insult to inflict on a small boy than to accuse him of behaving 'like a girl'. Where does it start?

Watching violent cartoons disguised as 'fun' and 'humour' inures children to the concepts they illustrate – that violence, killing or obliterating your enemies or people who annoy you, is an acceptable way to behave, and a means of coming out on top. Constant reference to beating, knocking about, raping or generally rough-handling women sanctions the idea that women are to be, even have to be (and what is more, like to be) treated in this way. Cartoons of the 'Tom and Jerry', 'Mickey Mouse' or 'Donald Duck' era appear to be aimed at children generally rather than either sex particularly. But take a closer look at the principal characters: almost without exception they are male and active. They may run the entire gamut of the animal world, but the sex remains the same. Female characters are restricted to two stereotypes. They are either brainless but decorative like Minnie Mouse, Penelope Pitstop and Daisy Duck, or pushy and nagging like the 'matriarch' – the female head of the house who beats Tom over the head with a broom whenever she gets the chance.

Cartoons can therefore be condemned on two counts: first there are almost no positive female characters for girls to identify with, and secondly, all the active characters are male, leaping about, running, jumping, zapping anyone who gets in their way (ever seen Minnie Mouse zap anyone? – her eyelashes would probably trip her up).

So little girls learn by the age of early-morning cartoon watching a number of hard facts to set them on the road to childhood (never mind adulthood). They learn that little boys do not like them very much, and they learn that most get-up-and-go characters are male – including the mice! They also learn that any female characters to be found are grown-ups and therefore boring, or are tiresomely, inactive, heavy on the lipstick, long on the eyelashes, high on heels and low on energy. And if the cartoons have advanced to space-age scenarios, the females are tight of costume and large of bosom, but still not very bright and/or active. The one exception is witches, who get about quite a lot, but they of course are wicked – and ugly.

Thus do we all have our roles set – who does what, and who does not: to whom comes later.

One very commonplace medium for low-key violence against women is the male stand-up comic: the laugh-a-line comedian. He is to be found everywhere: radio, television (count how many shows per week have one, and consider how many people are watching), the equivalent in strip-cartoons in magazines and newspapers, live shows such as cabaret, 'working-men's' clubs and so on. Though he does not often overtly encourage men to hit their wives, just listen to the many other ways in which he suggests violence against women: car 'accidents', connivance in male doctors' assaults on female patients, how to get rid of mother-in-law or wife in many and various ways. The list is endless. We have only to ask how funny such jokes would be if the sexes were reversed to see how pervasive is this so-called humour in condoning male attitudes towards violence against women. That women are obliged to laugh at all at jokes which treat violence by men towards women so lightly distinguishes those who draw up the rules, and those who have little choice but to follow them.

Even that most august publication, the *Oxford English Dictionary*, offers further proof of the way in which society condones violence against women. Its definition of the verb 'to beat' is truly unbelievable (or is it?) in these supposedly enlightened days: 'to beat' – 'to strike repeatedly, as in beat one's wife'. Not only does this show the presumed sex of the reader (for at least one half of the population does not have a wife), but it also clearly demonstrates that beating 'one's' woman is an acceptable way for men to behave. Would it not otherwise have been struck from the 'thinking man's bible'?

There is a theory much discussed amongst women which finds a connection between the way in which physical violence against women is depicted in films, and women's current status in western society: the medium of film as social commentary or social control over women's lives. This theory can be demonstrated by looking at two periods in recent history: the immediate post-Second World War years and the re-emergence of the women's liberation movement in the late sixties and early seventies.

During the Second World War women emerged as a strong workforce, having to do the men's jobs in order to keep the country functioning while they were away at war. Women drove trains, worked at engineering, in munitions factories, on the land and so on. They were lifted out of the realm of non-rewarded, non-waged work (housework and childcare) and into the realm of valued, paid work, with promotion, responsibility and prestige. And they rather enjoyed it! As a result they experienced a rise in self-worth and self-esteem. In order to combat this female 'uppityness', the films of the day (the late 1940s) began to depict virtually the first on-screen violence by men against women. Not actual rape of course, since such an act would never have been permitted on the screen in those days. But enough rough-housing – slapping around the face, punching and kicking – to show who was boss. And the recipients, of course, invariably 'deserved' it.

Likewise with the upsurge of the contemporary women's liberation movement in the 1960s and 1970s – women getting 'uppity' again – films of the period responded in a similar fashion, becoming more blatantly violent as time went on. By the mid-1970s it seemed that no film worth its salt (i.e. male-critic acclaimed) was without its fairly explicit rape scene. However, by this time the woman was not only 'deserving' it, but in due deference to the so-called permissive sixties, was actually 'enjoying' it.

If this was the decade when violence in films was considered to have developed, violence in its parasite industry, advertising, certainly did so. To show explicitly violent films was not enough: the films had to be advertised everywhere advertising was to be found – television, billboards, posters, newspapers and magazines. Soon it became the thing among advertisers to try to outdo each other with the most violent posters containing or suggesting violent scenes which often did not appear in the films themselves. The big sell was the advertising – the film itself was often a 'letdown' (what, no woman being raped then having her legs sawn off?).

Again, we must ask who these films are made for?

The same pattern emerges in another recent development – record album covers. The imagery on them went from the supposed male fantasy of the good old sixties – 'tits and bums' – to much more explicit and implicit violence against women in the early 1970s. By this time, however, women had become conscious of what was happening. Complaints flooded in to the makers of the more offensive covers, and some of them were withdrawn from the market. But, as with the makers of film posters, the makers of record covers produced the usual excuse: 'It's not us, it's the advertisers/publicity people/client. *We* wouldn't dream of using such sexist imagery, but unfortunately we have no control . . . '

And what about advertising in general?

Anyone familiar with the advertising industry will verify that advertising these days is Big Business. It is a highly competitive industry where new advertising campaign details are guarded more closely it seems than military secrets. It is much sought-after as an 'artistic' and highly lucrative job. Budgets are phenomenal: Terrys' (of chocolate orange fame) 'Raiders of the Lost Ark' advertising account is worth about £2 million; Reckitt & Colman's pharmaceutical division alone earmarked £4 million in one year, 1985, for their new campaigns; Nike sportswear, on the other hand, was spending 'only around £400,000', according to the London *Evening Standard* in March 1985.

If advertisers are willing to spend so much money, they must believe that advertisements exert a very considerable amount of influence over public images, attitudes and opinions. In effect, they are a kind of large-scale brainwashing. The theory behind flooding the public market – by whichever medium – with the brand name of a particular product is that the name will eventually work its way into the public subconscious as being inevitably linked with the product. A particularly good example of how successful this can be is the vacuum-cleaner: not only is 'Hoover' the best-known brand, Hoover *is* vacuum cleaners. We buy 'a hoover'; we 'hoover' the carpet. How proud the original advertising agency must be to have achieved what is surely the advertiser's dream: literally to make their client's brandname a household word!

It is then a logical extension to apply this maxim of 'if they see or hear it often enough, they'll buy it' to the gratuitous use of women's bodies (or parts of them) in advertising of any kind, be it for a film, car, piece of industrial equipment or sanitary towels. If we are constantly surrounded by larger-than-life billboard posters depicting women as purely decorative sexual objects, will this not eventually be absorbed – even unconsciously – into most people's minds as an accurate reflection of the state of things? That is, women are 'at best' decorative. They support the central image – a man. They are draped over his car, or purr against his all-wool suit, the dewy-eyed recipient of his box of chocolates. And to reiterate a point often made by women fighting sexism in advertising, all the media are controlled by men. If further proof of men's self-indulgence and urge to self-gratification is needed, we have nude calendars, pornography and photography/pornography as 'art' to illustrate the point.

To cope with all the competition, advertisements are becoming much more subtle in their presentation. They now rely more on wit – word-play – and often on heavily symbolic images in their visual displays. Given that the unnecessary use of women's bodies in advertising is already so common, it is a short step to slipping in some (even implied) violence. For example the front cover of a 'Warehouse' catalogue for women's clothes showed a young, attractive woman in bondage. This insidious form of anti-woman propaganda links with the theory on the presentation of women in films – women need to be taken down a peg or two. Never before have advertisements been so blatantly male-fantastic in their connections between sex (underwear advertisements) and violence (gun-toting woman with fire in her eye – remember the 'Lovable' bra advertisements?). And, it may be argued, never have women needed so much putting down. These days they object to anything. They object to advertisements showing a 'nice bit of leg', to 'girlie' calendars in work-places, to being chatted up in the office . . . they really are – dare it be said – asking for it!

And so women are getting it; in films, videos and in advertisements. It is probable that a visit to any video shop would unearth more undisguised violence against women in the form of 'entertainment' than at any other time.

One of the most insidious examples of the objectionable way in which women are treated by the media is in newspaper reporting of sexual offences. Under the guise of responsible 'news' reporting, showing righteous concern for the woman and a proper censure of the attackers, newspapers (that is, the men who own and run them) are able to carry off the most devious anti-woman propaganda of all.

Titilating reporting of sexual offences has been around as long as newspapers have. Sex, especially sexual assault, has always been assumed to be a successful newspaper seller. Witness how often a headline reporting a rape appears in the advertising frame of a news stand, yet is nowhere near front page importance in the newspaper. What else motivates the media-makers but profit? The reader (as with the dictionary) is still assumed to be male; the media-makers are male; therefore it follows that most of the contents are aimed at male audiences. (If this were not the case, why the apparent need for a 'women's' page?) Reporting of rape and sexual assault is just another way in which men deliver ready-made thrills under the guise of responsible, professional, ethical reporting.

The two main ingredients in such reporting of crimes against women are already there: sex and violence. Then there are photographs of the 'victim' (a word condemned by many rape crisis centres as pernicious because it traps women in the role of the 'eternal victim'). Identikit pictures of the assailants depict them as monsters with little resemblance to human beings. There are even the contrived photographs, the 'simulations', showing for example a dark alley with anonymous female and male figures posing. Most deplorable of all is the language, unique to this kind of reportage. Assailants are always 'sex fiends', 'monsters', 'crazed maniacs', that is, not ordinary men (like the reporters who produce such garbage. Women are invariably 'girls' until well into their thirties; 'attractive', 'blonde/brunette/redhead', 'blue-eyed', 'vivacious' (for this read 'provocative'), 'mother-of-four' and so on. Men are rarely described in terms of their appearance, and never as 'father-of-four', unless they have recently lost their jobs. Near or opposite the article there is often a photograph of a semi-naked woman or one of a clothed, smiling, young attractive woman. Photographs of actresses are often used. Any intended connection between photograph and article is always hotly denied by the editors, though the intention is clear. By association the message is 'on the one hand you (women) flaunt yourselves like this (the photograph), and then you have the nerve to be surprised or indignant when this (the article) happens'.

Reporting of these crimes in this way helps to perpetuate many dangerous myths:

● that it is only young, pretty women who are raped or assaulted;[2]

● that it is always strangers who rape;[3]

● that men who rape are abnormal;[4]

● that men cannot control their sexual urges, and will rape when provoked;

● that women need protecting by some men (the goodies) from other men (the baddies, all of whom look like those identikit pictures, and are thus easily recognised);

● that it is therefore up to women to limit their lives to 'non-dangerous' or unprovocative behaviour (as defined by men) and that if they do not, they ask for and deserve to be raped.

Over and over comes the message: men can't help it, and even if they could, women deserve it anyway. Apart from murder, rape is the ultimate act of social control of women by men ('See what we can do to you if you don't behave') and the constant reportage of it in all types of newspapers, every day, never lets us forget. To keep women frightened makes us more controllable. Even the 'quality' papers get in on the act, though more subtly. By producing verbatim accounts of cross-examinations in court cases, they manage to include all the sordid details, often straight from the woman's mouth. There is not even the need to embroider in order to provide the necessary titillation.

So we see the 'creeping effect' of the way in which we are all brought up. What begins in 'innocent' childhood ends with violence against women receiving society's sanction through the media. Such a vicious end-product of the presentation of images of women by men cannot be permitted to continue. Women must and will have the right to self-respect and the respect of all members of society.

Jennifer Peck

Notes

1 For further discussion, see *Sexual Violence* by London Rape Crisis Centre, The Women's Press, 1984.
2 *London Rape Crisis Centre Annual Report*, 1978, found women of all ages (6 months to 90 years old).
3 *ibid;* found 60 per cent of men who are convicted of rape are friends or acquaintances of the women.
4 *Criminal Statistics for England and Wales 1976*, states that less than 2 per cent of men convicted of rape are referred for psychiatric treatment.

Pacific Comics – neither pacific nor comic

In the United States in the fifties, as everyone knows, a general climate of repression prevailed. Sex and violence in comics did not escape the view of a paranoid state, especially following the publication of a book called *The Seduction of the Innocents* by Frederick Werthman, which maintained that comics caused a whole range of undesirable behaviour. Numerous prosecutions followed, which almost ruined one of the two comic giants, EC Comics.

As a result the comics industry drew up the Accepted Comics Code, a voluntary code of practice which sought to avoid future crackdowns. Until recently comics generally adhered to this code, which restricted the graphic depiction of sex and violence, and certain forms of 'immorality'.

In the last few years, however, following the emergence of 'underground' comics in the sixties, new publishing companies have been ignoring this (admittedly outdated) code. In this new brand of comic, anything goes.

One of these new US companies was Pacific Comics.* Their comics range from science fiction through cosmic mini-epics to grisly horror stories and thrillers. Artwork is sometimes fairly crude, but more often executed with talent. Dialogue and storyline are in the traditional mould, but with flashes of wit and originality. They aim at an adult male audience – in fact, some have 'For Mature Readers' on the front cover. But what supposedly appeals to 'mature' male minds is disturbing, to say the least.

The depiction of the female characters in these comics has much in common with the depiction of women in the media generally, and also in pornography. Pornography is not fundamentally about sex but about power; 'erotica' on the other hand depicts sexual activity between equals. None of the female characters represents 'real' women, in either body or personality; rather, together they represent a male fantasy based on an unequal power relationship. In order for power to be perpetuated to the extent that it is, women must be dehumanised, they must be objectified in terms of the male fantasy so that they can be manipulated.

---

* The company has subsequently gone bankrupt and ceased trading, but most of its titles have been taken over by other publishers.

It is also necessary that women be made to appear vulnerable so that ultimately they can be dominated. This is done by posing them in certain ways, by attiring them in scanty and revealing clothing – not just for titillation (because cartoon women are parodies of women's bodies), but because this makes them more vulnerable. Women appear in these scanty clothes and unsturdy postures in contrast to fully and sensibly clad men with their feet firmly on the ground. (The fashion world also does this to emphasise an empowering 'masculinity' and a disempowering 'femininity'). Women are constantly shown in need of protection and rescue, and are often behind or looking up to the men.

Even if a woman appears to be dominating in the first place (for example the Hill Hag (*Edge of Chaos*), the revealing clothing still suggests availability and their ultimate defeat is more titillating. For it is the power relationship which provides titillation, not the female body itself. Take away the elements of power and the attributes that the male fantasy has put upon women, and a female body is simply a female body. It is often said that graphic depictions of sex are somehow 'liberating', but when they embody sexist attitudes and the disempowering of women, this is the *opposite* of liberation. They merely make the sexist distortions of our world more graphically visible.

The women in the Pacific Comics are not only depicted as sexually available or vulnerable, they are also represented as a source of evil (a common theme in our culture). This is most clearly shown in the story 'Christmas Carol' (*Demon Dreams* No.1) where a woman gives birth to a huge litter of demons. Fear of women and women's power is of course the other side of male power over women – a fear which provides a keen edge to titillation, and a justification for keeping women down.

Keeping women down often means subjecting them to violence. The violence perpetrated against women in these comics is set in a context of all-pervasive, mindless, gratuitous and graphic violence against everyone. But men suffering violence are not depicted as inherently 'victim-like' in the same way as the women are (except the black man who is killed and eaten in the disgustingly racist story in *Twisted Tales*), nor are they sexually objectified – the violence is not eroticised. Examples of this violence against women include: women being struck for being disobedient to the male will (*Elric* No. 1 and *Edge of Chaos* No. 2); female bodies, some with bits chopped off, hanging in a freezer awaiting consumption (*Alien Worlds* No. 2); women murdered one after the other in a 'comic-horror' (!) story (*Demon Dreams* No.1); a naked woman embracing a giant thorny rose stem (*Ravens and Rainbows* No.1) – also a common image in pornographic works; a woman being constantly pursued and threatened by an unknown male enemy (*Somerset Holmes*).

It is sometimes said of such stories, 'It's just a fantasy, it's harmless.' But in real life *every day* women are subjected to oppression, to rape, to murder, to humiliation and degradation, to dispossession from the world's wealth, decision-making and culture on the basis of their 'inferiority' and 'weakness'. These are facts, not fantasy. Sex and violence in comics or other media are not the root cause of 'unhealthy attitudes towards women' (as Mary Whitehouse might put it) or sexual abuse or violence – these things would not disappear if comics were abolished – but they do reflect and reinforce these attitudes. They contribute to the prevailing climate of acceptance of the mistreatment of women, they help provide a rationale for it, they make it seem somehow 'natural'.

It might be worth pointing out here where a 'Mary Whitehouse' position differs from a feminist one. The moral 'majority' suppose that if all 'sex, violence and immorality' were removed from the media and we returned to good clean Victorian 'family' virtues, the world would once again be a safe and wholesome place for our children. They *are* concerned that women be treated with respect and decency – as are feminists – but they fail to understand that it is *precisely* the sexism of their rigidly fundamentalist view, a view which has prevailed in our culture for centuries, that causes the behaviour and images that they deplore. It is pointless trying to eradicate the effects of sexism if you don't eliminate sexism itself.

The violence in Pacific (and other) comics is a graphic reflection of the way the male mind has been brutalised. The brutal sexist conditioning undergone by boys leads to a separation of men from much of themselves, and from other men; to a glorification of only one aspect of their masculinity, unbalanced by other (gentle and nurturing) aspects; and to the domination of women and 'weaker' men. These imbalances within men's psyches, and between men and women, are ultimately annihilating. The habit of domination that sexism (and all other oppressions) bestows is the root cause of aggression, war, and the desire to conquer not only our planet and all its resources, but also other parts of the universe. The nature of the future, and of future developments in space as depicted in the science fiction comics, represent a vision of the future which is the logical outcome of the male world-view of the present.

It is just as well women know that this is *not* the way *we* intend the future to be!

Julienne Dickey

7
Women in the Public Eye

Introduction

'The exception that proves the rule' is still very much the attitude of the UK media to women in the public eye. Whether we are active in politics, sport, public service or entertainment, as women we are ill served by our media.

Our achievements are trivialised or ignored – 'PM puts husband second'[1] ran a headline on Norway's Prime Minister. 'Into orbit – with no lipstick'[2] made the front page when Sally Ride became the first western woman in space. 'Avon calling'[3] described a women's tennis final (for the Avon trophy). When a national supermarket chain appointed its second-ever woman to the board (in a non-executive capacity), the press reacted as though it had appointed a weird new category of being. And saw fit to note that the previous woman director had retired in 1982. When did we ever hear of a previous male director retiring?

It is important that we read about or see women in public life. Younger women need a wider choice of role-models when thinking about jobs or careers or both, and we all need to know where progress is being made, barriers broken down. We also need to be able to monitor that progress to make sure that it isn't mere tokenism. But it is also important for us to be aware of the ways in which women in public life are presented to us by the media. Why are these 'extraordinary' women given a packaged personality? What effect does that have on the rest of us? Why should it always be so astonishing when a woman reaches the top – or even gets half-way – or even redefines 'the top'? If women are always shown as exceptional or peculiar when we achieve anything, we will limit our own horizons by thinking that we can never make it ourselves – we who are 'ordinary women'.

These articles look at the ways in which women's achievements in some areas of public life have been present, and how the women themselves have been given media-packaged personalities. They raise questions about the present role and future possibilities for women in public life, and they demonstrate some of the ways in which women's choices are still limited, in spite of our living in a land of so-called equal opportunity.

We include a special case study of the way in which the media consistently derided the work of the Greater London Council's Women's Committee. The GLC was the first local authority to set up a women's committee. Its pioneering work for women in London led the way for other women's committees around the UK. Sadly, it no longer exists, but its work continues.

We also include a case study of how the media treat women who are brought to our notice because of their involvement in a particular political struggle – the 'Irish question'.

1 *Observer*, 8 February 1981.
2 Scottish *Sunday Express*, 19 June 1983.
3 *Observer*, 29 March 1981

Women, Media and Pop

All the little hoops were set up for me to jump through, and when you jump, you get a reward – an image. But it's the image *they* supply . . . you become the Perfect Couple, or the Faded English Rose, or the Wronged Woman, or the Rock And Roll Slut, or whatever. It has very little to do with real, manageable emotions.
(Marianne Faithfull talking to Cynthia Rose in *City Limits*, December 1981.)

Welcome to the wonderful world of pop, where the ladies are always young, lovely, slim and white (or at least as pale as possible). Lesbians do not exist in this world, and although the singer especially must give the impression that she is hopelessly in love, lost without love, nothing before love came, and lost when it is gone, although we are led to believe that love is her life, she is allowed to express her own sexuality only within certain, carefully drawn limits.

In the wonderful world of pop, women do not write songs, they do not produce or engineer them, they do not play on records nor do they create their own image or begin new musical trends. They are, poor things, frequently exploited, manipulated, and theproducts of men: Important People such as producers, managers, video makers, entrepreneurs. Their role as women is to sing and look pretty, for they are capable of little else.

This is not true of course, and in the emancipated eighties few express such 'dated' ideas outright. Yet the impression still lingers and it can be conveyed in the most subtle, most apparently trivial ways. Publicity shots, posters and record sleeves rarely show the woman in action – they are usually seen posed, pretty and passive under studio lights rather than on stage, actually at work singing, playing, writing or recording. The looks come first, the music a poor second. One of Tina Turner's great strengths, and part of her appeal to women, is that she is often shown sweating and dishevelled: we see she works hard for the money, unlike cool Carmel or stylish Sade.

Attention can be drawn away from the music in endless ways. There's the radio DJ who temporarily forgets his mythical 'housewife' audience and advises listeners to buy your record because you look so gorgeous on the cover. ('You have to ignore them, they're just stupid. They don't mean any harm' – Carroll Thompson, singer.)

Or there's the journalist who criticises your single on the grounds that you're overweight/too old/dressed wrongly, or simply not his type. ('Before I was well known, people on building sites would say, "Look at the state of her, fat cow!" They don't any more because they think they recognise me, but what happens is that the so-called educated men and women of the press have taken up that role. It annoys me that it makes something I'm singing so much less worthwhile than it should be.' – Helen Terry, singer.)

A pretty woman can always be used to draw attention. The band Eighth Wonder received an extraordinary amount of coverage for their debut single due to the presence of seventeen-year-old Patsy Kensit, who starred in the Birds Eye pea advertisement as a child, and who played Crepe Suzette in *Absolute Beginners*. 'The English Madonna!' cried the headlines, accompanied by photo-

Above
Beecham used this illustration in the medical press to promote Paramax, a migraine treatment, to doctors who prescribe it. More women than men get migraine; the image is meant to reflect the age group which suffers most.

Left
Guinness are aiming for the female market by advertising in women's magazines. These two advertisements were placed in *Company*, March 1987, to dispel the notion that you have to be a tweedy rambler to drink dark beer.

WHO WILL INHERIT YOUR TIFFANY JEWELS?

Everyone can apply for a share of the shares.

Left
Two images of youth from Tiffany and *Mizz*: the child-woman and the tomboy, but neither image is limited by age; indeed, the young woman dreamily gazing at herself in a mirror is an image from pornography.

Above
British Gas used this advertisement at the time of their share flotation in 1986, to show that anyone – even racial stereotypes – could buy a part of the company.

Above
The right to reply. Spray graffitti has become a
feminist art, and Jill Posener has recorded examples
like this from walls, hoardings and bus shelters all
over Britain.

Left
Two images of domestic life, used by the Electricity
Council to advertise their cookers to readers of
women's magazines.

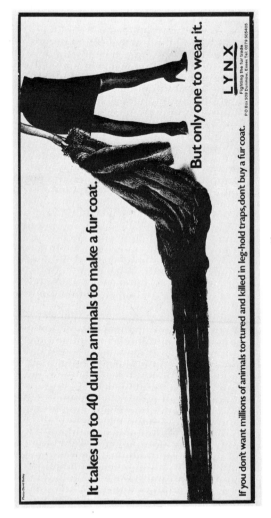

Photo: David Bailey

It takes up to 40 dumb animals to make a fur coat.

But only one to wear it.

If you don't want millions of animals tortured and killed in leg-hold traps, don't buy a fur coat.

LYNX

Fighting the fur trade
P.O Box 509 Dunmow, Essex. Tel: 0279 505405

Above

Advertisement used by Lynx in their campaign against the fur trade (previously used by Greenpeace before Lynx took over the campaign). The photograph by David Bailey has caused some controversy, because of its alleged sex stereotyping.

graphs of Peapod Patsy posing half-dressed in front of her boys, although nearly all forget to mention what one assumes most music fans wanted to know – could she sing?

Although this can be an advantage in gaining publicity, it can also leave women unsure as to whether they're invited along because of their looks or because of their abilities. Whereas most horn sections are made up of anonymous session musicians usually kept out of camera range on TV, trombonist Annie Whitehead is well used to lingering shots if she happens to be in the line-up. 'Cameramen on programmes like *The Tube* and *Top Of The Pops* should be working for the *Sun!*' she asserts. 'Which is why I prefer studio work – at least you know you've been asked because of how you sound rather than how you look.'

All too often, moralists and, unfortunately, some feminists are quick to blame the woman herself for leering press coverage, and to imply that she somehow 'asked for it' by exploiting her sexuality. Reverse the gender, however, and the absurdity is clear. Is Sting – who seems ever willing to whip off his shirt for a photo session and has a strange penchant for placing a phallic object such as a saxophone between his legs whenever possible – ever accused of 'flaunting himself'? Are Duran Duran ever called whores or accused of using their apparently endless stream of leggy model girlfriends to garner publicity? Image is undeniably important to male stars as well, but although many male musicians find their work trivialised (particularly those, like Duran Duran or A-Ha, whose music is seen as appealing to a mainly female – and therefore, it is assumed, rather gullible – audience) it is rarely because all media attention is focused on how they look.

Pressure on women performers to conform has increased in the eighties, with Fleet Street's renewed interest in the pop aristocracy. Writers such as John Blake (who began the *Sun's* 'Bizarre' column, and now collects salacious titbits for the *Daily Mirror*) scrutinise their behaviour more closely than ever before, and an exclusive on a pop star's sex life is almost as good as a Royal or a soap star. The last five years have also seen the rise of glossy magazines such as *The Face, i-D, No.1* or the world's best-selling pop paper *Smash Hits*, which tend to exclude those deemed 'unhip' or 'unattractive', while the video has become so central to commercial success that artists may be signed on the basis of looks and acting ability alone.

Although this may be manipulated by a (glamorous) few such as Annie Lennox or Grace jones, on the whole there is far less room for those who fail to conform to artificial standards, or who try to bend the rules.

This affects men too, of course, but for women those standards are so much higher, the range of acceptable images much less flexible. It has always been true that if a male star sleeps around, gets drunk, crashes his car or sinks a yacht every now and then, it may even enhance his image, but a woman involved in such activities is considered a case for pity, showing evidence of a deep psychological problem. In eighties pop, very little is uncontrived, but women especially have to think carefully about how they behave, what they wear, and how this may be interpreted.

Wearing a skirt on stage rather than trousers may mean that your performance is taken less seriously; baggy clothes may start a wave of pregnancy rumours, while tight ones provoke catcalls or criticisms of the slightest 'unseemly' bulge; mini or split-side skirts may offer freedom of movement and give an impression of strength and fluidity to a live audience, but look totally different when frozen, out of context, in a reviewer's photograph.

As a result, performers can put an enormous amount of time and thought into the most trivial of details: Alannah Currie, percussionist and singer with the Thompson Twins, developed her exaggerated comic book hats and hairstyles in an attempt to attract attention away from her body and to make herself appear taller – 'People have funny ideas about small blondes'. Even so, she is rarely taken seriously, and like many women in mixed bands, finds that journalists prefer to direct questions at the male members and fail to quote her even when she *does* reply. For an all-woman band, however, it can be even more difficult.

With 'Rough Justice', Bananarama became one of the few pop groups ever to push a single which dealt with Northern Ireland into the charts, yet only one paper – *NME* – really tackled them on the subject. More usual is the reception given them on *Saturday Superstore* at the time, when they were interviewed in a set crawling with wind-up toy babies. Did they like babies? asked inane presenter Keith Chegwin, offering them one each to hold. Didn't they once share a flat? Who was the untidy one and who did the housework? Even for children's TV (which usually says more about the puerility of adults than the needs of younger viewers), this was plumbing new depths of banality.

TV, of course, is only offered in the first place to those who look 'right'. Definition of what is 'right' varies according to fashion, culture, the type of music performed. In India, the highly respected film soundtrack singer Lata Mangeshkar continues to record film and sing live well into her sixties, as does New York-based salsa star Celia Cruz, but rock and pop music especially is considered only for the young. At the grand old age of forty, soul singer Millie Jackson is often asked how much longer she can keep on ('Why, are you tired?' seems to be her stock reply). Tina Turner is tolerated, but only because she doesn't *look* any different from younger performers. She is 'fantastic – for her age', with those trademark thighs 'still in good shape'. Rock guitarist/singer Vi Subversa, however, celebrated her fiftieth birthday in 1985 and finds much of the press unwilling to cover her band Poisongirls:

> The *NME* deal with us at the end of tongs from time to time, but if you want to get into the area of *The Face* or *Smash Hits*, there's a huge resistance. 'Oh, but the kids don't want to see old women.' Which is precisely why I think we *ought* to be in there.

Weight is another crucial factor, and female stars are pounced upon at the least sign of a bulge. Chaka Khan's 'thunderthighs' were one of the running jokes of 1985, because the singer had the effrontery to wear a leotard on stage and on TV appearances: something apparently unacceptable for anyone not a perfect size 10. Similarly, Alison Moyet and Helen Terry suffered constant comparisons as they embarked on their respective solo careers simply because, in Alison's words, 'We're both fat birds from Essex.'

Attitudes appear to be changing, however. US disco duo The Weather Girls successfully exploited their size as a gimmick, asserting at the same time that large women have a sexuality and a right to pleasure too, and shouldn't have to wear 'floral tents' all the time. Helen models for Body Map; Alison's stylish Betty Jackson dresses are admired in magazines such as *Just Seventeen*; and although there is usually a touch of condescension ('fat girls can look good too!'), progress is being made.

Alison's public pregnancy – she was number one in the charts when her child was born – followed on from that of Paula Yates, who had also continued to work as presenter on *The Tube*, challenging the unstated rules about the slim, sexually available female entertainer. Pregnancy even became a tabloid fad in 1985, and both Sade and Madonna were surprised to discover from the media that they were due to become mothers.

Such constant scrutiny, coupled with the already claustrophobic, controlled world in which they work, can put stars under enormous pressure: Karen Carpenter died, aged thirty-two, of a heart attack induced by anorexia, and Lena Zavaroni also spent a time in hospital recovering from the same condition. And although the slightest hint of flab seems cause for comment, the media seem unconcerned by the painful, almost skeletal fragility of UK soul singer Haywoode or US star Whitney Houston.

For black women such as Haywoode or Whitney, however, the fight is often to be visible at all. The renewed interest in soul has recently put many black singers into the pop charts, yet black artists are still invariably given a lower promotion budget than white rock acts. A video is rarely made until the single looks sure to be a success, and journalists are told less and so write less about them.

Thus, jazz pianist/singer Nina Simone is asked by her *NME* interviewer whether she likes the Sex Pistols, but is portrayed as difficult and unfriendly when she is angry that he in turn has not heard of her close friend, the exiled South African singing star Miriam Makeba. Reviewers covering Carroll Thompson's work with pop band Floy Joy or Ranking Ann's contribution to the Scritti Politti track 'The Word Girl' expressed surprise at their professionalism, only dimly aware that in their own field of reggae, both women have two albums apiece and numerous self-penned singles to their credit.

Black women are assumed to have a looser, more animalistic sexuality than their white counterparts, a view often perpetrated by the adjectives used to describe black performers, and the images used to promote them ('Tina Turner – captured live!'). Yet sexism is also used *against* black music, with (white) writers smugly dismissing whole areas of black music on the grounds that it is 'sexist' – a liberal excuse for their own antipathy. Reggae particularly has suffered in this way from writers apparently unaware that Rastafarianism, for those women who have chosen it, can offer an essential sense of history, dignity and pride.

For those performers who *do* break through such prejudice and ignorance to success, retaining a black identity can be a struggle. For black women are expected to conform to western ideals of beauty even more than their white sisters: to be thinner, prettier, to have a pale skin, straight hair and a straight nose. Clever lighting, wigs, airbrushing and even the surgeon's scalpel are used to create a media image that tells young black women that to get ahead, become as like to white as you can.

Conventional good looks are not the key to success, however, even though they help. Talent counts a little, hard work counts even more, and it takes an awful lot of hard work to sound as effortless as Sade on record or look as blasé as Madonna on stage. Yet the media are still surprisingly quick to credit this work to men.

In the fifties, Larry Parnes changed the face of British pop by taking a stable of pretty boys with names like Tommy Hicks, Ronald Wycherley, Clive Powell and Reg Patterson and transforming them into Tommy Steele, Billy Fury, Georgie Fame and Marty Wilde. Yet no one thought of these men as puppets. Marty Wilde was never accused of being manipulated as his daughter Kim was to be later.

What this puppet theory does is to portray women who may be talented, strong-willed, intelligent and ambitious as passive: as dollies for the boys to dress up. And so Sheena Easton was manufactured before our very eyes on the TV programme *The Big Time*, but what the cameras *failed* to show was how she fought to be featured by the BBC in the first place, nor how she successfully kept her career going afterwards. Grace Jones is viewed as a product musically of her producers, and visually of her former lover Jean-Paul Goude; Debbie Harry was described as a product of boyfriend Chris Stein; Sade Adu is assumed to have been helped significantly by her journalist friend Robert Elms, etc, etc. This is rarely~ stated: rather implied, but amid such insinuations a woman's work and abilities disappear almost by sleight of hand.

Which brings us to the pop phenomenon of 1985 (*Live Aid* aside), to Madonna Louise Ciccone. This is from *The Face*, February 1985:

The story of her rise to fame has such a mechanical inevitability, you'd think it was written in Hollywood. In New York, she met a boy named Dan, who persuaded her to join his rock band and move in with him. He taught her to play guitar and write music. Then a boy named Steve, an old boyfriend from Detroit . . . inspired her to take her music in a disco direction, and to make some demo tapes. Her next boyfriend introduced her to New York's thriving 'new wave' nightclub scene. Madonna developed an interest in trendy fashion and became one of New York's 'night people'.

The sales of Madonna's two albums, the numerous singles culled from them and her record-breaking live shows have probably made her the most successful female artist of all time, and the eagerness journalists have shown to credit her success to her boyfriends has been almost as incredible as her meteoric rise to fame. The piece quoted is typical both in its inferences and its omissions. For what we are *not* told is that before she joined Dan Gilroy's band, Madonna trained as a dancer and worked in Paris as a singer/dancer in disco singer Patrick Hernandez's revue. In mentioning her writing partner Steve Bray, the writer forgets to mention that he didn't just happen to be in New York, he came to join Madonna's own band Emmy as a drummer, and that as co-writer and co-producer of her 'Into the Groove' single, he's done pretty well out of the association. Writers frequently express surprise that Ms Ciccone's ex-lovers still seem quite fond of her; what they stubbornly refuse to see is the boost she may have given *their* careers, or her own contribution to her success.

So what happens is that women are written out, their achievements credited instead to their looks/lover(s)/manager/producer/another (male) member of the band. Songs they helped write, long months of rehearsing and recording all vanish, and young women are fed the Mills and Boon formula for success: look good and get the right man. In spite of their wonderful voices, The Ronettes and Darlene Love are remembered solely as Phil Spector's pawns. Those who see instrumentalists such as Annie Whitehead as pioneers do not know about the Tracey Sisters (friends rather than relatives, who took their trombone double act around Europe in the fifties), or Ivy Benson's all-woman showband (who in fact gave

Annie, aged fourteen, her first taste of professional touring). Both have long since been written out as novelties, filed under nostalgia, and when the critics come to pick over the past, they are not included.

When the early seventies were resurrected and reclaimed, Marc Bolan, Sweet, even the ridiculous Gary Glitter were put back on plinths and lovingly restored to a position of 'influence' or at least remembered. Yet the magnificent Suzi Quatro – who played her own bass and was a leather-clad tough woman long before punk – is forgotten, occasionally referred to as a product of Mickey Most's RAK stable. Many women honestly do believe that punk was the first time women ever played in rock bands; women younger than I am, those who read *Smash Hits* and *Just Seventeen* now, perhaps already see Siouxsie as an old hippy singer fronting yet another male band and don't know that Poly Styrene, Patti Smith, Pauline Murray, Gaye Advert or The Slits were even there at all.

It is too easy, however, to see conspiracy theories in all this. It is, in a way, inevitable that men should identify most strongly with the men they see on stage, and recall their male heroes more strongly when writing about the past. What is encouraging is the number of female writers now making their own museums, keeping their own heroines alive. The music press puts a premium on youth in its writers, and many of those working there now – women *and* men – grew up with slightly different attitudes to those Real Men who wrote about booze and birds in the early seventies. A 'lady writer' is no longer considered a freak or a groupie by another name, and she may even be given support – as I have – and stimulus from her male colleagues. Ironically, just as the influence of the traditional rock press has begun to wane, it has finally begun to take women seriously. When *NME* prepared their memories of punk ten years on, they automatically commissioned a piece on the women involved. *No. 1* can interview Suggs of Madness on his views about feminism and sexism for their 1986 Valentine issue without looking at all odd, and when Feargal Sharkey appears on TV with two female drummers, it excites little or no comment. Even the trade press has largely stopped draping bikini-clad women over the guitars and amplifiers, because it simply doesn't help sell them any more.

There are many signs of hope, much to encourage women to work both in the music industry and the media which services it. What we must fight for, however, is a time when terms such as 'woman producer' or 'girl drummer' will sound archaic, when 'Women in . . . ' articles will no longer be necessary, and women won't be novel, special or exceptional at all. They'll just be *there*.

Sheryl Garratt, January 1986

Greenham and the Media

Press Statement
Women are here today to express their objection to the sexism, racism and war-mongering in the press, including the gross misrepresentation of the women's peace camp.
We accuse the press of creating a climate of distrust and prejudice against women working for peace. Our voices are silenced and facts are distorted in ways which incite more violence and bigotry against us. We demand fair and honest reporting for all women, including peace workers and victims of male violence.

This statement was handed in to all the newspapers, in a demonstration in Fleet Street in September 1983. It was produced in response to an avalanche of slanderous articles in the popular press which seemed to reach a peak at the end of that summer.
It started on 14 December 1982: 'Pigs jibe at police after gays hit nukes demo' (*Sun*). This inspiring headline, containing all the key words to instil fear and loathing in respectable citizens, marked a significant change in the press coverage of Greenham. Only the previous day the same paper had described 30,000 women surrounding the base as 'peaceful' and 'jubilant', and the *Star*, somewhat patronisingly, remarked on ' . . . ordinary suburban housewives clutching little children'. When it became obvious that so many women were prepared to be arrested the next morning for blockading, the right-wing press saw it as a serious threat – as in the article *The Bully and the Bomb* (*Daily Express*, 14 December 1982).
Here, however, we are not concerned with this early period;

it has been covered in *Greenham Women Everywhere* by Gwyn Kirk and Alice Cook (Pluto, 1983). Nor are media other than the national daily newspapers considered.

A few attempts were made in some papers to go into detail about the arguments put forward in the courts; 'Who's afraid of wimmin?' (*Observer*, 13 March 1983) and 'Greenham women to fight cruise in U.S. court' (*Guardian*, 19 September 1983). An analysis of the non-hierarchical structure was covered in 'Leaderless peace movement keeps law at arm's length' (*Guardian*, 31 March 1983) and a tentative questioning of why it's women only in 'Women Power' (*Guardian*, 10 December 1983) and 'The camp that will not go away' (*The Times*, 2 May 1983). But most feature articles, regardless of which paper, fell prey to an obsession with details on the conditions within the camp, the appearance of the women, their age, sexuality and background. They ranged from being embarrassingly adulatory: 'The Frontier Spirit' (*Observer Magazine*, 12 February 1984) to despairingly pessimistic, 'Harder lines dig in round the peace camp fires' (*Guardian*, 21 March 1984).

Far worse were the distortions of 'inside stories'. The *Mail on Sunday* sent an 'undercover mole' to the camp, resulting in a scandalous article (13 March 1983). The *Daily Mirror* too, 'joins the Greenham gutter press' (*Tribune*, 13 July 1983) in another diatribe against the camp – surprising coming from a paper purporting to be supportive. In the first week of April 1984, the *Daily Express* managed to string out five days of tedious revelations. The first day coincided with an important Crown Court trial at Reading, which prompted the judge to adjourn, because of the libellous nature of the article.

As with any group opposed to the government's policies, certain papers took every opportunity to insinuate communist infiltration: 'Soviet "spy" on demo' (*Sun*, 14 December 1983) 'Reds tune into cruise signal' (*Daily Express*, 31 October 1983) and 'Red mole shock at Greenham' (*Daily Express*, 20 August 1983). They criticised the women for never protesting against Russian bombs, but only the *Guardian* covered a trip to Moscow (25 May 1983).

Stories were often grossly exaggerated and distorted in an attempt to alienate and quell support. The most blatant example was when Michael Heseltine visited Newbury Conservatives on

7 February 1983. He had to be escorted through protesting women and apparently stumbled. Mr Heseltine said at the time, and it was later confirmed in an official MOD statement, that he was pushed by a policeman. A local reporter was emphatic that the Minister did not fall to the ground. Yet the next day's headlines were: 'Jeering peace protesters punch minister' (*The Times*), 'Peace camp women mob Heseltine' (*Daily Telegraph*) and 'Angry peace girls rough up Heseltine' (*Sun*).

Babies became the next target for attack. In May there was 'The CND baby scandal' (*Daily Mail*, 11 May 1983) which attempted to criticise the birth of a boy at the camp. As it happened, it took place on a sunny afternoon in a clean and comfortable shelter which had been specially prepared. Two midwives and a doctor attended and were astonished at how quick and problem-free the birth had been.

At the eviction in May, the *Daily Mirror* took exception to a mother holding her little boy during a blockade. 'Small face in a sea of protest' (13 May). There were less than twenty women sitting down in the road. May-Day celebrations involved children's parties both inside and outside the base, much to the horror of the Newbury *Weekly News*, 'Naked babies thrust into front line of peace battle' (5 May).

In August, a three-week old baby boy was brought to the camp by his mother after a care order had been placed on him by a Welsh local authority. When the police came to collect him, newspapers confused (deliberately?) the story by implying that Jak (the baby) was the same as Jay (born at the camp in May). 'Peace camp baby found starving' (London *Evening Standard*, 24 August).

Local opposition to the camp united when rumours spread of squalid conditions. 'Dysentery drives peace campers out' (Newbury *Weekly News*, 18 August). In fact it didn't. Many people did not bother to read that 'local Health officials remained confident that the dysentery victim was merely passing through Greenham Common, carrying a disease she caught elsewhere'. She was the only woman to suffer from it. Two others had gastro-enteritis. But the damage was done and more Newbury retailers closed their doors to the camp and vigilante attacks increased.

On 17 July while the camp was having a meeting to discuss the Air Show due to take place shortly, an angry and concerned Lady

Bader appeared. (The Air Show was to be dedicated to her late husband, Sir Douglas Bader.) She was upset because of a story that had appeared that morning in the *Sunday Express*. Apparently Lady Olga Maitland (founder member and chairman (?) of Women and Families for Defence) had written in her diary column 'women intend to disrupt a tribute to wartime fighter pilot ace, Sir Douglas Bader'. Lady Bader was quoted as replying: 'I am not surprised that they plan to do something. It will just show what sort of people they are. What do you expect of them?' Eventually she left, reassured that there was no intention of showing disrespect to her husband in any way. She in turn insisted that the first she had heard of it was that morning in the paper.

By the end of August the tabloid press had exhausted all avenues of attack, 'It's time to go home' . . . 'they have a duty to the families they left behind and the children they took to share the hardship' (*Sun*, 26 August). The *Daily Express* opinion was 'Sweep away this tip', and 'official feebleness is disgraceful' (20 August).

Meanwhile, crucial talks were taking place in Geneva, the last chance for some agreement before Cruise missiles were due to arrive in England. About fifty women from Greenham went to Geneva to put pressure on the talks. While other protesters were blockading the front of the building, women scaled the wall round the back and got into the grounds. Six women managed to reach the entrance and deliver a statement to two delegates from the talks, one Russian and one American. They promised to read the statement to the meeting inside. While it got coverage on West German TV news, and in the Swiss national press, absolutely nothing of the event was reported in Britain.

As Cruise missiles were due to be deployed in England by the end of 1983, a large demonstration was planned at Greenham to coincide with Halloween (29 October). Four miles of fence came down, but women decided not to go inside the base, which took the police and soldiers completely by surprise. It was a powerful statement of defiance. 'The Government asks us to take down the Berlin wall. This fence is our Berlin wall. We can only begin to tackle the concrete and barbed wire that divides our world, when we start with that on our doorstep and in ourselves' (part of a statement given to the press). The *Daily Mail* (31 October) totally misrepresented events: 'Demo flop for "Peace" women', and 'They were relying on a report in the *Guardian* that Cruise missiles were about to arrive . . . after cutting down 1000 yards of wire perimeter fencing, the women drifted away.'

Equipment for the Cruise missiles started to arrive at the beginning of November, but Michael Heseltine's warnings got far more prominence: 'Cruise intruders could be shot' (*The Times*, 2 November), 'Shoot us . . . if you dare' (*Daily Mirror*, 2 November). It was almost forgotten that the Geneva talks were still in progress, making a mockery of the theory that Cruise was to be used as a bargaining tool. The dramatic climax came when the missiles finally arrived on 14 November. Only the *Sun* and the *Guardian* noted that the latest MORI poll showed 59 per cent of Britons either opposed Cruise or wanted to delay its installation.

December 1983 saw another large gathering of women at Greenham, and some sections of the fence were pulled down. Predictably, the *Daily Express* reacted with 'Storming of Greenham' (12 December) and the *Daily Mirror* with 'Fury at the fence' on the same day. The strength of opposition to Cruise missiles was unquestionable, but the media insisted on promoting a story that was never substantiated. Apparently a horse had been whipped with barbed wire by a woman. No evidence was ever produced, nor was anyone charged. The most newsworthy story of the day was a policeman who had been knocked unconscious by a falling post, but the many women who had been injured by soldiers were ignored.

Most papers expressed concern when three women got inside the flight control tower. They remained until they got so bored they flashed the lights to attract attention. The *Daily Mail* described it as 'The most flagrant and potentially dangerous breach of security' (29 December). The Newbury *Weekly News*, however, considered it was not as important as when a woman kicked a door in court: 'Resentful Peace woman damaged court dock' was followed by a story four times longer than that about the control tower (30 December).

In early 1984, a series of nuclear and chemical alert exercises occurred inside the base. American children were still wearing their nightclothes as they were driven into the base in the back of their parents' cars. Sirens wailed as armed American soldiers guarded the perimeter, and others rushed around in 'chemi-suits' and gas masks. In an attempt to disrupt these deadly war games and attract publicity, women blockaded the gates. One woman was seriously hurt while being dragged out of the way and an ambulance was called. The next day's headline in the *Daily Mail* was 'Demo halts ambulance' (12 February 1984). Apart from the story being completely false, there was no explanation as to what the 'demo' was about.

1984 was the year Greenham was supposed to die and 'pass into legend, like . . . the sufffragettes' (*Guardian*, 21 March). While the press diverted their attention to the miners' strike, Greenham continued, largely ignored. But women continued to irritate the government every time the Cruise convoy came out, belying any assumption that the 'exercise' could be done in secret. 'Ministry outwits Cruise protest women' exclaimed the *Guardian* (10 March) as though 100 policemen surrounding 12 sleeping women was a great tour de force. 'Arrests as Cruise convoy returns' (*Guardian*, 30 March) was yet another effort to spare the Americans embarrassment when a launcher broke down for half an hour, and had to be towed back the last 100 yards. Only two women were arrested out of hundreds of protesters, but neither was charged.

There were further red faces in Parliament on 9 July when Tony Benn asked how two women were able to remain inside the base undetected for a week.

Another two women got inside the base at the end of September, in broad daylight, and walked around with a pram, in and out of buildings. They managed to smuggle out documents which related to such matters as the high level of training against biological and chemical warfare, and the failure to maintain equipment. 'USAF praises Cruise base' (*Guardian*, 2 October).

Margaret Thatcher finally acknowledged publicly that the camps still existed when she personally wrote to local Tory MP Michael McNair-Wilson, pledging her support for the camp's final removal. A High Court hearing quickly followed which accepted an application by the MOT to widen the road at the main entrance of the base. It did not cover a 20-foot wide piece of land which the women managed to prove was not owned by anyone. This modest success was acclaimed by the *Guardian*, 'Greenham campers beat bailiffs again' (13 September) but *The Times* gave a totally confusing headline and photograph, unconnected with the High Court story underneath, 'PC knocked down during No. 10 protest' (13 September). A policeman was shown lying on the ground, while a second picture showed a woman being led away. In an apology the next day, *The Times* admitted that they had not intended to suggest that the woman being led away had actually knocked the policeman down. But of course the damage was already done.

Evictions continued almost on a daily basis, as did incursions into the base. On 4 November, twenty-one women boarded an USAF bus in the middle of the night and drove half-way round the base, unnoticed, as far as the silos area. They got out and cut through two sections of wire fencing before being stopped. Although it was reported on radio news there was nothing in the papers apart from reference to it in a more general article in the *Guardian* (5 November).

It has become increasingly clear that the protest at Greenham Common no longer focuses on the single issue of Cruise missiles. It has become linked with other struggles, such as supporting Women Against Pit Closures during the miners' strike; setting up the Women's Network for a Nuclear Free and Independent Pacific; initiating the Mountain Movers campaign which drew attention to the massive stockpiles of surplus food in Europe; and investigating the possible use of low-level radiation waves by the base against Greenham women.

This progression of ideas was cynically put down in an article in the *Guardian* (9 December 1985). 'Widening the Web . . . ' (referring to the theme for the forthcoming demonstration) ' . . . sounds very like breaking the thread', arguing that the lack of direction could only dissipate the movement. 'They are Utopians without a political programme.' But Greenham has never purported to be a political party.

1986 was heralded with a front page 'Spetznaz Infiltration' story published by *Jane's Defence Weekly* (20 January), and given much publicity by the tabloids. 'Russian Spies at Greenham' blazed the *Western Daily Press* (21 January). But how many people took notice of the *New Statesman*'s article on 24 January which revealed that the allegations come solely from an Israeli freelance defence consultant who was under investigation for espionage against the United States. *Jane's* own news editor admitted the next day that no British source could corroborate the story.

In the aftermath of America's attack on Libya, and the Chernobyl nuclear reactor accident in April, there was a dramatic swing of public opinion in favour of the anti-nuclear campaign, and Greenham women. In July, however, the *Sun* and the *Daily Express* reprinted a story that had appeared in the *Mail On Sunday* a few days earlier and devoted two whole pages to 'How Greenham Killed my Dream' – revelations of three ex-Greenham campers who ' . . . had to leave in order to grow up.' The *Daily Mail* and the *Daily Express*, however, after much pressure, eventually agreed to print, as a right of reply, a letter from one of the women, pointing out the considerable distortions and misrepresentations in the article. Surprisingly the *Sun* acknowledged that Greenham was 'one of the most powerful protests in British history'.

But it has not stopped. September 1986 was the camp's fifth anniversary, and while the media continues to speculate on the numbers of women at Greenham Common, evictions, actions, trials and convoys are now regular events.

Women everywhere have been photographed and written about by male journalists, who are subject to the whims of male editors, who in turn are accountable to a media empire owned entirely by men.

The most accurate comments about Greenham have come as direct quotes, from the few letters to be published, or from articles and books written by women themselves.

As a result of their experiences with the media at Greenham, women have become aware of the extent of bias and misrepresentation, and find themselves taking a far more critical stance towards the media. To this extent the bias has been self-defeating, and casts doubt on the interpretation of all events covered. But in spite of the reports both biased and unbiased – Greenham continues.

Carola Addington

Women in Public Life

The way in which women in politics are depicted by the media reflects their rarity and, hence, their novelty value in terms of what makes A Good Story. After the 1987 election still only around 6 per cent of MPs are women. MP for Barking, Jo Richardson, says: 'Women constitute over half the population, yet their views continue to be represented by a male-dominated and deeply chauvinist House of Commons' (*SHE*, January 1981). The words, actions and *looks* of the few who manage to progress beyond the Selection Committee, stand out in bold relief against the serried ranks of sober-suited males.

Should (as seems likely) the proceedings of the House of Commons be televised, women MPs will doubtless be judged, and sometimes berated, on their appearance, in the same way that women newsreaders and presenters are. What you actually need to get into Parliament, says Gwyneth Dunwoody, MP for Crewe, is not some preconceived notion of female attractiveness, but 'the constitution of an ox, very strong feet, the temperament of a saint and the persistence of a ferret' (*SHE*, January 1981).

Margaret Thatcher, when asked for the secret of her stamina, replied: 'Either you've got it or you haven't (*SHE*, January 1981). In her case, stamina has helped create her Iron Lady persona, which has been promoted by image-hungry media and capitalised on by the Tory Party.

Since she became Prime Minister in 1979, Mrs Thatcher's intransigence has given ample scope to Britain's political writers and cartoonists. Anthony Barnett called her 'Iron Britannia'. The *Daily Mirror* (leader, 28 February 1984), following her decision to ban union membership at GCHQ, referred disparagingly to Her Upstairs, and to her Iron Heel: 'She has added a brass neck to her iron image, and it makes her intolerable.' Accompanying this tirade is a cartoon of an immaculately coiffured Mrs Thatcher, a finger in each ear, symbolising her typically unresponsive stance.

She has been likened to Boadicea (or Woadicea) and to Queen Elizabeth I. To *Daily Express* columnist Jean Rook, she is Wonderwoman. Woodrow Wyatt even admitted to being a bit in love with her (*Sunday Times*, 9 June 1985).

The *Sun* is predictably obsequious in its praise of her robust style of leadership, her apparent invincibility – never more so than during the Falklands War in 1982, when her jingoistic rhetoric provoked new depths of gutter-press reporting.

Unlike most other women in the House of Commons, Margaret Thatcher has turned an unflattering image to her advantage – aided and abetted by Saatchi and Saatchi. It's a giant step from the Grantham grocer's daughter schooled in simple home economics to the uncompromising right-wing demagogue of today. The machinations of the media have brought about a staggering change from Thatcher the Milk Snatcher (when she was Education Secretary during Ted Heath's government) through the early months at Number Ten, to TINA ('There-is-no-alternative') in her second term.

Her very appearance is a contradiction; the scrupulously groomed, 'feminine' exterior masks a macho opportunism, a reluctance to listen or to admit personal fallibility – traits encapsulated in her reputation for 'No U-turns'.

Journalist Melanie Phillips observed: 'The gender factor seems to have been utterly erased by the Thatcher factor, a phenomenon undreamed of in feminist philosophy' (*Guardian*, 8 June 1983).

This is surely the supreme irony: that such a significant historical landmark should be associated with some of the most reactionary and anti-women policies this country has ever known. 'Her identity is that of the men's club, and she shared its reaction to the "peccadillos" of Cecil Parkinson . . . It is a hard-faced party, with the leader looking the hardest of them all' (Barbara Rogers, *Guardian*, 2 November 1983). The only chink in this matriarchal armour was the revelation – in the Autumn of 1984 – that a Scottish MP, the worse for drink, had propositioned her, and been suitably rebuffed. The prospect of the Iron Lady *in flagrante delicto* was, of course, irresistible to Fleet Street, and may even have boosted her popularity ratings. Sex appeal was not part of the original Prime Ministerial 'package', though Anthony Burgess alludes to her 'sexuality' as inseparable from the 'charisma of leadership'. She is 'Venus at the prow . . . a rather mature Venus, but she is slimmer than the one of Milo and, as the song says, she has arms. We may fear these weapons but we cannot help being seduced' (*You*, 10 February 1985). A characteristically middle-class male fantasy.

Yet, to the majority of women, Mrs Thatcher has proved to be

Bad News. Feminists regard her policies as an act of betrayal, the antithesis of sisterhood. The archetypal Queen Bee, she presides over a team of passive male minions and an increasingly divided society. Patriarchy remains safely intact. The Token Woman is at the top. The Tory conference hall may traditionally be seen as a blue sea of Lady Bountifuls in hats, but their leader's doctrine is geared to the needs and aspirations of the white heterosexual upwardly mobile male.

The most potent illustration of her strident authoritarianism is in ITV's satirical *Spitting Image* series, where the Thatcher style is captured in the mean, angular features and brisk, headmistressy manner of her screen 'alter ego'. To her team of shuddering syco-phants, she is portrayed as the mythical Nanny figure, She-who-must-be-obeyed. Roger Law, of Fluck and Law (the puppets' inventors) sees *Spitting Image* as a useful outlet for unexpressed spleen when feelings run high about a public figure's behaviour or actions. 'People say we're too savage, but you never hear of any-one going to Saatchi's to complain they're being grossly benevo-lent' (*Radio Times*, 20 – 26 July 1985).

At the opposite end of the political spectrum is Valerie Wise, past chair of the Greater London Council's Women's Commit-tee and daughter of Labour MP Audrey Wise. Feminist politics has long been a popular target of scorn in *Private Eye*, which delighted in ridiculing Ms Wise and the former GLC Women's Committee (sneeringly referred to as 'Wimmin's Committee'). Anthea Hall of the *Sunday Telegraph* described her thus: 'That morning, wearing a high-necked frilly smocked blouse and a smart suit, she looked like a high-powered secretary or business woman' (3 March 1985). The night before, we learn, Ms Wise had spoken to a group of top professional women who had been 'agree-ably surprised by her and the reasonable profile of the Women's Committee which she presented'. A case of 'Look no horns!' Acceptable images of femininity dilute the strong poison of socialist feminism.

When she was an MP, Shirley Williams cultivated an air of sar-torial indifference; her hair was in permanent disarray, and she was also notoriously unpunctual. The media used her lack of 'dress sense', her scattiness, as convenient sticks with which to beat and berate her.

To the female electorate, however, these were presented as engaging attributes. Shirley Williams was portrayed as One of Us, as Shirl the Girl. Her lack of vanity gave her a homely, unpretentious image. Recently, this image has become smarter, more sophisticated, but to what degree this was really necessary, or indeed desirable, is a moot point. 'The PR men failed to understand that her enormous appeal to women was based on her rushing around trying to cope, and under constant criticism for lack of glamour. Magic! But now the trenchcoat and careful hair have spoiled it all' (Barbara Rogers, *Guardian*, 2 November 1983). To thousands of her female admirers, who were able to identify with her physical 'ordinariness' while admiring and respecting her intellectual astuteness, it must have seemed as though she was selling out. Instead of simply being herself, she was seen to be jettisoning her apparent earlier disregard for her appearance, shedding an old skin for a new, neater, more pristine image. Such media preoccupation with the superficial trappings of celebrity smacks of our society's obsession with the cult of the personality.

Personalising policies sanitises them for public consumption, vicariously fuelling the appetite but detracting from the real issues. There are Thatcherite clones – women like Edwina Currie, MP for Derbyshire South, whom the media project as a *femme formidable*, arrogant, ambitious, a ruthless maverick. Denis Pitts in the *Sunday Express* magazine pays predictable homage to Edwina Currie's physical qualities, ending with a key phrase: 'Tough indeed, but still feminine' (3 March 1985). This remark encapsulates the kind of criteria by which any woman in public life is deemed socially 'acceptable'. Traditional ideas of femininity stave off the threat of emasculation, though Currie has de-sexed herself to the extent that, like her mentor, she alienates herself completely from very many women. 'I think that Margaret Thatcher and I would both say that we're not women MPs. We're MPs. I don't represent women; I represent 76,000 people' (*ibid*). Clearly, the only woman with whom she feels any empathy is Mrs Thatcher herself. As she delights in telling 'chat show' hosts, they even share the same birthday.

One woman whose style is very much her own, untrammelled by outside influences, is Glenys Kinnock. The media portray her as the Power Behind Neil's Throne, yet as a woman who enjoys an equal relationship with her husband and is not content to play second fiddle. She is seen both as a major asset to the Labour Party and as a liberated, multi-talented woman: teacher, mother, feminist, campaigner. Young and attractive in a non-stereotypical way, warm but assertive, witty but with forthright views, she is difficult to typecaste.

In the final analysis, how the media choose to depict women in the political and trade union arenas depends primarily on the political leanings of the writer concerned. The sex of the writer is generally immaterial. We expect a more responsible, considered approach from the *Guardian*, and rightly so. Jeremy Seabrook, discussing ideology rather than personality, defines Mrs Thatcher's government as 'the most unflinching and barefaced representative of the Enemy Within' (*Guardian*, 10 December 1984). Salman Rushdie attacks the Prime Minister's 'ideology of impotence masquerading as resolution . . . Maggie's sting' (*Guardian*, 23 May 1983).

If you are a woman and a political high-flier, the pressures to conform are very great indeed. The sheer dearth of female competition sees to that, together with the double standards of social behaviour which continue to keep women 'in their place' in all areas of public life. Step a fraction out of line and the media will spring into action and judge you.

Ex-Labour MP Helene Hayman chose to breastfeed her baby at the House, a deed for which she was roundly castigated by Parliamentary colleagues, backed by the media.

In 1977 Maureen Colquhoun chose to be forthright about her lesbianism – but at a price. She was promptly rejected by her constituency party at Northampton North.

When first appointed, after the 1983 general election, as personal assistant/'minder' to the Leader of the Opposition, Neil Kinnock, Patricia Hewitt was taken to task in the media for being 'overprotective' (*sic*), when in all probability she was only doing her job.

The reality of Margaret Thatcher in 1987 is worlds away from the quasi-cosy 'good housekeeper' image of her early days in power. To promote this image, she colluded with the popular press, giving 'homely' interviews, for example, 'I could not have been an MP if I'd had to leave the family' (Alison McDonald, *Woman*, 27 September 1986). Several years on, 'the Prime Minister no longer wheels out her femininity to win hearts and minds. She relies instead on an image of steely resolution' (Melanie Phillips, *Guardian*, 8 June 1983). Mrs Thatcher is proof positive of the media's ability to manipulate 'hearts and minds'. By dominating her Cabinet and her party, she has manipulated the media, reinforcing their right-wing bias and revelling in their projection of her as a strong leader. She has turned into a caricature, the extreme manifestation of the cult of the personality.

Veronica Groocock

Media facts and fictions – a case study

In 1986 the Greater London Council was abolished by the Conservative government. Why was it that the Women's Committee of the GLC, the officers who worked for it and the work they did were subjected to hostility and vilification by the media?

There were various reasons why the media coverage was so negative: partly political, partly because women's issues are not treated seriously by men who are mainly responsible for decision-making in the media, partly social prejudice and so on. The end result is that the Women's Committee was constantly described as controversial, its members denoted 'virulent viragos' by the *Daily Star* and its grants invariably described as handouts.

Hostility to grants

Selective reporting of grants by certain national newspapers perpetuates the image of the loony left which they so like to pillory. An £800 grant to a mother and toddler group who wished to discuss peace is still, years later, being reported in derisory and mocking terms as a way of putting down the Committee – all because the group had the eye-catching name of Babies Against the Bomb.

The establishment press howled that any initiatives taken by the Committee to fund work with lesbian, black and minority ethnic women and women with disabilities, was a waste of ratepayers' money, conveniently forgetting that many of the women who benefited from them are ratepayers too. They further undermined the Committee's work by stories which whipped up a sense of outrage. 'Now it's babies against racism' screamed a *Daily Mail* headline on a story which began 'Toddlers, some as young as two years old, are to be "cured" of their prejudices against blacks and women –with the help of a £95,000 GLC grant.'

The grant enabled the Lewisham Mobile Crèche project to get under way and provide good quality anti-racist and anti-sexist play activities for under-fives. The story didn't seem to know about the principle of 'You're never too young to start', never mind uphold it.

Expense was a favourite way of Committee bashing. The £500,000 which the Committee set aside for a week of events to celebrate International Women's Day in 1985 caught the media in two minds, however. Some coverage was carping and critical of the Committee for going over the top, and some was straight ('GLC salutes women in a week of events around London', said the London *Evening Standard*). But only Loretta Loach of *Spare Rib* had her finger on the button. She wrote: 'At first sight half a million may seem extravagant spending for an International Women's Day celebration in London. But if one pound was to be given to each woman in London there would still be three million who had to do without.'

Paper fantasies

Distortion of facts, usually to comply with a newspaper's own political bent, was something we had to live with too. Nevertheless, it still came as a surprise to find in the *Daily Mail* that 'Militant GLC feminists are launching a £700,000 campaign challenging the idea that sex between men and women is normal.'

The story confused three things: the money for International Women's Day activities (open, of course, to lesbians); an estimated £100,000 for a women's handbook; and a report from the Women's Committee to the Council on GLC policy as it affected lesbians and gay men. It rounded up the sum for good measure, all of which just goes to prove you shouldn't believe what you read in the newspapers, particularly the *Daily Mail*.

The rose story

The story which obtained our most widespread coverage, and was picked up by papers from Belfast to Portsmouth, from Edinburgh to Gwent, wasn't anything to do with our unique survey of public transport and women's needs, or the women's perspective we introduced to the Greater London Development Plan for the first time, or the £250 million we've spent on childcare projects. It was about roses.

The *Local Government Chronicle* accused the London *Evening Standard* of starting off what it called the silliest council story of 1985. It all began when promoter Raymond Gubbay planned to give a single red rose to every woman in the audience for a St Valentine's Day concert at the GLC Royal Festival Hall. Valerie Wise, half serious, half tongue-in-cheek, tabled a Council question asking whether the roses 'represent a cutting comment on the difficulties this Council's Women's Committee face in their work to combat sexism, racism and heterosexism in our society.'

Unfair Wise cracks

Since the media are forever accusing the committee of being 'kill-joys' and 'lacking a sense of humour', the media didn't see the joke. Indeed, the *Shropshire Star* declared 'Ms Wise is undoubtedly serious about the rose. If you think she might just be joking, forget it.'

'Spare me from this nonsense', cried a woman writing in the Southampton *Evening Echo*. 'Lunacy in full bloom', said the *News of the World*. 'Blooming nonsense' said the Worcester *Evening News*. 'Well girls, do you like receiving roses or are they really a sexist symbol?' asked the Hitchin *Express*. The *News and Weekly Argus* in North Gwent said that Ms Wise was most inappropriately named, and the dear old *Daily Mail* said that 'Gubbay's floral brainwave is suffering a withering attack of blight from the militant feminists on the GLC Women's Committee', adding that its gardening expert, Percy Thrower, was 'outraged' by the incident.

Brian Walden raised the issue in his syndicated column which appeared in newspapers all over the country, including Belfast and

Newcastle. The Oldham *Evening Chronicle* blamed Audrey Wise for the whole thing; you should never trust newspapers to get their facts right.

The *Daily Telegraph* thought the issue of sufficient importance for an editorial and said anyone could be excused for treating Ms Wise as the fit subject for facetious humour. It remarked upon 'the extreme crudity of this preposterous episode' and advised its million or so readers that 'sensible race relations will be learned not from the GLC Women's Committee but from the Lancashire (cricket) leagues'. The Chester *Observer* confessed that what tickled them was 'Ms Wise's innocent suggestion that daffodils, shamrocks and thistles should be thrown in, and to at least make sure that some men have a leek'. Innocent?

Slowly, the light began to dawn on the media. They'd been well and truly had. But not before Valerie had a field day accepting bouquets from the *Daily Mail* and the *Standard*, which admitted with a half-page picture and story (on page 3) that 'Ms Wise has the last blooming laugh!'

The only other issue to attract such a lot of media attention was the ban on sexist advertisements on the buses and tube introduced by London Transport after pressure from the Women's Committee. The press response included personal attacks on Valerie Wise and focused on sex rather than sexism. It also tended to play down the fact that the ban included advertisements which portrayed violence against women, and the context of women feeling vulnerable when using public transport at night.

Changing attitudes

As chair of the committee, Valerie Wise had much of the flak from the media directed at her. *The Times* caught the mood in its headline over a personal profile to mark the committee's third birthday: 'Wicked witch or power for good?' *Daily Express* Women's Editor Katharine Hadley wrote: 'The Committee hasn't worked and has brought mockery to perfectly respectable issues like the care of elderly parents and a host of other concerns both sexes take to heart.

'The imminent demise of the GLC can only be a good thing as

far as this Committee is concerned. And for Miss Wise.' With a total lack of finesse, she goes on to wonder 'what lies in the future for Mrs Gow?' Could she be thinking 'back to the home' perhaps?

Increased personal contact with journalists brought interesting results. *Ms London* noted that 'the press have always given Ms Wise a rough ride, the picture left in the average reader's mind being a cross between Edwina Currie at her most tiresomely imperious, and a humourless harridan!!'

But, enthused their reporter Jane Butterworth, 'The thing that astonished me, when talking to her, was how absolutely ordinary an image she presented. I kept thinking of the millions of pounds, directly or indirectly controlled by her committee, and found it hard to relate to the quiet, well-dressed woman before me . . .'

The headlines in *SHE* magazine were in similar vein: 'Isn't she the Marxist-feminist nut? The woman from the GLC who gives away millions to black lesbians? Sue Arnold was pleasantly surprised by the real Valerie Wise . . .'

Media coverage wasn't always biased or inaccurate. Sometimes there was no coverage, or less than was hoped for. It was usually publications from the alternative press such as *City Limits* or *Spare Rib* which seriously examined the committee's work. Women's magazines were a little wary of us, but various issues were covered in a factual, straightforward way by the national, local and ethnic press.

Accurate ethnic reporting

When Valerie Wise closed down a section of the Tomi Ungerer exhibition at the GLC Royal Festival Hall, acting on complaints from women that it was pornographic, reporting was generally fair. The London *Evening Standard*, local and ethnic press, and radio all ran stories about the Women as Carers conference in County Hall in 1985. The *Asian Times* devoted more than half a page to a story and picture about the women's transport survey, while Thames TV gave it extensive coverage on their main news bulletin. The 'signing on' campaign to encourage women to claim benefits which are right-fully theirs was also widely reported in the local press.

The ethnic press, including *West Indian World* and *The Voice*, regularly carried stories about committee initiatives and activities, and a *Daily Jang* photographer was a familiar figure at many of our open meetings at which representatives of the establishment press were noticeably absent.

Indeed, reporting of the committee by the ethnic press and the Scottish press was more consistently fair and accurate than any other section of the media. Could it be because they are removed from the whims and politics of Fleet Street? Just look at the following comments about Valerie's speaking tour of Scotland:

'*Women's voices must be heard*', said the headline in the *Aberdeen Press and Journal*. '*New committee "a vital step"* ' said the Lothian *Courier*. '*Front-line fighter for female issues*' said the *Glasgow Herald*, while the Edinburgh *Evening News* reported '*Women leading the way.*'

Jennifer Simon
Reprinted with permission from the GLC
Women's Committee Bulletin, issue 25, 1985.

The media, women and political violence in Ireland

'Her Irish eyes may be smiling, but her trade is fear and death . . . Consider this female of the species . . . But keep well clear. For Margaret McKearney is certainly more deadly than the male.' Thus the *Daily Express* contributed on 5 September 1975 to a massive press campaign initiated by Scotland Yard against the woman who briefly became famous as 'the most evil girl in Britain', 'danger woman', and the ' "most dangerous" IRA blonde'.

British media coverage of Irish women is conditioned by the British establishment view of Ireland in general. Stories about Irish women display the same biases as stories about Irish men and Irish political developments generally: the IRA are portrayed as the main devils, the alpha and omega of the problem in the North; the conflict is described as religious, irrational, the product of an innate Irish propensity to violence; loyalists – Britain's embarrassing allies – with their sectarian violence and bigotry are generally ignored; the British are presented as sane, civilised, non-violent, and their responsibility for the conflict and abrogations of human and civil rights is suppressed or avoided; the only truly 'good' locals are those whose actions flatter the British perspective, by trying to 'bridge the sectarian divide' without challenging British rule in the North of Ireland.

Thus for the media the villains are those who support, or are accused of supporting or promoting, republican armed struggle against British rule: women like Margaret McKearney, Dolours and Marion Price, Maire Drumm, Annie Maguire (who was in fact a Conservative!), and Evelyn Glenholmes. Media heroines are women like Mairead Corrigan and Betty Williams, stars of the short-lived 'peace people' whose campaign was primarily directed against the IRA. Other acceptable, because unchallenging, Irish women include the singer Mary O'Hara and author Edna O'Brien, both of whom in different ways feed the 'other side' of the British stereotype of the Irish – charming, musical, feckless, romantic, emotional, rustic.

But the women who are victims of British violence never become media stars, even though their stories are as full of 'human interest' as even the tabloids would wish: women like Emma Groves, housewife and mother of eleven children, blinded by a rubber bullet at the age of fifty-one, and Nora McCabe, a thirty-three-year-old housewife with three children, killed by a plastic bullet as she went to the local shop; nor has the campaign against the strip-searching of women prisoners won media support.

Within this general framework of vilification of republicanism and support for the British establishment line, the national media exploit the fact that some of the 'characters' in their stories are women to provide extra piquancy, drama, titillation or shock value. The extent to which the women conform to or depart from the patriarchal version of the feminine ideal is used to give additional zest to the message about the British political ideal.

The rapid transformations in the coverage of Bernadette Devlin-McAliskey demonstrate the intimate links between political position and media portrayal. Her election and arrival in Parliament in April 1969, at a time when the British establishment and media both favoured removing the sectarian excesses of the Northern Ireland state and sympathised with the civil rights activists, delighted the press – especially since she wore a mini-skirt. 'Swinging – that's petite Bernadette Devlin', trilled the *Daily Mirror* But when she joined in the defence of Derry's Bogside in August that year against a police invasion, she became, in the *Daily Mail*'s eyes, the leader of a 'sinister army' of 'revolutionary extremists'. After Bloody Sunday, when British soldiers shot dead fourteen people in Derry, Bernadette hit Home Secretary Reginald Maudling and received a torrent of abuse from the media: the *Daily Mirror* called her 'Miss Bernadette Devlin of the long, lank hair and nasty left hook'. For the media, her glamour had evaporated when the situation polarised and she aligned herself with the oppressed nationalist community.

The media often indicate their loathing of republican men by invoking animal images – 'Mad Dog', 'The Jackal', 'Bald Eagle' – to demonstrate their distance from 'human', 'civilised' society; republican women are treated not as animals but as deviants from their prescribed roles in the family.

Thus Maire Drumm, vice-president of Sinn Fein, was dubbed 'Grandmother of Hate' for her denunciations of British rule in the North. 'Hate Granny Shot Dead' was the *Daily Mirror*'s headline when she was murdered by loyalist paramilitaries as she lay in a hospital bed in 1976: an approach shared by the rest of the press, which treated her death as the 'wages of sin'. 'Aunt Annie's Bomb Kitchen' was how the press headlined the story of Annie Maguire, who was wrongly convicted along with five members of her family and a friend for conspiracy to cause explosions and spent a nightmare nine years in prison. Dolours and Marion Price, convicted of bombing the Old Bailey, were 'The Evil Sisters Who Smiled As The Bombs Went Off': how, one wonders, did the *News of the World* know that they smiled? 'The Sisters of Hate' was the *Daily Mirror* headline for a December 1984 double-page spread on four women described as 'petticoat Provos' and 'ruthless women warriors': these included Rita O'Hare, head of Sinn Fein's women's department, and Evelyn Glenholmes, who was the most recent target of a Scotland Yard scare. Like Margaret McKearney, Evelyn Glenholmes was dubbed 'Britain's most wanted woman' and a 'blonde bomber', and was, it seems, likewise in Ireland at the time Scotland Yard said she was committing offences in Britain. Both women were convicted by the police and the media without trial, and, if arrested, would stand no chance of a fair hearing in Britain.

It is perhaps worth asking, by way of conclusion: what are these women *really* like? To take just one example, Margaret McKearney – though not, the evidence suggests, involved in bombings in Britain – was a republican in outlook. She was brought up in County Tyrone, just north of the border, in an area where the effects of British colonisation centuries ago are still very apparent: Protestants hold the best land and the best jobs, while Catholics – descendants of the native Irish – hold the worst. Her mother's side of the family are traditional republicans – Margaret's great-great-uncle was a Fenian rebel against British rule and was arrested and sent to Van Diemen's Land, now Tasmania. Margaret had eleven 'O' Levels and an 'A' Level. She applied for a job in the chemistry department of a bakery, was politely told she 'wasn't suitable', then found out afterwards that the young woman who got the job, a Protestant, had three 'O' Levels. It was experiences like this, common to many Northern nationalists, that made her a republican – experiences that are never told by the British media.

Liz Curtis

8
Romance

Introduction

Romance may be considered by some to be a bourgeois notion – but life without it would be immensely duller. So would popular culture.

Our argument is not with romance per se, *but with the stereotypes presented, the motivation behind them, and their disempowering effect on women.*

From romantic fiction to advertisements, the fairy-tale narrative depicts a woman being completed and fulfilled through union with a man. Any initial independence of spirit shown by the woman merely adds spice to her eventual conquest. Sometimes romance involves a confusion of love with physical as well as emotional conquest, which further decreases the woman's power.

The use of romantic innuendo in advertising and the constant clichés in romantic fiction debase the reality of human love and caring. The exclusive heterosexuality denies validity to lesbian and gay love. Characters are inevitably white ('fairness' is a virtue) and physically 'perfect'. (Romance occasionally comes to the lucky woman with a disability – so the tabloids would have us believe – in spite of *her 'handicap'). For working-class heroines the pinnacle of success is to be rescued by a wealthy man.*

Romance is strewn throughout media intended for a female audience. Focusing on romantic relationships to the exclusion of other kinds of relationships and other pursuits may be good indoctrination for women's servicing role – especially when the narrative stops short of describing the drudgery and conflicts of 'afterwards' – but it cannot be said to be in their best interests.

The constant encouragement for women to seek fulfilment in a union with a man disguises the reality that she is already *complete and perfect, that her primary relationship needs to be with herself, that passionate love does not ultimately enable an escape from anything, that she has every right to demand an equal relationship, that she does not have to collude with men's sexism – and that at all times she has a choice about how and with whom to express* her *sexuality. None of this is easily incorporated into media which support the idea of limited (subordinate) roles for women.*

Women in their millions consume media romance. This is hardly surprising given our conditioning, the escape it offers from the far-different reality of our lives, its addictive properties – and the paucity of cheap and easily accessible alternatives, such as might be offered by women's publishers.

And, although popular romance may distort and divert attention from reality, offering a panacea, and inhibiting the development of women's powerfulness and unity, at least it is about human beings (albeit cardboard ones) relating to one another (albeit unconstructively). Media products aimed at men never *include romance – only sex devoid of human involvement – and are immeasurably duller for it.*

Brand of possession[1]

Paperback romance novels are a modern marketing success. Sapphire, Minstral, Harlequin, Silhouette, and, of course, Mills & Boon, are widely advertised, easily available, and immensely popular. A new Mills & Boon title has a print run of nearly 100,000, a figure which exceeds that of many best-sellers. Most of these books are bought (or borrowed from libraries and friends) by women. Few of them are sold through bookshops. Instead, their outlets are station news stands, chain-store stationers, and supermarkets. For those readers who are isolated or house-bound, there is the Rose of Romance book club, which promises 'the pleasure and security' of receiving new titles through the post, and offers six free stories as an introduction. Such confidence in the appeal of their novels is justified by their sales figures: 20 million books (or 'units' as the company terms them) sold in the UK during 1985, to an estimated readership of 8.5 million.[2]

Romantic fiction marketing is largely dependent on advertising, mainly in shops and women's magazines, as only the glossier, and more expensive romance novels – Shirley Conran's *Lace*, for example, or Judith Krantz's *Princess Daisy* – are reviewed in newspapers and journals. The cheaper books are not regarded as having sufficient individual identity as texts,[3] a view which, judging by their advertising, Mills & Boon seem to endorse. It is the imprint which is emphasised, not the individual title, author, or story. This type of advertising is common to the cheaper romance imprints. It was used in 1981 to launch the new Sapphire series: the reader was encouraged to trust Sapphire to provide consistent romantic storytelling.

The romance publishers tend to use the same image in their advertisements as on their book covers: a picture of a couple below the title, author and publisher's logo. The couple may be embracing, but seldom are they actually looking at each other. The man is usually gazing down at the woman (she is smaller, of course), and she is looking coyly in another direction: an indication to the consumer of the roles she will find inside the book.

Romance novels depend on dramatic plots with exciting events, usually in far-away places (favourite locations are Africa and the Caribbean, though Devon and Scotland are also popular – presumably considered to be far-away enough from most readers' homes). The chronological events are dramatic and often dangerous, setting a tone of nervous tension which is further increased by the vexed relations between the female and male characters, particularly the principal ones. Though unquestionably heterosexual, these people are not, it seems, relaxed in each other's company; in fact, they seem to function on completely different levels from each other. What is presented to the reader is a polarisation of gender roles. The heroes and heroines are presented as archetypes of feminine and masculine behaviour.

In the traditional romance novels, the men are tough and the women are vulnerable; the heroes are dominant and the heroines are like children in their lack of self-determination (sent away by her father to Tanzania, for example, Claire is 'taken up' by an older man, Rod.[4]) This reaches its extreme form in the 'bandit story', a popular theme in which the heroine is literally captured by a man with whom she cannot resist falling in love. The implication that women like men who tie them up and imprison them has unpleasant overtones of bondage pornography. The 'bandit' motif might suggest behaviour which psychologists call the Stockholm syndrome (in which hostages find sympathy with their captors through a need to alleviate the alienation they feel)[5] – but this would destroy the romantic mystique; no, our heroine is simply falling in love.

The heroines of these novels fall in love under the most adverse conditions, not least of which are frequently their own feelings of unwillingness. But one of the most glaring differences between women and men in these romances is that, while the men keep such a tight control over their emotions that their feelings are not revealed until the final page, the women are completely ruled by emotional forces. This is particularly true of the less recent titles: being alone in a car with the hero can be simply too much to bear.[6] The lack of harmony between cognitive and physical response is bewildering (to the reader, as well as the heroine): it was 'frightening, the way her body responded to him'.[7] Evidently, more than emotional submission is going on here; in these books, women's physiological responses are completely unpredictable. As Lucy is kissed by Philip (for he does the kissing, she is kissed), there is a 'strange singing noise' in her ears.[8] Is this tinnitus perhaps? No, it is true love.

A woman portrayed in this way is so passive, even her body chemistry needs to be activated by a man (not any man, the hero). The traditional idea of feminine beauty on which romance novels depend is young, unconfident, naive – and white: a blank sheet on which a man can design the woman he wants. Politics are, of course, taboo in these books, but the heroine's class position is crucial to the plot. She tends to be from a lower social class than the hero, and if she is working it is in a low-status occupation: nannies, secretaries and nurses are popular. Her lack of social or economic power is therefore due not only to her gender, but also to her social class, making marriage to the lawyer/doctor/farmer/ businessman/freelance adventurer all the more understandable and desirable.

An intriguing new heroine has developed recently, however: the career woman, evidently a response to the positive images of professional women in magazines such as *Cosmopolitan*, *Company* and *Woman*. She tends to be older than the traditional heroine, though younger than the hero, of course. She is middle class (often upwardly mobile from a 'sad' start in life), professional and, with depressing certainty, white. She is allowed to be experienced; in fact, her experience is vital to her current predicament, which is one of disappointment and cynicism. All the money and status in the world cannot compensate for the emotional hollow she feels inside. She may have been hurt by a married man, like Romily, [9] or she may be, like Eleanora Jassamine, 'a typical victim of the modern career-woman syndrome',[10] an apparently serious disease, for which the cure is, conveniently, the hero of the story.

The main symptom of their emotional lack is the cynicism with which these women build their emotional defences against the unrewarding world of men. This gives the hero the challenge he needs to prove himself, as, like the knight cutting through the forest of thorns to reach the Sleeping Beauty, he sets himself to win her. Invariably he succeeds. His prize is her release, for he knows what she really wants. 'I could show you pleasure,' murmurs Colby to Eleanora Jassamine. 'Let me be your fantasy.'[11] To do this, however, more durable qualities have to be brought into the story: trust and mutual confidence. For these older, more worldly-wise heroines cannot be expected to respond purely with their aroused hormones and their fluttering hearts; cognitive appeal is required. So, with a vulnerability not previously permitted romance novel heroes, Lucas begs Emily, 'Don't refuse me, not when I need you so much',[12] and Colby asks Eleanora Jassamine, 'Give me the chance to be the man I know I can be.'[13] This is a big step out of the cave for the romantic hero.

In almost all the stories, the hero has to possess all the qualities the heroine will need for companionship and support, as well as romance, as friendships hardly feature in these books. Sometimes the heroine is allowed some friendly male colleagues or neighbours, but the absence of female friends is striking. Women are rivals, not friends. The lack of potential for friendship is spelt out in the unflattering, often unkind, ways in which other women are described in contrast to the heroine. Romily's rival, Carol, has an 'artificial laugh' and a 'cat-with-the-cream' smile.[14] Mon, in *Beloved Captive*, is dark, a gypsy and also Russian: a sinister rival to the blond, younger Seranne.[15] It is the old virgin/whore contrast.

Sexual competition is used to divide and categorise, and to prove that only the virginal can win (that is, get the man).

Setting women against each other distracts from the more serious conflict in these books: between the women and men, and particularly between the heroine and hero. This is sometimes resolved with some brutality. It is hard at times to see the dividing line between the traditional strong male qualities and bullying domination. Who would go out with a man who has eyes which gleam 'narrow and ruthless' as he twines his hand 'rather cruelly through a swathe of her [your] hair'?[16] Or how about one who 'sank his teeth into the fleshy curve of Lucy's cleavage'?[17] There seems to be more pain than romance in descriptions like these.

The more recent imprints tend to resolve the conflict with less graphic physical discomfort, but one point remains unaltered: the terms are his. Whatever the heroine had achieved in her life B.H. (Before Him), she leaves it. Modern romance writers have a problem making their career-woman heroines still seem plausible as they discard generous salaries and city apartments for men whose restless adventuring distinguishes them from all the others yet makes them improbable as husband figures. In *Treasure Hunt*, the only way round the problem was to make Lucas the owner of an island; in *The Straight Game*, it was to make Colby the long-lost son of the boss.

With impossible heroines and implausible plots, the popularity of romance novels may seem inexplicable. Why do women keep on buying them?

One immediate impression is that they are easy to read. Many women find their undemanding styles relaxing. But there is more to this than short sentences and a limit on length. There is considerable appeal for women in the persona of the hero. The notion of having a masterful man to take care of you reaches back into women's early childhood memories. It is the father figure who is being evoked here, with all the associated notions of being cared for and having decisions made for you. This is why the heroes often seem more like parents than lovers. ('Will you keep quiet for a moment' says David in *The Winds of Winter*, 'Here am I trying to tell you that I love you, and you keep interrupting me.') Vulnerable, alone, often in unknown foreign places, these heroines are in evident need of a father figure to take care of them. Some of them are described as having been orphaned, or abandoned, as infants.[18] But the need is specific: it is, apparently, for a male parental figure, not a female one, for seldom do these books acknowledge a mother, sisters, or other female relatives.

Ask women who buy romance paperbacks if they believe them and they will laugh at you. They know they are buying fantasy, and the women who write them (far more women write these than men) know that fantasy is what they are producing. It is very reliable fantasy: the imprints keep to similar story lines with predictable character roles. The books are cheap, and women can pick them up at the supermarket. But are these the only kinds of books that can sell to women in these quantities? Is there a place for different types of romantic fiction? Feminist writers have only recently addressed themselves to the business of romance.[19] Yet several feminist authors use the romantic tradition in their own work.[20] Would these sell in their thousands if cheaply priced on a station news stand?

Teresa Stratford

Notes

1 The title of a novel by Carole Mortimer, Mills & Boon, 1980.
2 Deborah Phillips, 'Marketing moonshine', in *You Are What You Buy: Essays in Consumption, Identity and Style*, ed. Alan Tomlinson, Pluto Press, 1986.
3 Ken Worpole, *Reading by Numbers*, 1984.
4 Kay Thorpe, *No Passing Fancy*, Mills & Boon, 1980.
5 Linda Laushway, 'Trust, the key to hostage incidents', *Liaison 2*, vol. 13, no. 1, February 1976.
6 Sandra Field, *The Winds of Winter*, Mills & Boon, 1980.
7 Margaret Way, *Flamingo Park*, Mills & Boon, 1980.
8 Caroline Standish, *Sweet Temptation*, Minstral, 1981.
9 Sally Wentworth, *Tiger in his Lair*, Mills & Boon, 1986.
10 Rebecca Flanders, *The Straight Game*, Harlequin, 1986.
11 *ibid.*
12 Maura Seger, *Treasure Hunt*, Silhouette, 1986.
13 *The Straight Game.*
14 *Tiger in his Lair.*
15 Iris Gower, *Beloved Captive*, Minstral, 1981.
16 *Flamingo Park.*
17 *Sweet Temptation.*

18 *Treasure Hunt*.
19 See Rosalind Coward (ed.), *Female Desire*, Paladin, 1984; and Germaine Greer, *The Female Eunuch*, McGibbon & Kee, 1970.
20 Those who have written in this tradition include Sara Maitland, Margaret Drabble, Alison Lurie, Zoë Fairbairns.

Feminism and soap opera

Liking soap opera has always been a risky business. Wooed by the television companies with an endless stream of character-centred publicity – for the soap watcher is that most desirable statistic, the regular and committed viewer – the fan is frequently abused by both the quality and popular press.[1] Even those involved in the production of soap operas, from actors to producers, are frequently apologetic about their occupation and their product.[2]

The advent of the new 1980s soaps, *Brookside* and *EastEnders*, with higher budgets and determined appeals to a wider and younger audience of both sexes, has to some extent improved the public profile of soaps. Similarly, the recession chic of the American prime-time serials, *Dallas* and *Dynasty*, which have exported padded shoulder fantasy worldwide, have to some extent allowed the particular pleasures of serial viewing to be more publicly acknowledged.[3] Still trash, soaps have, in some circles, been elevated to good trash. As a recent article in *The Times* rather exquisitely put it: 'It was Sir John Betjeman who made it respectable to admit to an addiction to *Coronation Street*.'[4]

It is in this context, one in which fans are frequently ashamed of their pleasures, that we have to place the contradictory feminist response to soap opera. Initially predominantly one of fierce rejection, feminist response was partly determined by the way in which soaps were seen as women's programmes. Feminists in the 1970s were particularly aggressive towards 'women's genres' – the feminine ghetto of soap operas, fashion, romances and women's magazines.[5] I have been ticked off more than once at feminist conferences for even watching the programmes. (I say this not to draw attention to my daringly *outré* tastes, but as evidence of the way in which many feminists *assumed* that soaps were such a bad thing that erring sisters should be pointed back to the right road.)

Soaps were criticised for offering stereotypical and unrealistic images of women which confirm us in our subordination. To a certain extent there is a truth in this argument – what I want to do here is tease out some of the complexities and problems that this simple political criticism ignores.

Like much political criticism, the argument was a realist one. It was assumed that there were (readily available) more realistic representations of women which would better serve a feminist argument. There are at least two kinds of realism in a soap – an 'external realism' created through reference to the outside world, through set, modes of dress, discussion of contemporary events, etc., and an 'internal realism', whereby characters conform to our knowledge and expectation of them, which is derived from having watched the serial. To call for more realistic female characters involves a rather complicated negotiation of these realisms. As soaps grow old, instead of wrinkles, they get a lack of fit between these two types of realism. Thus although *Coronation Street* has conformed to the demands of 'internal realism' over the years, its 'external realism' has become much more obviously constructed in comparison with the fresher conventions and representations of *East-Enders* and *Brookside*. The 'lack of fit' between these realisms means that, paradoxically, it can be argued that the female characters in *Coronation Street* are much 'stronger', more independent figures than those in the more (externally) realistic recent soaps.[6]

Thus firstly we have a feminist rejection of soaps, which although couched in different terms, is, in effect, almost homologous with the traditional high cultural contempt for soaps. This was followed by a certain revaluation which coincides, across the women's movement, with the revaluation of conventionally feminine skills such as embroidery and the admission of enjoyment in some of the pleasures of traditional femininity, like dressing up. More positive attitudes – and I don't want to claim that these necessarily apply to all feminists – have been based partly on a recognition of the strength of female characters such as Meg Mortimer in *Crossroads*, Bet Lynch in *Coronation Street* and Sheila Grant in *Brookside*, and partly on the revaluation of women's genres as such. Perhaps soap opera has such low cultural status, not because it is any more trashy than war movies or westerns, but because the people who watch it have less cultural power?

The argument about realism is a tricky one. Soaps have very

strong *generic* features – rules and conventions which all soaps share – like the idea that these people carry on living even when we're not watching them. It is partly conformity to these generic rules which produces the 'internal' realism of the serial. The 'external' realism is not so much a matter of direct comparison with the Real World (i.e. 'I live in Liverpool, and it's not like *Brookside*') but of the way in which the soap opera partakes of, and contributes to, all the different ways in which we make sense of the Real World. Soaps are dependent on already existing discourses – in the papers, on the news, about law and order, about young people – to represent the Real World to us. But the representations they produce also contribute to our understanding of what that world is. Feminists have argued that dominant discourses in this culture are ones which both devalue women, and repeatedly insist on the social power of sexual difference. It is these dominant definitions which are most powerful in constructing our image of what the Real World is. Thus for feminists to call for more realistic images of women is to engage in the struggle to define what is meant by 'realistic', rather than to offer easily available 'alternative' images. Feminists are not just quarrelling with soap opera, but, fundamentally, with the Real World there represented. Arguing for more realistic images is always an argument for the representation of 'your' version of reality. 'Realistic' to a feminist will often seem propagandist and thin to a political opponent. The image will precisely lack the sedimented 'concreteness' of a dominant image. This problem – of the lack of credibility of alternative and oppositional representations – is particularly pronounced in a form like soap opera which is mainly pleasurable in its predictable, conservative, repetitive elements, and its necessary generic commitment to realism. It is extremely difficult to construct plausible, but challenging and different, characters and situations.

A good example of this is the women's screen-printing co-operative which appeared on *Brookside*. Unlike the years of television living rooms, and mums getting the tea, this location and these characters have almost no television history at all. Although it may, in one sense, be more realistic, in that it shows representations of women doing things other than servicing men – what one might call 'feminist-realism' – it is also deeply implausible.

Charlotte Brunsdon

Notes

1 The recent Radio Rentals Advertisement for a video tape recorder is a good example. 'It can take 8 hours of *Crossroads* if you can.'
2 People involved in *Brookside* are a noticeable exception here. The *Soap City* day, organised by Dorothy Hobson as part of the 1985 Birmingham Film and Television Festival demonstrated many of these attitudes.
3 See Ien Ang, *Watching Dallas*, Methuen, 1985.
4 Elizabeth Walton, *The Times*, 25 November 1985, p.12.
5 Both Rosalind Coward in *Female Desire* (Paladin, 1984) and Elizabeth Wilson, *Adorned in Dreams* (Virago, 1985) take these issues on in different ways.
6 See Christine Geraghty's discussion of *Brookside*, 'No common ground', *Screen*, vol 24, no. 4-5, July/October 1983, pp.137-141.

Soap: Diana and the Royals

The engagement and subsequent marriage of Diana Spencer to Prince Charles in 1981 took the British royal family into a glare of publicity of a more intense and inquisitive nature than had ever been focused on them before. The stable, homely image which had pre-vailed when the Queen and Prince Philip had been the focus of media attention gave way to a more exciting and changeable scenario. The royal family, it seemed, had needed an injection of youth and romance, and it had got what it needed in Diana, a blonde nineteen-year-old with a pretty face and a willingness to please.

Moreover, along with these ingredients came the practicality of less publicised qualifications for the job. As Diana's father attested, she had no 'past'. She was young, virginal, fair (white, of course), aristocratic and not too clever. Already suitable for the role, she could be made perfect for it with some expensive grooming, diet-ing and clothing. Diana's impressionability seems all the more marked in comparison with Sarah Ferguson, who married Prince Andrew, complete with her own career, past lovers, and a robust body. Sarah herself has evidently lost weight since her wedding, and it remains to be seen how much of her own life she can hold on to as a royal wife.

The key to Diana's success lies in the anomaly of her role: as the epitome of wifely perfection, she represents an ideal which none of us will ever reach, yet she serves the basic purpose of supplying the royal family with appropriately 'well-bred' heirs to the British throne. In fact, there is little that is romantic about this marriage: a suitable match between two members of the aristocracy, meeting the needs of both families, as well as both partners: a serviceable and predictable arrangement.

Put this way, the reality sounds harshly pragmatic, and hardly the stuff of national fantasies. Some dressing-up was imperative in order to create a sense of mass involvement. The media played a very large part in the creation of this fantasy, and why not? They had only to gain. Princess Diana sells papers. (To a lesser extent, so does Sarah Ferguson.) The Features Editor at *Woman* believes there are three women whose faces on the magazine cover will sell more copies than anyone else: Joan Collins, Linda Evans and Princess Diana. How long Collins and Evans will continue to sell out magazines depends on the popularity of the TV characters they play and the series in which they feature. Princess Diana is likely to outlast them, not only because she has youth on her side. Her position will assure her magazine covers, newspaper headlines and TV specials for the rest of her life.

It may seem surprising to find a princess alongside two soap opera actresses in readership popularity, but it is logical in a press which increasingly blurs the difference between fantasy and reality. This is most obviously the case in the tabloid papers, which chronicle the stories in TV shows as if they were real news items.

In fact, the media in general and the tabloids in particular, presented Diana's story like tear-jerking soap: poor but winsome Nobody weds rich, charismatic Somebody at publicly witnessed extravaganza, then blossoms into attractive and confident Personality. It's just like Krystal and Blake in *Dynasty*: or the Cinderella story come to life.

Cinderella may seem a far-fetched role for the daughter of an earl to play, but this is just one of the fictions energetically maintained by media determined to cast Diana in a role to which we, the readers and viewers, can relate. Media presentation of the pre-wedding Diana made her seem like the girl any of us could have been: the giggling, shy teenager whose unsophisticated charms captivated a prince. It was an image of accessibility not limited to her shaking people's hands at fetes; we were made to feel that, because of her apparent shyness and inexperience, this aristocratic young lady, brought up on a country estate and educated at private schools, was just like one of us. (Sarah Ferguson's image has been given similar overtones of ordinariness, and she, moreover, is a working woman still.)

Even since Diana's transformation into a far more assured and stately figure, we can still, it seems, relate to her, because now she is a mother, and can be seen displaying the care and affection for her children that mothers everywhere feel. The human side of the princess's image retains our interest, and in fact this human ingredient is vital for the whole royal family: without it, they run the risk of losing public sympathy. Their collective image has popular appeal because it is homely and unaffected. They are 'The Royals', the ideal bourgeois family, featuring in the tabloid press and on the news almost daily with their cast of endearing characters: smiling granny, handsome young sons, doggy pets. The relationship between the media and the royal family is reciprocal, and, at present, extremely rewarding to both sides.

What could be a better selling point for a newspaper than the nation's very own real-life royal soap opera? Unlike TV series, this one is guaranteed to run and run. For the other side, the royal family have the constant problem of maintaining interest and support from a populace who have so little in common with them. On the most practical level, we have to be persuaded that they are worth financing, and the whole apparatus of royal ceremony requires crowd audiences: how embarrassing it would be if the Queen went to a public function and nobody had turned up to cheer. There is, at present, no danger of losing any of this public support; the royal family's popularity is widespread among young and old, and to most people their cosy stability represents a kind of bulwark against unknown political threat.

Collaboration between the royal family and the media dates back a long way. The Queen's coronation in 1953 was the first major royal event to be televised, and this was done at her express wish. It is an arrangement which keeps them in the forefront of public attention and interest. There are other roles possible for royalty, as the Scandinavian monarchs demonstrate, but most people in this country are so used to royal stardom, any such alternative would seem unacceptably drab.

Teresa Stratford

9
Health

Introduction

*Over the past ten years, health has become a major focus of media
attention. Health issues feature in TV dramas and front page headlines. It is rewarding to devote air space and newspaper columns
to health issues, for they can provide enough melodramatic ingredients to hold an audience fascinated. There's suspense (will the
operation work – only a 50–50 chance), joy (it did), tragedy (it
didn't); there are tales of 'everyday folk', and of wondrous deeds
far too clever for us to fathom (the press loves medical miracles);
and, with the recent emergence of AIDS in Britain, there is fear
and trembling.*

*With few exceptions,[1] we receive a highly dramatised, action-
packed picture of illness and health care through our media. It's
understandable: crisis and drama is attention-grabbing. Yet the
pattern of disease in this country does not live up to this exciting
media picture; our health problems are predominantly ones of an
insidious and chronic nature. The diseases which are particular
problems for industrialised countries such as Britain are heart disease, cancer, chronic bronchitis, hypertension and diabetes.[2] The
treatment for these conditions involves long-term care and support
with appropriate medication. There is no startling headline material here, unless a famous person is involved.[3]*

*Reportage of health issues relies on various assumptions, one
being the standard of health considered acceptable. In Britain, for
example, dental caries are considered to be compatible with
health, but intestinal parasites are not; thinning hair is healthy for
men, but not for women.[4] Another assumption is the wisdom and
reliability of the medical profession, which is held in very high*

esteem in this country. This has encouraged the medicalisation of our health: local, homely remedies have been superseded by treatments which are prescribed for us by a doctor.

This has had a profound effect on women's role as society's carers. We are expected to take responsibility for the health of our partners, children and elderly relatives as well as (in fact, more than) our own. Yet we are not supposed to know anything beyond the most basic skills of caring; anything considered 'medical' is the domain of the 'experts', who are still mostly male. The media reinforce the message with their fondness for stories about wives, girlfriends and mothers in supportive, caring roles, while medical experts handle the technical side of healing women's partners or children. Women, it seems, should have the emotional dedication to nurse sick people, but it is usually men who have the intellectual knowledge to save lives. Despite an increased proportion of women doctors in recent years, this stereotypical message also permeates the medical professions, in which nurses (still mostly women) are seen as 'angels', and doctors (still mostly men) are scientific wizards.[5] In this context, Wendy Savage's campaign was particularly striking, partly because she was fighting for women's increased control over their pregnancies and births – and partly because she was a woman who won her case. Even so, one of the issues she stressed – that midwives should be considered as central to obstetric decision-making – became lost in the media reportage, which focused on the doctors in the case.[6]

The focus of media attention on health has changed over the past few years. In the 1970s, there was a strong focus on personal psychology and self-awareness. Since the early 1980s, the emphasis has shifted on to physical health: while people still explore their neuroses, it seems more imperative to worry about blood pressure, heart rate or posture. What is seldom made clear in the media is that these worries are essentially middle-class preoccupations. The industry of keeping healthy (including whole-food shops, gymnasia, books, magazines, equipment) thrives on the support of people from the healthiest section of society. Surveys of mortality indicate that working-class people (that is, social classes IV and V) have the highest mortality risk at every age.[7] Of course, they are the people who do not have the financial means to jump the NHS queues and pay for private treatment. Since women usually earn lower

*wages than men, and tend to live longer, this is a situation of
particular difficulty and potential distress for us.*

*There is an abundance of information available in the media to
guide women on staying healthy (notably in women's magazines).
Unfortunately, it tends to link health and beauty in an emphasis on
health as the key to remaining desirable. There are a few exceptions,
however: concern about cervical cancer, side effects of the contraceptive pill, venereal diseases and AIDS seem to be topics for which
magazines abandon their beauty-conscious angle,[8] encouraging
women to take care of themselves for their own sakes, not for a
man's. But we have still to see media acceptance of women's own
standards of health. At present, our health (especially our mental
health) and strength is still measured against men's.*

*The following articles explore further some implications of
current media attitudes to health for women.*

Notes

1 For example, Denis Potter's *The Singing Detective*, broadcast in
1986, in which the hero suffers badly from psoriasis; also *SHE*, October
1986, which included an article giving help and advice to incontinence
sufferers.
2 L. Doyal, *The Political Economy of Health*, Pluto Press, 1979.
3 For example, Elton John's possibly cancerous nodules of the larynx,
January 1987.
4 P. Brearley *et al.*, (eds) *The Social Context of Health Care*, Robertson
and Blackwell, 1978.
5 J Salvage, *The Politics of Nursing*, Heinemann, 1985.
6 W. Savage, *A Savage Enquiry*, Virago, 1986.
7 L. Doyal, *The Political Economy of Health*.
8 For example, *Cosmopolitan*, January 1987, which included an article
on AIDS which posed some fundamental questions about what women
get out of sex.

Women and Fitness

Keeping fit is an exhausting business. The relentless pursuit of the
ageless physique demands unflinching dedication. One slip, one

weak link in the chain of discipline and that blubber of flesh swamps us in pounds of guilt. Like a dropped face lift, the years of decay race back, turning us all into forlorn Cinderellas.

Or so the experts would have us believe. As with all growth (shrink) industries, there's just enough truth to get us hooked before we become exploited. And there *is* plenty of truth in the notion that keeping fit means keeping alive. As the workout manuals tell us; exercise fights heart disease: 'There is good evidence that regular vigorous exercise can have a protective effect on the heart.'[1] It also guards against early death and strengthens muscles to support the back. 'Strong abdominal muscles are the best insurance against lower back pain. Exercise helps to reduce weight, strengthens supportive muscles and increases circulation of nutrient-carrying blood to the spine.'[2] 'A strong, supple back can *prevent* strain and damage.'[3] Exercise acts as antidote to a sedentary desk life, relieves pre-menstrual tension and facilitates childbirth. 'By toning up your muscles and your pelvic area, stretching will help prepare you for birth. It may also help to relieve backache and other minor discomforts.'[4] 'Poor posture can be corrected by strengthening back and abdominal muscles',[5] 'a strong thigh muscle helps protect the fragile knee joint',[6] 'aerobic work-out plans improve the circulatory system.'[7] 'If a joint is stiffening up it's essential to keep the circulation going by actively exercising the joint yourself, and so disperse the fatigue-causing aches and pains in your muscles and joints.'[8] 'Aerobic exercises like jogging, swimming, walking and running increase stamina and exercise heart and lung muscles.'[9] The list is endless.

Any incentive towards preventive health care must be encouraged. But the new body boom is not just concerned with perfecting the physique, it's more to do with refining the psyche. Slimming down one's aspirations in an anorexic bid to transcend the body is now what it's all about. 'Exercise releases a natural hormone to give a natural high. Physical fitness gives a sense of well being, alertness and high spirits and these in turn bring inner feelings of calmness, strength and assurance which will not only make your everyday activities more enjoyable but will give you a new approach to life itself.'[10]

And now that we have been brainwashed into asceticism, the axe falls even more deadly. 'Shapely arms are as important to a beautiful body as are shapely legs. Overweight, sagging arms are a sign of premature ageing.' 'A pretty ankle can still turn plenty of heads.'[12] Shocked into the realisation that it's not enough to achieve the new, trendy 'optimum health',[13] – you've got to be pretty too. Are we now sufficiently broken down to yield to the barrage of exercise machines, running shoes, vitamin tablets, workout manuals and records, dance and sportswear, health and beauty centres and other accoutrements of an advertising machine that will coax us all into achieving that goal? Willing accomplices to a benevolent industry? Isn't it simply combining our interests with . . . its own?

Even the ideal of just a beautiful veneer is now *passé*; we've got to have *inner* muscle too. Magazine models bloomed 'shapely' in the fifties, shrank waif-like in the sixties (from which emaciated bondage they've never fully recovered), and after a brief flurry as dishevelled rape victims have now begun to glow Olympian-like in the eighties. Weight training is the new fitness boom. Muscle building is all the rage. 'Strong and sexy embodies the new feminine ideal. Luscious Deborah Diana in a seductive pose.'[14] Does the boom correspond with the trend to Amazonian models, or does the trend, with a keen eye for profit, lucratively follow the craze?

And who are we becoming more shapely for? 'Shapely' with its fifties, film-starlet connotations, throws up an image of beckoning passivity: women waiting to be looked at, or looked over, by men. Objects, rather than subjects in our own lives, as Simone de Beauvoir would say. *Are* we so free from pressures of stereotyping that we are, in fact, doing the right deeds for the right reasons – acting freely for ourselves, rather than being locked into collusion, confirming ourselves as the second sex?

At a women-only workout gym in Hackney, London, women agreed that exercise made her feel not just fit but 'better, more exhilarated and energetic, more aware of my body as strong and powerful, not just something you happen to be lumbered with'.[15] Prime athletes reveal that running helps their track record in childbirth, too.[16] Forty-seven-year-old ballet star, Doreen Wells, talks of the transformation aikido has brought to her life as a working mother.[17] Glance at the timetable of even the glossiest workout gym and you'll find circuit training, karate, yoga or Tai chi along with the aerobics. 'Who for?' seems to be the key issue.

It's not the act itself that's ideologically in question, but its lack of integration with the rest of one's life. The dislocation is caused by pitting one's body against a hostile and scrutinising consumerist society in which we as women are encouraged to market ourselves ever more proficiently.

And who is this fitness industry aimed at? The targets of those insidious institutionalised and unchallenging midmorning radio programmes[18] are not men, but women who are already trapped and isolated in domestic monotony.

If fitness is meant to be so ingenuous, why all the pazazz, the shining cheekbones, the high-cut, low-plunge leotards, the impossible waistlines? Jane Fonda and Raquel Welch may be doing a service to the health industry by promoting life After Forty, but they're not doing a lot for Ms Average, slogging away on the exercise treadmill, feeling too big, too small, too fat, too shapely, too gauche amidst the sea of Covent-Garden-coordinated hype that equates fitness with glamour.

And inevitably, the Fondas and Welches are exceptions in the cult of the Body Chic that otherwise tends only to cultivate the under thirties. A letter to a current fitness magazine points this out. 'I am slightly irritated by your assumption that only the under-30s are interested in health and keeping fit. Many older women . . . sadly receive scant attention in the pages of your magazine. The maximum age in your "Meet the Guinea-pigs" feature is, after all, only 30.'[19] Primed to appeal to men as a good catch, women can be discarded as scrap, once that dubious dream has been (in theory) realised.

The new fitness boom brings other, more overt dangers. With the New Puritans comes the New Masochism manifested in the shin splints, stress fractures, joint strains and sudden heart attacks that can be the new casualties of the aerobic/jogging syndrome. In the struggle to cross the pain barrier – colourfully called 'the burn' – it's not unusual to see women drop exhausted. I've nearly collapsed myself during factory-schedule aerobic sessions, and not only in horror at seeing others falter first. And more insidious still, isn't there something faintly Hitlerian about that obsessive striving after the perfect physique?

The doubtful pleasure of disciplining our minds and bodies demands the leisure time to relax, meditate, take classes and prepare a corresponding *cuisine minceur*. A class-bound, luxury. 'Women are so busy caring for everyone else that we feel terribly guilty about spending time, energy and money on ourselves', says a massage teacher in south London.[20] A double bind. Exercise is, on the one hand, a necessity, on the other an indulgence.

These contradictions evade men for whom jogging, badminton and other activities appear sublimely unproblematic: sport without a conscience. If a man suddenly undertakes to 'go public' in a television charity keep fit bid, he's treated as a guinea pig to be marvelled at and applauded. But for him, it's not so much a case of fighting the flab as of 'realising his own, innate potential'.

For women, this kind of fight throws us into competition with other women, and eventually ourselves. It's a kind of preoccupation that can become a madness: a desperation born of frustration, whose goal, by definition, can never be fully realised. Disregarded as the shape that can never quite conform to the glossy magazine, Bond Street dummies staring us out, we learn, in humiliation, the art of disguise, slurring over our own outlines and blanking ourselves out. Seen as imperfect, we see ourselves as grotesque and unlovable: objects in our own lives. The quest for eternal beauty, that evanescent elixir of zest, youth and glamour, becomes all-consuming. On a life-long, low-calorie diet of ersatz nourishment, we end up trailing after a mirage in the desert.

Norma Cohen

Notes

1 *Beating Heart Disease*, Health Education Council, 1984.

2 *Jane Fonda's Health and Fitness Diary*, Allen Lane, 1984.

3 Diana Moran, *Get Fit with the Green Goddess*, BBC Publications, 1983.

4 Maxine Tobias and Mary Stewart, *Stretch and Relax*, Dorling Kindersley, 1985.

5 Valentine Fox, *Aerobics Stretch and Shape Workout*, World's Work Ltd, 1983.

6 Olive Smithells, *Fatness, Figures and Fitness*, Thorsons, 1967.

7 Patrick Holform, *Vitamin Vitality*, Collins, 1985.

8 *Aerobics Stretch and Shape Workout*.

9   *Jane Fonda's Health and Fitness Diary.*

10 *Aerobics Stretch and Shape Workout.*

11 *ibid.*

12 *Get Fit with the Green Goddess.*

13 *Vitamin Vitality.*

14 *Muscle magazine*, USA, 1984. (Others include *Flex*, *Body Building*, *Sport and Fitness*.)

15 Interview with women at Sequin Park Gym, London, *City Limits*, September 1985.

16 'Running for Women' supplement to *Running and Fitness* magazine, October 1985.

17 *Fitness* magazine, January 1985.

18 Bryan Hayes phone-in, LBC radio; Bobbie Vincent phone-in, Radio London; Tony Blackburn, BBC Radio 2.

19 *Fitness* magazine, October 1984.

20 Interview with Fiona Harrold, *City Limits*, September 1985.

The Shape of Slimming

Good news – well, quite good. The casual observer may not notice the subtle changes in attitude about women and weight which are surfacing in the press. After all, following Christmas one still expects to see the 'Slim into your swimsuit' and 'Our ways to slim' features. There are still the advertisements and articles featuring flabby and depressed 'before' photos with radiant and trim 'after' shots. But something new has been happening too. Compulsive eating, bulimia nervosa, and anorexia have become topics for regular discussion, particularly in women's magazines. More notice is being taken of why women eat (or don't) rather than what they eat – not a lot of notice, but enough to make a difference. And assertiveness is creeping into the language of the slimming magazines.

There are seven magazines devoted to slimming. The largest, *Slimming*, had a circulation figure of 248,640 for January 1986, while in 1980 it sold 343,969. Despite a few new slimming titles since 1980 the overall trend in sales shows a small decline.

Of course the pressure is still on to be *slim*. However the angle here has changed. We're now meant to be *fit* and slim. Flick through a slimming magazine and you'll notice that many of the advertisements for slimming products would do equally well for sportswear. The first specific fitness magazine was launched in 1984 and in the second half of that year already had a circulation of 77,984. Monthly magazines have produced fitness supplements. But if the emphasis is on exercise and fitness rather than quick-slim diets then this can possibly be seen as a positive step, because 'fitness' should be aimed equally at both sexes.

Obesity and poor diet are problems in developed countries. They're not limited to women. However, a man can be obese yet still be seen as successful, while for a woman that's far more difficult. To be successful, a woman is also meant to be attractive, and attractive in the present fashionable shape.

The language of slimming is the language of 'success' and 'failure'.

'As you triumphantly reach your target weight'
'I'm 5' 4'' and I was going on 12st, hopelessly brainwashed into believing that I was a total failure . . . '
'Here are a reader's very real reasons for her failures . . . '

These are all quotes from *Slimming*, July/August 1985 issue. Success, for women, is about control – of weight and food.

While one side of the food industry tempts us into being 'naughty but nice' with cream or suggesting we do 'disgracefully indulgent' things with bacon, another section insists we shouldn't be able to pinch more than an inch and to achieve this they'll help us control and so be successful.

The confusion over 'food that's good for you', let alone what weight you should be, has spread. Findus, in a recent press release, quotes Dr Vernon Coleman saying at a 'Lean Lecture' set up by them that 'the main reason for all this confusion is that there is an enormous number of people with vested interest in promoting particular types of food. Commercial forces influence the sort of information we get and the way in which it is presented.' Presumably one infers from this that Findus isn't one of those commercial concers trying to influence us. The government's Food Standards Committee might feel otherwise.

In its 1980 report on 'Claims and Misleading Descriptions' the

FSC criticised the names and implied promises given by products saying that ' . . . the effects on general public understanding resulting from the food industry's incursion into this [weight loss] area are not encouraging . . . We consider that the public should move away from the delusion that by eating a particular food weight can be lost.' They continued: 'Names for foods containing the word "slim", "slender", "weight watchers" etc. should not be permitted and we recommend accordingly'. Not much notice was taken of that. We still have 'slimming products' called 'Slim-line', 'Slender', 'Shape', 'Waistline', 'Slim-a-meal', 'Trim-line' and 'Lean Cuisine' (new from Findus).

Industry isn't discouraged that easily. According to a Euromonitor Report (1983) the slimming foods market was estimated to be worth around £545 million. This included crispbread, skimmed milk, low-calorie substitutes, artificial sweeteners, natural yoghourt and other not solely 'slimming' products but aimed primarily at that market. Specially produced foods to help 'serious' slimmers were worth £28.5 million. Add the money spent on joining slimming clubs and buying slimming magazines and you're talking business, big business. They're not likely to roll over and die(t?) just because the Food Standards Committee say 'the expression "slimming foods" is a contradiction in terms and it can be argued that any claims related to food being an aid to slimming are inherently misleading'.

The Euromonitor Report also noted:

the market has been disappointing in its growth . . . new products generally get a good reception and help to keep up the total market but in real terms sales have grown little since 1970. The reasons may be summarised as follows:
— the products are perceived to be expensive;
— the results achieved are often disappointing (this is not necessarily the fault of the products but may be due to over-expectation on the part of the consumer and/or lack of rigour in applying the diet);
— the products themselves are varied enough within the limits but must be boring in comparison with the tremendous variety offered by a normal diet.

Perhaps there is yet another reason. I know, from my postbag as Problem Page Editor of *Woman's Realm*, that women are changing their ideas. They will still ask whether the 'Cambridge Diet' is the miracle weight-loss theory they've been waiting for, but they're just as likely to ask why they're compulsive eaters, bulimics or anorexics and what they can do about that. In a help-line phone-in *Women's Realm* set up with the Women's Therapy Centre 210 calls were taken on three constantly occupied lines in two days. Virtually all the callers responded to the idea that they might by over- or under-weight, or holding a precarious balance through a harsh physical regime, for a reason. Many had begun to accept that no diet was going to solve their emotional problems, no diet would wave a wand over special pressures or problems, that dieting and all that goes with it might actually be encouraging them to think of themselves as failures with no will-power or control over their lives.

Slimming magazines carry features that look realistically at ways of life which encourage eating disorders and their physical ramifications. Slipped between diets and 'success' stories – which it has to be said, readers love – you're likely to find the psychological approach. In *Slimming* their consultant psychiatrist wrote 'I know that the people who will stay dissatisfied with their shapes, weight and personal relationships are those who believe or hope that at some magical unspecified time in the future a sudden wondrous change will make all their problems disappear'. In this case he omits to say that women are encouraged to do this right from our first children's stories. Girls are reared on damsels being rescued while boys are bred on overcoming difficulties and slaying dragons to get what they want. Women are meant to wait for it, at least so the stories go. Though not explaining the educational process which has conditioned women to this state of waiting, the psychiatrist for *Slimming* does say that 'wishing, you see, takes the place of action' and 'your emotional well-being depends on the realisation that surplus weight does not mean failure, just as being slim does not guarantee success'. Mind you, he doesn't advocate abandoning dieting as a way of life, in fact says that 'looking as good as you can is a wonderful incentive to carry on a diet – and life – with growing confidence'. Notice diet comes first, life second – no wonder we feel failures if we fail to diet.

In a recent, much publicised, booklet on *Slimming and Nutrition* from the British Medical Association thirteen facts about weight loss are cited. Two, I think, are of particular importance:

'Due to their lifestyle most women have more opportunities to overeat than men.
'Many people need to eat to make up for something lacking in their lives. A fresh interest in life may lessen the craving for food.'

The psychological and social pressures theories about weight gain and loss are gaining ground. Surely, that's good news.

The BMA booklet, written by Dr Dennis Craddock, also releases some 'encouraging news'. 'The increased risks to life due to overweight have been over-estimated in the past. For most there is no appreciable increased risk until a woman is about 30 per cent overweight. For a man it is 25 per cent.' He says that 'No one is going to come to any harm from being five to ten pounds overweight. In fact only 10 per cent of the adult population carries less than five to ten pounds of unnecessary fat. Young men in particular should watch their weight if they exceed this.' So, it's men they should have been aiming the advertising at all this time! Well, that's good news too . . . isn't it?

Gill Cox

'Smoke gets in your eyes' – Women and smoking[1]

Thirty-two per cent of women in Britain are smokers, and increasing attention is now being focused on the growing intensity of the smoking problem amongst girls and women.[2] Ten years ago research showed that more teenage boys than girls were smoking, but over the decade the pattern has changed. In a number of recent studies the proportion of girls smoking in their mid-teens has now caught up with or overtaken boys.

Anti-smoking campaigns seem to have had more effect on adult men than women – between 1972 and 1984 cigarette smoking declined by 31 per cent amongst men but only 22 per cent amongst women (who are now only 4 per cent behind men, 36 per cent of whom smoke cigarettes). The female death toll from smoking-related diseases is rising – nearly 30,000 British women died as a result in 1983 – and for the first time, in 1984, lung cancer killed more Scottish women than breast cancer. Smoking brings increased risks for young women. Those who smoke and take the contraceptive pill have an increased risk of coronary heart disease and stroke; smoking has been linked to cancer of the cervix, is known to harm the unborn baby and is also linked to an earlier menopause.

In the face of these problems, the tobacco industry, which spends at least £100 million on its promotions, has increasingly aimed its product and its advertising at women. A leading tobacco trade journal has even openly stated that 'women are a prime target . . . '

The potential of women's magazines as a medium for promoting smoking has clearly been recognised by the tobacco companies. The audience for these magazines is massive – they are read regularly by half the women in Britain. They reach women of all ages and social backgrounds, and since many of the more glossy magazines lie around for a long time after publication, their readership is far higher than their circulation figures.

With these advantages, it is not surprising that women's magazines have increasingly become one of the more important media outlets for cigarette advertising. Between 1977 and 1982 revenue from tobacco advertising in women's magazines increased from £2.4 to £6.2 million, and by 1984 their total earnings had reached £6.9 million.

Not only do women's magazines reach an enormous number of women, they also have a long tradition of acting as sources of advice on a wide range of topics including health. It is widely believed that because of the close relationship cultivated between magazine and reader, women are more likely to trust and value the information offered by these magazines compared with other media. They have an agenda-setting role in defining ideas about health. If articles about smoking and ill-health do not appear in magazines, is it because the topic is not considered to be important? And if cigarette advertising does appear in a magazine, does this mean that cigarette smoking is OK? *Vogue* has pointed out how the magazine itself acts as an image-giver which endorses products advertised in it: 'If an ad is seen in *Vogue*, this is as good as a stamp of acceptability.'

Between August 1984 and February 1985, fifty-three magazines were surveyed for the BMA and the Health Education Council. All had a predominantly female readership, usually 75 per cent or more. Most were targeted at women but in an attempt to cover major magazines read by young women the survey also covered *Smash Hits*, *The Face* and *No. 1*. (These three are not specifically aimed at women but have a large young female readership.) The survey looked at cigarette advertising policy and coverage of smoking and health in the magazines. Amongst its findings, the survey showed that those magazines which derived above average revenue from cigarette advertising were much less likely to devote any major attention to smoking and health.

It has been suggested that the use of glamorous models smoking cigarettes in editorial pages as well as in films has contributed to the growth of smoking among girls and young women. The survey found that although magazines such as *The Face* (September, October 1984, May 1985) and *Company* (January 1985) recently portrayed glamorous models smoking, they seem to be the exception rather than the rule.

As far as the effect of cigarette advertising is concerned, the tobacco industry defends cigarette advertising by claiming that it neither increases sales nor creates new smokers, but merely persuades established smokers to switch brands. Yet in a comprehensive review of the evidence, the BMA has argued forcefully that cigarette advertising plays a key role in creating an environment where smoking is seen to be desirable, and that this along with other social factors acts to encourage people to start smoking, and may defer a decision to stop. *Campaign* magazine, voice of the advertising industry, has said, 'Everybody agrees that the aim of advertising is not to produce memorable work but to improve sales . . . ' The tobacco industry would be unlikely to spend £100 million a year if advertising was ineffective. A recent government survey[3] showed that in the opinion of the public, cigarette advertising increases the social acceptability of smoking. In the BMA survey it was discovered that at least one million female non-smokers aged 15-24 are exposed to cigarette advertising through the magazines selected for the survey alone.

Amanda Amos and Bobbie Jacobson

PS In April 1986 the government published its new voluntary agreement with the tobacco industry on tobacco products' advertising and promotion.

Included in the agreement was a new rule (1.18) which states that 'no advertising of cigarette or hand-rolling tobacco brands will be placed in magazines or periodicals published in their own right when it is apparent at the time the advertisement is placed that the publication has a female readership of more than 200,000 and more than 33 per cent of those female readers are aged 15–24'. Whilst this new rule is but a token gesture in the right direction (magazines such as *The Face* with 190,000 readers are excluded as are magazines such as *Woman's Own* which has over 1 million readers under twenty-five but they count for less than 33 per cent of the readership), it will mean that the following magazines can no longer take cigarette advertisements.

	Readership
Cosmopolitan	1,815,000
Vogue	1,668,000
True Romances	1,077,000
Options	1,041,000
Woman's World	834,000
Company	701,000
Over 21	694,000
Ms London	267,000
Girl About Town	217,000

Notes

1 Adapted with permission from *When Smoke Gets in Your Eyes*, written by Dr Bobbie Jacobson and Dr Amanda Amos for the British Medical Association Health Education Council, 1985.
2 Much of the information contained in this section is derived from *General Household Survey 1984*, Office of Population Censuses and Surveys Monitor, GHS85/2, London, 1985.
3 A. Marsh and J. Matheson, *Smoking Attitudes and Behaviour*, OPCS Social Survey Division, HMSO, London 1983.

10
The Domestic Sphere

Introduction

The confining of women to the domestic sphere has proved useful to the male establishment in limiting the influence of women in society. This is reinforced by systematically devaluing everything connected with that sphere – and simultaneously aggrandising those spheres dominated by men.

The media collude with this process. They continue to perpetuate the myth that the domestic sphere is the one of greatest relevance to women – with only token attention paid to the fact that a large proportion of women not only work outside the home but also participate in other activities. This myth operates more especially for working-class women, whose paid work is devalued in the same way as women's unpaid work.

The media also collude with the myth that women and domesticity are linked by nature – *this is their* natural *role. This of course provides a rationale for continuing to expect women to do most of the household work, and enabling men to escape its confines. There is virtually no recognition in any part of the media that men do (or could, or should) play a role in the domestic sphere; in fact presenting men in non-stereotyped ways (e.g. as 'househusbands') is often cause for comedy, the humour being generated by the perceived incongruity of the situation.*

Since things domestic are portrayed as part of women's nature, it is not surprising that they are also seen as unimportant, incidental. This allows society to continue to exploit women's unpaid labour. Child-rearing, perhaps the most important activity undertaken in any society, is accorded low prestige. Even those male right-wing moralists, including politicians, who make a career out of denouncing 'sex and violence in front of the children' on television, have little to say on the subject of family support or the provision of child-care facilities.

Yet at the same time 'the housewife' is being wooed as a consumer. This function too is of vital importance to the nation's economy. Advertisements directed at 'the housewife' assume that she is white, relatively affluent, heterosexual (and married), able-bodied – and above all, passionately, intimately and contentedly devoted to the minutiae of household life. She is considered susceptible to the male 'voice of authority', and her intelligence is insulted at every turn.

The articles that follow are in no way meant to devalue the nurturing and home-making that most women do with considerable skill and few resources. They attempt to place the issues within a framework for further discussion.

We include an article on women and food production in the Third World because we feel that this is one very important area where the media ignore women's contribution. Our ignorance of the reality of women's lives in large parts of the world results from the media's judgement that this is not a newsworthy subject. We believe it is.

Radio Times – private women and public men

Switch on your radio set and listen: there's a subtle, but pervasive, gender apartheid going on. If it's daytime, the broadcasters (mainly men) are speaking to women, and women firmly situated in the domestic realm. If it's evening, we're offered a seemingly ungendered world in which political and social concerns are debated, and culture celebrated or scrutinised (still mainly by men), but with rarely any sense of the listeners' immediate context. When darkness falls, the domestic world falls away.

Radio offers us private women and public men. Women are addressed in the singular, in their individual homes going about their daily tasks. The evening audience – apparently Anyone, but at times suspiciously like Everyman – is addressed in the collective, as listeners abstracted from the imperatives of labour. They're engaged in the world out there but almost no reference is made to the world at their feet or in their living-rooms.

Presenters don't buttonhole them with 'Going to pour yourself a sherry, and put your feet up?' or 'Relieved that a hard day's nearing its end?' They're appealed to as listeners in their leisure, as men of the world. And this even happens where, unusually, the evening broadcasters are women – high-fliers like Mary Goldring, presenter of Radio 4's 'Analysis' programme, generally deny any connection with their gender, and speak to a similarly ungendered collectivity. There's rarely any acknowledgement, by the mediators of this 'after work' world, of their listeners' or their own gender, class, or ethnic group, or that different perspectives come out of different social placings.[1]

Back in the daytime, it's a very different story. Comments about the chores to be done are common, on Radios 1 and 2, local radio, and even to some extent on Radio 4. The radio which begins with the houseworking day, and accompanies every stage of it until the television goes on in the evening, has a domestic ideology, a sexual division of labour, threaded into its very fabric. Therefore it occupies a very special relationship with women's lives – a commentary or counterpoint.[2]

As Lesley Johnson has suggested, writing about the introduction of radio in Australia in the 1920s and 1930s, 'programmers had adapted their timetables to the imagined pattern of a woman's life. Through this process radio stations set out to regulate the work and rhythms of daily life of all women to this pattern . . . Listeners responded by altering their domestic arrangements to fit in with their favourite shows'.[3]

The frequent allusions which daytime broadcasters – especially on Radios 1 and 2, and local radio – make to the time, and what's currently going on in their listeners' schedules, have the effect of normalising the domestic routine: doing the washing to 'Jimmy Young', or baking to *Woman's Hour* become fixed points, which have an almost independent, natural life of their own.

But actually, the programming is the result of a particular set of ideas about the listener. Its clearest expression came in the mythical prototype listener coined by the commercial local radio station, Essex Radio. 'We call our average listener Doreen . . . Doreen isn't stupid, but she's only listening with half an ear and doesn't necessarily understand "long words".' She's also a housewife with a working husband (this may already make her atypical) and children at school. She doesn't work outside the home and is generally content.[4]

Doreen is the butt of broadcasters' advances. Here's David Hamilton, BBC disc-jockey, 'I try to talk to one person. I've got this picture of a woman, a housewife, young or young at heart. She's probably on her own virtually all day. She's bored with the routine of housework and her own company and just for her I'm the chatty, slightly cheeky romantic visitor.'[5]

With this notion of Doreen, it's not hard to appreciate why there is still no weekday female disc-jockey in the daytime on Radio 1. As Radio 1's Executive Producer, ironically herself called Doreen Davies, explained,

I think the housewife at home would rather hear Tony Blackburn than a girl [*sic*] . . . If a girl in some studio in London starts talking about getting your washing and ironing done – you're going to resent it. It just sounds personal to another woman. She'll feel, 'Why should I? That girl's not doing housework and washing'. It's different if Tony Blackburn says it; that's just light-hearted.[6]

One gets a marvellous vision here of executive terror that the BBC might inadvertently incite the housewives of Britain into a housework strike. More seriously, it illustrates the consensual, non-disruptive dimension of daytime broadcasting, and its reaffirmation of the normality of women's domestic labour.

Moreover, Davies implies that while a DJ couldn't manage without mentioning housework, one who talked about it seriously and perhaps questioned its ideology would be unacceptable. It's certainly not surprising that commercial radio in particular, dependent as it is on advertising revenue, needs to foster a cheery image of women contentedly polishing the floor, or whipping up a chilli con carne. Who'd want to advertise soap powder between programmes urging listeners to domestic insurrection?

But if broadcasters' ideas about women are structured round domesticity of a kind, they're also overlaid with notions of sexuality. Radio critic Gillian Reynolds recognised this and suggested that a woman presenter would threaten the assumed sexual relationship between broadcaster and listener.

If a man came on the phone to dedicate a record to his wife, could she [a female presenter] say things like, 'All on your own, then? I pass your house on my way home, I'll nip in for a cup of tea. Ho, ho'? She could not, she would not. Men can, men do, and women expect them to, even if it's all fantasy. Men in broadcasting are expected to be surrogate lovers, all bold flirtation and innuendo. Women are not.[7]

A classic example of this, from an afternoon DJ show on BBC Radio London, was cited by Women's Airwaves (a collective of London women who make radio programmes about, for and with women), when they monitored a week of London's local radio.

Man presenter:	But right now, looking as beautiful as ever, it's . . . Oh aren't you nice ha ha. Well, old flatterer that I am, I've forgotten what you're going to talk about today. Er yes of course, fruit and veg. time isn't it?
Woman presenter:	That's right, yes, we've had lots of nasty weather . . .
Man presenter:	Let's just talk about you and forget the fruit and veg.
Woman presenter:	I'm sure no one's interested in me.
Man presenter:	Yes they are, yes. All right, we'd better talk about fruit and veg.
Woman presenter:	'Cos it's quite sad really, we've had some quite nasty, frosty weather all over the country . . . It's destroyed all the blossom on the English cherry trees and pear trees, so of course . . .
Man presenter:	Has it interfered with your *pears* then?
Woman presenter:	Yes it might do later on in the year. These things show later on in the year. We shall have to see, won't we?
Man presenter:	Your *pears* show later on in the year do they?
Woman presenter:	Yes they do.
Man presenter:	Yes, because of the cold weather is it?[8]

The only way in which the woman copes with the male sexual innuendo here is by ignoring it, by deliberately accepting only the surface meaning of the man's questions.

Helen Baehr and Michele Ryan argue that the stereotypes about women which local radio perpetuates, most notably in their conception of Doreen, are lamentably outdated. In 1980 there were 10.4 million women in the labour force, including more than half of all mothers (54 per cent) with children under sixteen. Almost two-thirds of all married women are now either employed or looking for work. Three-quarters of a million women now head single-parent families, and only 5 per cent of British households conform to the traditional nuclear family (with working husband, housewife, and two children). Baehr and Ryan ask, 'does the "contented housewife" only exist in the minds of ILR [Independent Local Radio] programme controllers, presenters, and advertisers?'[9] Are our radios broadcasting to a fictional character from our culture?

Certainly, it's likely that the real listeners are a much more mixed bag, with plenty of men – students, unemployed, those on shift work, self-employed, retired – as well as women who don't conform to the stereotype. And given that working-class women at home with small children have been found to be the likeliest of all to suffer from depression,[10] the jokey banter between DJ and listener, together with the golden oldies music, has clear narcotic properties – Valium taken aurally.

Yet daytime radio is more complex in its appeal, and appealing it certainly is, attracting listeners in their millions. Researchers into mass media are increasingly revisiting popular culture, and greeting its pleasures and ways of meeting real needs as well as its diversionary and controlling aspects.

Dorothy Hobson, who interviewed women in the home about their radio preferences, suggests that it's precisely the way that radio helps to structure their day and their work which those women who are housebound as mothers and housewives find appealing.

In some cases switching on the radio is part of the routine of beginning the day; it is, in fact, the first *boundary* in the working day. In terms of the 'structurelessness' of the experience of housework, the time boundaries provided by radio are important in the women's own division of their time.[11]

She also argues that the disc-jockey, as well as providing relief from isolation, links the isolated individual woman with the knowledge that there are others in the same position, in a sort of 'collective isolation'. The music played may well be the kind that was fashionable before they got married or had children. And 'since listening to music and dancing are the leisure activities which they would most like to pursue, radio is also a substitute for the real world of music and discos which they have lost'.

Hobson sees their liking of disc-jockeys as a way in which these women negotiate and manage the tensions caused by the isolation in their lives. So the romantic role played by DJs may be a way, a safe way, in which the women can re-enact the dance of sexual attraction.

She goes on to contrast the women's television preferences with men's. The women consistently avoid programmes which they think are important, but can't relate to (like the news), and opt instead for soap operas and other such genres which present a world which, symbolically at least, resembles theirs, i.e. is organised around the family.[12]

We can take this further. It's precisely because DJs and other daytime presenters do, implicitly, acknowledge women's domestic obligations – however jokingly and condescendingly – that women can recognise in these programmes a simulacrum of their world. DJ and listener are united in a nexus where the conflicts and ructions of political life are blanked out, save the odd allusion to newspaper headlines, and where domestic life is ordered and comfortingly predictable. It's perhaps the one area of broadcasting where housework is no longer invisible, where the daily minutiae of the domestic round are spoken of, and even celebrated, where home is a place of work, and not just of leisure and consumption. Can we wonder that it's irresistible?

The contradictions of radio addressed to women – that it both acknowledges the constraints in their lives and simultaneously denies them – have been evident over the years in *Woman's Hour*. Like Radios 1 and 2, this forty-year-old daily programme (now on Radio 4) speaks to women at home, its original function 'to lift the load of loneliness borne by women facing misfortune and to help them realise in time of trouble that they are not alone, that others are having to keep a home running, despite the despair and discouragement of unalterable circumstances'.[13]

At times *Woman's Hour* has seemed like a soothing lozenge. An anthology published to celebrate its twenty-first birthday was divided into eight sections which give its flavour: Children, Happiness, Adversities and Triumphs, Abroad, About the House, Animals, The Human Comedy, and Miscellany.[14]

In the letters section of *Woman's Hour* many of its older listeners in particular express their anger and bewilderment at the changes which have destabilised traditional female roles, and their conviction that the programme has become the channel for every modish, radical idea, and a loudhailer for feminism.

For these listeners, *Woman's Hour* has become a reference-point in their day and their lives: its continuity provides a link with the past and the future, a sense of the durability of domestic and public life – much as the Royal Family does. In the tempest of contemporary society, dole and bomb-ridden as it is, they want *Woman's Hour* to map out a known and safe terrain.

At the same time, the programme developed something of a pioneering reputation, braving the airwaves with frank talk of abortion, contraception, divorce, and other hitherto taboo subjects long before other media – let alone the evening programmes – took them up. In the mid eighties, it again started taking risks, broadening its agenda, adopting a more explicitly pro-woman approach, and running items on older feminists, lesbians, men and violence, and other gritty topics. Its editor in this new phase, Sandra Chalmers, says, 'I believe totally in equality for men and women, and to be honest I don't think anyone could work for *Woman's Hour* if they didn't at least have very strong feminist tendencies.'[15]

Though its tone is still often Home Counties bungalow, *Woman's Hour* is the closest thing we have on national radio to a feminist programme. It negotiates the conflicts in broadcasting to and for women, at times unsure how far to examine and interrogate the 'outside' world, without losing its focus on and validation of the domestic world. It's a rare programme which does both, engaging with domestic and emotional subjects, but also scrutinising issues like transport, housing, and defence for their effects on women's lives (and entertaining us into the bargain) – broadcasting to straddle the breach between daytime and evening radio.

Anne Karpf

Notes

1 Even where evening broadcasters speak mainly *to* one social class, they rarely speak explicitly *about* social class.

2 Anne Karpf, 'Women and radio' in *Women's Studies International Quarterly*, vol. 3, no. 1, 1980, republished in Helen Baehr (ed.), *Women and Media*, Pergamon Press, 1980.

3 Lesley Johnson, 'Radio and everyday life. The early years of broadcasting in Australia, 1922–1945', in *Media, Culture, and Society*, vol. 3, no. 2, April 1981.

4 Helen Baehr and Michele Ryan: *Shut Up and Listen! Women and local radio: a view from the inside*, Comedia, 1984.

5 Quoted by Mileva Ross in her chapter on radio in *Is This Your Life? Images of women in the media*, ed. Josephine King and Mary Stott, Virago, 1977.

6 *ibid.*

7 Gillian Reynolds, 'Women's place', in *Broadcast* magazine, 19 February 1979.

8 'Women's voices', in *Nothing Local About It: London's Local Radio*, by Local Radio Workshop, Comedia, 1983.

9 Baehr and Ryan, *op. cit.*

10 George W Brown and Tirril Harris, *Social Origins of Depression – A study of psychiatric disorder in women*, Tavistock, 1978.

11 Dorothy Hobson, 'Housewives and the mass media' in *Culture, Media, Language*, ed. Stuart Hall, Dorothy Hobson, Andrew Lowe, and Paul Willis, Hutchinson, 1980.

12 *ibid.*

13 Joanna Scott-Moncrieff, Foreword, in *The BBC Woman's Hour Book*, The World's Work, 1957.

14 *Woman's Hour*, BBC publications, 1967.

15 Quoted by Sarah Dunant in 'Current affairs shapes Chalmer's finest Hour', *Broadcast* magazine, 31 May 1985.

Women and Food

All our affluent society's guilt about food is focused on women. Our society admires, but cannot achieve, abstemiousness. Thin women are fashionable partly because they seem to represent this elusive quality of self-discipline (and also because the apparent powerlessness of their emaciated bodies suits a patriarchal society like ours, in which men are the ones with strength and power). Women have little control over these values, but they cause us great anxiety about food. Advertisers, supported by fashion, beauty and cookery writers, play relentlessly and profitably on this anxiety.

The advertisements which are designed to provoke the greatest anxiety are at either end of the calorie spectrum: slimming products on the one hand, and high-calorie foods on the other. Outline spread tells us we can 'push the boat out once in a while', use 'a little licence', but only if we've been good all week. Meanwhile, cream cakes are 'naughty but nice', and women are encouraged to 'be a devil' with fresh cream from the Milk Marketing Board.

Many of these phrases have another connotation: the (wicked) involvement in sexual activity. Not only are advertisers making women feel guilty about eating, they are linking their messages with the age-old feelings of guilt women feel about their own sexuality. 'What are you getting up to these days?' asks an advertisement for BN French Toasts.

Overtones of sin and immorality appear in many advertisements: 'Even the most dedicated dieter reaches the point where she'd sell her soul' (Outline). Are we really wicked to eat margarine and cream? Compare these with beer advertisements aimed at men. Beer is hardly slimming stuff, yet the spirit of enjoyment being promoted is unashamed, and the emphasis is on taste and enjoyment.

These feelings of guilt are underlined by cookery articles. Unless it's a salad you're preparing, the implication is that you're cooking for your family. When a writer says, of banana recipes: 'Indulge in some utterly sinful delights', s/he knows that the delights are only sinful for the woman; for Dad and the kids, they're simply nice things to eat.

Home and cookery articles in magazines and newspapers support the role in which food advertisements place women: that of nurturer and provider, the hands that cook and feed. So rare is it to see a picture of a woman actually eating, that when the Women's Monitoring Network held a monitoring day on women and food only one out of hundreds of cuttings sent in showed a woman enjoying food, and this one was an advertisement for denture powder.[1]

A recurrent advertising image is that of Mum waiting passively, ready to serve the next meal, while Dad and the kids enjoy themselves. Moreover, in a world which considers a man and a family to be a woman's real security in life, it is assumed that it's also her responsibility to ensure their good health. The Flora Margarine advertisements show this most clearly, with their 'To have and to hold' and 'thanks to Mum' campaigns, but other examples abound, like the Fresh Fruit and Vegetable Information Bureau's leaflet on how to 'Save Your Man'. They are supported by cookery and health articles in magazines and women's pages.

But it's hard to get the balance right when your cooking is supposed to be *tempting* your man, as well as keeping him healthy. For, in male-defined terms, a woman has two roles to maintain: she must be both sex-object and nurturer. A lot of advertisements for kitchen equipment play on the double image by showing a glamorously dressed woman preparing dinner in an immaculate kitchen. 'It's hard to say who will enjoy your AEG most', says the cooker advertisement; the enjoyable results may be waiting for guests, but they are primarily for the male partner, and are certainly not for the woman who did the cooking. Women must seduce men with their food as well as with their bodies.

But there is another aspect of food's seductive effect. Rosalind Coward has discussed the presentation of food as pornography in her book *Female Desire*.[2] Food pornography is a display of luscious, succulent things (in fact often created out of crêpe paper and paint) to be drooled over. What is most disturbing about this is the use of women's bodies as part of food pornography so that the distinction between woman and food becomes blurred in an image of tempting sensuality. Both the poster advertisements for Crunchie bars and the TV advertisements for Cadbury's Flake feature the chocolate and a woman's lips in long close-ups full of sexual innuendo; the women's luscious lips are as consumable as the chocolate bars. This unpleasant approach is not confined to advertising foodstuffs; an advertisement for Dr White's sanitary towels recently used in women's magazines featured a woman posed on a slice of cucumber, like a party canapé, ready to be consumed. It is also disturbing to see the presentation of women as meat (a common device in pornography) used to sell cosmetics in women's magazines. Yet this is the suggestion behind, for example, Cocoa Butter Sun-Tan Cream, which is to be 'spread' on your body 'before browning' (slogan accompanied by a close-up photo of a woman's naked back).

Food pornography indulges a pleasure which is linked to servitude and therefore confirms the subordinate position of women. It is immediately accompanied by guilt, however, because of the pressure to diet. This is most explicit in slimming magazines, where all the 'no-no's' glare at us from the pages, with the numbers of calories emblazoned near them. As Rosalind Coward says 'The way images of food are made and circulated is not just an innocent catering for pleasure. They also meddle in people's sense of themselves and self-worth . . . '[3] Either way, whether emphasising the serving of food or the self-denial of luscious treats, food pornography confirms the subordinate position of women; it is a masochistic sort of media consumption.

Men generally appear in food advertisements as judges and consumers of food which women have prepared. Sometimes they feature as experts, instructing women on how to do household tasks, from using a food mixer to cooking pasta. Most professional cooks featured both in advertisements and in articles on food are men, be they Robert Carrier promoting food blenders, or Paul Levy writing in the *Guardian*.

What an insult it is to wheel out these male 'experts' to tell women how to do work we've had to do for years! Food production world-wide is women's responsibility (see Sheila Dillon's article below), yet this is rarely acknowledged in the media. As *Spare Rib*'s issue on food [4] pointed out, between 50 per cent and 70 per cent of the world's farmers are women. In Africa, this proportion is even greater: according to the UN Food and Agriculture Organisation, 90 per cent of the rural food supply is provided by women in some parts of Africa (*African Times*). [5]

For most women, feeding their families is work which has to be done, day after day; there's no alternative. Because men are not involved in this day-to-day work, it lacks the status and authority which men generally demand from work they do. The male experts featured as our guides and judges have made cooking into a 'science', with certificates and commercial interests – devices to increase their feelings of worth and satisfaction? For them, the emphasis is on cooking as a skill; for women, it is on service. It is a service which we are expected to continue providing whatever other work we do, and for which we are given only as much respect as the titles 'mother', 'wife' or 'housewife' bestow. It seems that this essential and hard work will only receive the respect it deserves when men become 'wives' too.

from: *Women's Monitoring Network Report No. 6*

Notes

1 'Women and Food' – Report by the Women's Monitoring Network
(see p.217 for address).
2 Rosalind Coward, *Female Desire*, Paladin, 1984.
3 *ibid*.
4 *Spare Rib*, 31 May 1984.
5 *African Times*, 25 May 1984.

Women and Food Production in the Third World

The United Nations Food and Agriculture Organisation estimates that more than 50 per cent of the world's food is produced by women. In Africa the figure is between 60 and 90 per cent. That is the reality. If you wanted to be simplistic you could say that the famines of 1984 and 1985 are the price Africans paid for the West's refusal to recognise that reality (though a reality that ruling elites in Africa – as elsewhere in the Third World – were mostly happy to ignore).

The African famine had an unusual amount of coverage in the developed world. Through coverage of Band Aid as well as documentaries, the plight of the peoples of the sub-Saharan countries of Africa touched millions of people. Unsurprisingly, the reasons for the famine have not had a comparable amount of air time or column inches. Even in the news pages of the serious press, the images of the famine dominated the coverage: gaunt, hollow-eyed women holding dying babies. Those *are* the most stark images of famine, but it is an imagery of helpless victims – victims not only of the famine, but of the failure of their menfolk's livelihoods. They were women who appeared to suffer silently, images in a long line of acceptable female roles: the wife, the mother, passively suffering on the sidelines of wars and depressions. Deeply disturbing to the conscience, but unthreatening to accepted notions of women's roles.

Our perceptions of Africa and Africans were deeply affected by these images, mostly from television. But it was rare in any of the news coverage to see those women as productive individuals who had until this disaster, played a large part in the production of the crops that had now so spectacularly failed. Here it seemed we were witnessing an act of God, a consequence of too many babies, a consequence of being primitive in a harsh world; not, here is the heritage of colonialism and the consequence of the development policies that we in the West have supported wholeheartedly.

You would have to be an avid reader of the *Guardian*'s weekly Third World Review page or of specialist journals to understand that subsistence food on the African continent is produced on a very small scale, mostly by women. You eat what you can grow or barter for. The western model of buying one's food for cash is not relevant to the majority of the African population. Yet for the most part western agricultural aid has gone to already prosperous – male – farmers enabling them to produce food which can be sold to city dwellers at home or as an export crop.

According to the UN *Handbook on Women in Africa* women there do:

85 per cent of the processing and storing of crops
75 per cent of the weeding
60 per cent of the harvesting
50 per cent of caring for livestock
30 per cent of ploughing
95 per cent of the domestic work

But North–South agricultural aid has been almost irrelevant to the people doing that work. 'Women's work is undervalued in a society that is overwhelmingly interested in cash. The woman produces the maize, beans and vegetables to keep her family alive, but the governments are more interested in calculating the income from crops like coffee, tea and cotton which can be sold abroad,' said Lindsey Hilsum of the United Nations Children's Fund. She was speaking at the United Nations conference held in July 1985 in Nairobi to mark the end of the UN Decade for Women. And although what she was saying is not common fare in the general media (her remarks were quoted in *The Times*, 1 August 1985) this lack of aid support to subsistence food producers in Africa has been well documented at an official level since the beginning of the UN Decade. Since the opening conference in Mexico in 1975 innumerable official texts on the position of women in development have been written, published and ratified by governments and official bodies of all sorts – but all to very little effect.

A recent FAO report was blunt: 'In the Third World agricultural productivity cannot be substantially increased, nor can rural poverty be alleviated, unless women's access to key productive resources is substantially improved. The consequences of patriarchy for agricultural productivity are very expensive. Developing countries cannot bear their heavy cost.'

The reality and importance of women's role in feeding the Third World and in producing cash crops for export has been ignored for a number of reasons. First, development policies have been based on what the donors thought the recipients should have – and that has been an industrial and agricultural superstructure as much like the West as possible. Almost all the research and development effort in the Third World has been on the western model. This fact has been happily forgotten by most commentators on the current famine. In a highly acclaimed two-part article on the African famine in the *Financial Times* (3 and 5 April 1985), Anatole Kaletsky blames African governments and people for the 'nightmare of economic collapse' and the present famine: 'that nightmare's cathartic climax'. Kaletsky asks why Africa's ability to feed itself has deteriorated since 1960. He has no answer except crisis, corruption, disaster, but he has a solution: the conventional wisdom among today's aid donors is that something must be done. 'This "something" . . . may require cherished economic institutions and class privileges built up since independence to be swept away. "In a sense, we're talking about a kind of recolonisation – about sending *smart white boys* to tell them how to run their countries" admits one official' (author's italics). Some African governments are even now 'embracing new policies with gusto, apparently convinced that the white man's medicine can be adapted and Africanised to serve their country's needs'. This passes for serious, informed comment of the highest order in the British media.

Smart white boys have long viewed the fact that Third World women do farm as some unfortunate stage in primitive development that would, with the application of the right policies, become a minor historical fact. This is not so much a conscious decision, but rather underlying and totally unquestioned assumptions about 'progress', and what is primitive, and 'natural' for women's roles.

Most Third World governments have accepted these western assumptions as right. Government aid is after all dispensed from the top and in the Third World is received at the top – the top in both places is male.

But in the last five years there has been a change in the rhetoric and policies on 'top down' aid. The recent famines have concentrated a lot of people's minds on where the aid has gone. In fact it's now almost a liberal commonplace to castigate western aid-givers for putting their own commercial needs first in formulating aid policies. Thousands of useless 'cathedrals in the desert', as they've been called, now dot the landscape of the Third World – depressing monuments to decades of such policies. For example, all over Africa massive sugar refineries now stand empty or operate well below capacity (four are in Sudan, one of the countries most severely devastated by the recent famines). They were built in the 1970s with development grants and loans from western governments and banks to take advantage of the world shortage of sugar. Africa was to be a sugar-exporting continent. By the time most of these mammoths came on line there was a world sugar glut (mostly because the European Economic Community had at the same time encouraged subsidised sugar beet production within its own borders) and prices were at an all-time low. Since then the low has got lower. There are now massive sugar stockpiles and hundreds of thousands of acres of good agricultural land that was once used by small farmers are under sugar cane. And the African states are now paying a large portion of their annual wealth to repay these loans and others like them.

But just because it has become a commonplace to identify these capital-intensive, industrial, large-scale projects as the embodiment of the failures of western aid one would be mistaken to assume that it's now all change at the World Bank, the UN, the European Development Fund and the British Overseas Development Administration. The rhetoric has certainly changed: the role of women in development is mentioned everywhere and food self-sufficiency and food security are the new goals. But the realistic pursuit of those goals is almost as far away as ever.

There is a deep unwillingness at the policy-making level of government aid agencies to recognise that the role of women in development is not just today's catch-phrase, it is central in achieving food self-sufficiency.

For a country to achieve self-sufficiency in food it would need to support and improve its indigenous agriculture as a priority. Agricultural aid would be on tap to everyone from the bottom up – helping food producers do better what they already know a great deal about doing. But such a commitment is incompatible with western ideas of progress, with western notions of women's roles and totally incompatible with the conditions that have in recent years been imposed by the International Monetary Fund on most Third World countries.

In return for allowing indebted Third World countries to borrow more money to keep on paying their creditors and to renegotiate the timing of their debt repayments, the IMF (the West's monetary police force) has imposed complex conditions – these vary from country to country, but all include increasing exports. Exports usually mean food commodities. For the past decade most major food commodity prices have been low, so to keep up loan payments the pressure is on to increase exports – which increases stocks which keeps prices low. The cycle goes on and less and less land is available for subsistence agriculture. Unless the South puts together its own united policy on debt repayments, food self-sufficiency can never be more than rhetoric.

Thus, the thrust of western agricultural aid remains the same as ever: 'help' based on western models – large acreages, high inputs of fertiliser and pesticides, hybrid seeds, the use of farm machinery. (A pressure that is fuelled by the farm depression in Europe and the US – agribusiness companies are now making the Third World their major sales target as demand remains low at home.) For the most part aid policies are still being imposed from the top down – women, who economically make up the bottom layer of most Third World societies, are not part of the decision-making process.

The new double-speak is everywhere. In late 1984 the EEC signed its third aid and trade agreement, with the African, Pacific and Caribbean (ACP) countries (mostly ex-EEC country colonies). This five-year agreement, the Lomé Convention, is seen in the development world as extremely important because it is, unlike most other official North–South transfers, an agreement which links aid with trade and recognises the economic importance of South commodities, labour, and debt repayments to the prosperity of the North. In the publicity that surrounded the signing much was made of the new emphasis on the role of women in development and indeed in the section of the agreement called 'Operations to enhance the value of human resources', article 123 states that particular attention shall be given to 'access by women to all aspects of training, to more advanced technology, to credit and to cooperative organisations, and to appropriate technology aimed at alleviating the arduous nature of their tasks'. And one can't ask fairer than that. But women go unmentioned in the more specific articles on agricultural co-operation, desertification, the development of fisheries, and so on. The fear that these might just be fine words grows as one looks through the many photographs of the signing ceremony and the working parties that preceded it. There are no women to be seen.

But a more telling sign of the way the wind is blowing is what happened to the EEC's microproject programme while these men from North and South were arguing the fine points of the latest agreement. The programme is the one part of EEC aid that has operated from the bottom up – programmes are proposed at village or community level and the community must then contribute to the project either in cash or kind. A recent internal EEC audit found microprojects to be the most effective way of providing aid. There was minimum waste, minimum corruption and a positive change that seemed to last. However, though the recent agreement included increasing the money available for microprojects, the staff in Brussels exclusively concerned with processing and monitoring microprojects was disbanded. Microprojects are now the concern of country desk officers – men (and they are almost all men) who are responsible for approving and monitoring all the aid projects within one country. It is obviously much easier to approve and monitor one £1m project than 40 £25,000 projects. And a £1m project will have a much clearer, more conventional chain of accountability. Microprojects are the only part of EEC aid that has consistently reached women.

Anne Clarke, Michel Bo Bramsen and Lisette Caubergs[1] point out the profound changes that have to take place in the attitude of western development specialists if aid is to help women – and in doing that ensure that the Third World becomes self-sufficient in food. Two examples from their paper illustrate the problem: in

Burkino Faso UNESCO and the UN Development Programme were having no success in involving women in education programmes. In trying to understand why, project officials worked out that women had only 1.3 free hours in their first 14 waking hours, so three labour-saving devices were introduced: mechanical grain-grinding mills, carts for the transport of wood, water and crops and more easily accessible wells. The women then took part in the educational programmes.

In Benin, a project devised to increase the production of cotton and groundnuts as cash crops quickly ran into trouble because the project planners ignored the role of women in processing and marketing the crops. Cotton yields went up, but the quality of the cotton went down. The situation only righted itself when UNICEF set up agricultural training for the women.

What is unusual about both examples is that the failure to consider women's needs was seen and rectified. In 1975 a survey by the Economic Commision for Africa found that half of all non-formal education programmes offered to women were in domestic science. A Gambian woman quoted by Clarke, Bramsen and Caubergs said 'We are taught how to make scones. How could that help us with our farming? Flour was too expensive anyway.' In 1987 domestic science is still on offer. There are more agricultural courses open to women – but not very many. Agricultural extension agents are still 99 per cent male.

But even these minimal changes in aid policies toward women food producers in the Third World, or even changes in rhetoric are not reflected in the western media. What is most obvious is that western non-specialist media don't find the Third World very interesting at any level. And for the tabloids the Third World barely exists. During January, February and March 1985, some of the worst months of the African famine, the *Daily Mail*'s coverage was made up of occasional photographs of Bob Geldof at Heathrow. The three-line captions said he was returning from looking at the situation in Africa. *The Times*, however, showed a more serious interest, and during 1984 and 1985 there were several hundred news items either on the situation in the drought-stricken areas of Africa or, more commonly, on western aid agencies, and governments' reactions to the situation. During those two years, there was only *one* story that referred to the role of women food producers in the drought-stricken areas, and that was a report from the UN End of the Decade for Women Conference in Nairobi.

The British media – like the US, French, German, Australian – are not very interested in women. Other contributors to this book document the minute amount of coverage given to anything to do with women, apart from clothes, cooking, and beauty. To the British male editor, whether of the *Sun* or *The Times*, women are not serious news (however you define serious). Third World women have even more against them – they are also foreign, the wrong colour, poor and very far away. And these editors merely reflect the more general values of our society.

Cultural imperialism is a phrase to numb the brain. But in the Third World it has a precise, living meaning. The West's refusal to grasp that meaning and to see the South as a place where women hold up far more than half the sky, is killing people. And no amount of Band Aid concerts, or running for the world or real, tearful concern will make any difference.

Sheila Dillon

Note

1 *Will Lomé Reach Women?* Lomé briefing no. 16, available as one of a set on the EEC/ACP agreement, from Catholic Institute for International Relations, 22 Coleman Fields, London N1 7AF.

11
Work

Introduction

Men are traditionally dependent on the work they do for the structure and direction of their lives. Although unemployment has deprived many men of this, it has not altered the dependency a man has on his work role for the shaping of his identity.

The same cannot be said of women. The assumption in this society is that women gain their identity from emotional and domestic spheres, no matter what work they do outside the home. This has a severely devaluing effect on the jobs that women do. Despite constituting nearly 40 per cent of the work force, women at work are accorded so little of the respect unquestioningly given to men that they are expected to do all the domestic work as well as an eight-hour-a-day job. Their 'real' job is still seen as that of domestic and emotional carer. Through the media the consumer is constantly informed that the workplace is essentially a masculine arena, involving responsibility, decision-making and a degree of commitment not supposedly within women's capabilities. Women's work is seldom taken seriously. It is a a job, not a career. If a woman is married, her wage is called the 'second income', despite the growing numbers of married women who support their families financially.

One effect of this attitude is that the professions in which women dominate, such as secretarial and nursing (the service and caring industries), are greatly devalued. Accordingly, these jobs carry low status and offer low wages. That this is connected to the gender of those doing the work itself is exemplified by the high social position occupied by male secretaries in the past. As soon as women form the majority in any work field, it becomes downgraded.

*From TV serials to newspaper reports the social system presented
to the viewer or reader is one in which there is women's work
(cleaning, caring, teaching children) and men's work (the real,
the hard stuff). And different values are accorded to each. Overlap
is potentially threatening, so if a man chooses to do 'women's
work', he has lost masculinity; if a woman enters a 'man's field'
she is either a hard bitch or an amazing phenomenon.*

*By basing writing and broadcasting on these stereotypes the
media does much more than reflect what goes on in real life. It
actually teaches sex roles. It is an active process of gendering, to
the benefit of the 'dominant' sex, maintained by a set of myths.
Men who control the media know very well how to maintain the
mythological mystery; these are the very devices which prevent
more women from entering and making more successful careers in
film, broadcasting, publishing and printing – the workplaces of
the media.*

Images of tradeswomen

If you were asked to visualise 'a tradeswoman' – or, more specifically, a woman carpenter or mechanic – what sort of picture
would come into your mind? Chances are, nothing very definite,
or nothing based on any personal experience. Maybe distant
echoes of the film *Rosie the Riveter* or Second World War photographs would bring a picture of smiling women with headscarfs
and overalls to mind. Put the question another way – if you were
reading a building trade magazine, or a DIY magazine, or product
promotion material for industrial drills, what images of women
would you expect to come across? Pictures of women working on
building sites? Operating the drills? The 'nothing very definite'
becomes a resounding 'nothing at all' – at least as far as tradeswomen are concerned. What you would expect to see of course are
familiar images of women decorating the otherwise sensible,
manly, important but somewhat drab terrain. Pin-ups posing astride
sparkling new, unused Kango drills; sexy girls teetering around in
high heels distracting workmen, women in bikinis and hard hats,
women in bikinis and workmen's aprons, women in bikinis cling-
ing on to stepladders. They're all completely inappropriate –

because they're not dressed right, because when they're near or holding any machinery or equipment they so obviously haven't a clue what to do with it, and because they're women. Their poses are all heavily sexually suggestive – and the message for men reads loud and clear: 'these tools are for men; women, also, are for men – and doesn't our nice road drill make you think about your prick?' The underlying violence in this particular form of pornographic imagery is quite horrific. All of which livens up the advertisement, or article, reminds us how tough and macho this world really is, and entertains the men reading it not only because they might be turned on by these pictures but because they're amusing. The women look ridiculous. Women, images of women, in the 'literature' of the manual trades, are either idiotic or invisible.

Recently (over the last ten years or so) an alternative has begun to emerge. (Perhaps it's important to say *re*-emerged, in a different form.) This alternative now surfaces before our eyes in the one-off articles, the special feature, it's the personalised, all-talking, all-smiling, all-posing tradeswoman. We always know her first name, she's young, she's white, and *yes*, she's 'normal' (i.e. heterosexual) – or at least presented as such. We're expected to be intrigued as to why she's doing this dirty, difficult job, and then to be reassured that she can cope, that she's as good as, no, even better than, the boys. What she *isn't* is ordinary, either as a 'tradesperson' (which, at least, is true), or as a woman (which is untrue). Images of women working as canteen assistants, teachers, shop assistants, factory workers are all subjected to the general pressure for pictures of women to show them as pretty and young. Only in a news context (for example redundancies or strikes) can tradeswomen be shown as ordinary, middle-aged, working women – 'pretty' or not – and the impact can still be positive, without us having to be reassured that these women are married, or have boyfriends.

Those who are hostile or suspicious of women working in the trades can all too easily ignore, or marginalise and 'invisibilise' them. And now when images of tradeswomen do appear they're usually being very consciously presented as 'a good thing'. The result is an attempt to balance the job with the woman, her competence with her femininity and/or her individual personality. Far from being a deliberate attempt to demean the women concerned this is usually part of an effort to make tradeswomen both visible and acceptable to other women, and to men. So important is the visibility that in the job advertisement, for instance, the woman must above all be clearly identifiable *as* a woman – and once more femininity becomes crucially important; we want her clearly smiling at the camera, not bent, sweaty and bulkily dressed, over a shovel.

But however good the intentions, the end result is an impression of the exceptional qualities of the individual, or the artificiality of the carefully drawn equal opportunities job advertisement. There comes a time when you long to see tradeswomen just *there* – part of the background, part of the furniture, one of the workers who's illustrating the health and safety hazard or labouring in the background in a photograph. Of course tradeswomen *aren't* yet anything but extremely unusual, particularly in the mainstream construction industry. On a private firm's building site they're still 100 per cent shock value. So showing tradeswomen as an integral but ordinary part of working life, in trade magazines, product promotion material, trade union journals, job advertisements, and health and safety information, is not reflecting what we find in the everyday world, but trying to speed up the day when we do find it. And it is based on a reality – those individual tradeswomen who are already ordinary workers once the fuss has died down and the novelty worn off. Advertising, after all, is accepted by us all as presenting the world the advertisers think we would like, rather than the one that for most of us exists. Employers advertising jobs tend to make clear through pictures what they can't say in words – that they want clean, smart, respectable, white applicants who haven't dyed stripey hair or nose studs. Their version of the ordinary employee has very little to do with the majority of young people. A recent advertisement from the NatWest Bank is so aware of this that its sole purpose is to convince the 'undesirable' young that they too will be welcome to open an account.

Images of women in the trades could be used to persuade the construction and engineering industries that women plumbers, bricklayers, plasterers, carpenters, electricians, painters, welders, etc., etc., are neither an exotic exceptional species nor a joke. No one is going to be fooled in terms of what they expect to see around them now, but it is possible to create a sense of 'this is how it would be perfectly acceptable and normal for the world to look' – rather than 'wow, amazing, my god it's a tradeswoman, how does she cope with lifting zinc baths unaided up five flights of stairs all day long?' Images of women; lots of women of all different shapes and sizes and races and ages, women just getting on with it and working, could be used to tell other women that these sorts of jobs are perfectly possible and you don't have to be the outstandingly strong, one-in-a-million trail blazer to do them.'

Liz Allen, Paddy Stamp

Just my type – images of secretaries

Such is the demand for secretarial assistance that we are confronted daily with images of the 'typical' secretary. The message from advertisers is that the ideal secretary is young and attractive, white and heterosexual and of course female. Like most other images of women offered in the media, this hinges on a traditional idea of femininity.

In general, the 'perfect' woman is represented in two conflicting ways. First there is the 'fantasy' woman: the temptress who brings excitement to and diverts from a repetitive daily routine – the sexy women featured in the Bond movies or the Jojoba advertisements. Men dream about them, they may even have them as lovers, but often they are no more than unattainable idols. Then there is the 'real' woman: the home-maker – mother, wife, daughter – who offers companionship, security, comfort and a refuge frm the competitive world of work.

This two-dimensional image of woman, idealised in art and literature, is rooted in a particular idea of a physical and emotional life for which women are believed to be destined. Within these two extremes women play many parts, and the ideal woman, the media seem to suggest, is the one who can encapsulate all these qualities by being several women at the same time. But if she does not conform to established stereotypes, or does not come up to the set standards of perfection, she is criticised and derided.

This is nowhere more true than in popular images of secretarial workers. A secretary is expected to offer her professional and personal support in promoting her boss's interests. In her multiple roles, she services the predominantly male hierarchy: from confidante to coffee-maker, receptionist to advertisement ministrator, she teeters between flamboyant hostess and passive wife. Some advertisements call her job 'keeping calm in a crisis' or 'managing his day'. In others, realism wins the day with appeals for 'a saint with an appetite for hard work' or 'a pedigree dogsbody'.

The advertisements boast 'fascinating' opportunities for secretaries who are 'truly creative' and who are 'bored by the same old routine'. Occasionally they offer salaries to match these responsible jobs, but usually the rewards are short-lived perks: 'the most modern equipment on the market', 'a slap-up lunch', 'gifts from his(!) business trips' or simply the privilege of working with 'a charming man'. Generally she is offered no real prospects and little job satisfaction. The emphasis is on the employer's needs and his challenge 'are you versatile enough to cope?' offers nothing to the secretary but a route to frustration.

For those unfamiliar with the demands of secretarial work, the following advertisement makes it clear: 'Secretary/PA . . . must be lively, intelligent, industrious, articulate, mobile, competent, imperfect [*sic*], humorous, patient, alert, confident, well groomed with strong personality and expert in typing, shorthand, audio, car driving, entertaining, arranging, placating, forging, persuading and general duties'. Some advertisements are more succinct, stating that they want 'a first class executive secretary – the kind who used to be called "Private or Confidential" and who had hysterics if anyone else dared to make her boss's coffee'. In others a 'nice, humorous boss' seeks 'a patient shorthand secretary, willing to be good listener where necessary, to join him in ensuring everything runs smoothly and is carried out on time'.

The secretary, a permanent and reassuring feature of the office scenery, must be ready with 'charm, sparkle, vitality, initiative and smart, not to say elegant, appearance' to brighten up the humdrum working lives of her employers or to offer them a sanctuary when the going gets tough. All they really want is a touch of humour and sensitivity to distract them from the serious world of work, some light relief 'to put those smashing blokes out of their misery'.

The advertisement pages of the local and national papers bear witness to the fact that 90 per cent of low-status, low-paid jobs are done by women, that 70 per cent of all office workers are women and that almost all secretaries and typists are women.

Moving away from the classified advertisements to the rest of the media, however, the secretary is almost invisible. If she exists at all she is likely to be seen whiling away her empty day by filing her nails or reading *Cosmopolitan* (not that anyone we know has ever had time to do either).

Bristow's temp is man-mad. Dallas beauties, far from being the responsible skilled women one would expect of oil-kings' secretaries, moon over their bosses, eager to jump into bed at the drop of that Texan hat. Secretaries who use Datapost dream of the day when 'he' will declare his love. Exceptions to the 'young and pretty rule' appear in the form of James Bond's Miss Moneypenny – a quiet, mousey type, content to contemplate other people's lives from an anonymous corner of the office.

In British comedies, the secretary is frequently depicted as 'an old battle-axe', who frightens the boss and everyone around her. Otherwise she is 'a scatty young girl' typing dreamily: we see her sitting at her machine copying nothing in particular nor listening to any tape but typing constantly. It is only when she is working for a detective that her work suddenly becomes interesting and she is treated as a person with ideas and emotions.

Although there seems to be a difference between North American and British TV portrayals of secretaries, they are universally shown as appendages to powerful men. The American secretary appears stronger, more independent, and more readily invites respect. It is no coincidence though that secretaries in America, who have fought hard to improve their conditions of work, are streets ahead of their British counterparts in this. The secretary in US series and films is sometimes shown as a 'dumb blonde' stereotype, probably having an affair with her boss. More frequently though she is an attractive 35- to 40-year-old 'lady', the boss's right hand. He tells her his problems, consults her about professional and personal matters and takes her advice without argument. They always have a good relationship. Della Street in the *Ironside* series is a good example.

There are few realistic representations of office workers. Those that do exist are often rather negative, rarely acknowledging the value of secretarial skills or the indispensable role that secretaries play in the office. More often than not, they focus on the powerlessness of the secretarial worker and exploit the fears of secretaries.

The greater independence and freedom gained by women recently has been met with a whole new series of advertisements and images that ostensibly take into account the changing interests of women. Job agencies, for example, are waking up to the needs of office workers, and advertisements showing sympathy with the role of secretaries and typists are increasing in number. But, 'exciting news for all lively minded typists! Britain's brightest temp agency has come up with a new and daringly unique plan that can increase your status and your earning power . . . we will train you in the important new technology of word processing.'[1] Is this the best they can offer?

Media imagery may be keeping step with changes, but under the new make-up the face is the same. We are still looking into the eyes of a distinctly 'feminine' woman with 'feminine' preoccupations: in the shadow of each image lurks a boyfriend, boss or husband. And women remain prey to the power of advertising to cajole them into recognising themselves in its mirror.

To judge by today's agency advertisements in London's underground, secretarial work is glamorous, lucrative and exciting: temps are portrayed singing in a rain of banknotes or departing on a continental holiday, their pockets bulging with foreign currency. The same message booms out of the radio: so-and-so's temps get interesting assignments, paid holidays and endless perks. The racy world of temps is waiting to snap you up but if you dial too slowly you may get left behind!

The latest fashions in advertising seem to betray a reluctance to portray the typical agency 'girl'. We see gleaming electronic type-writers, hands, feet, never a face – but we can be sure that the average secretary is still young and carefree, attractive and fash-ionable, white and positively heterosexual. Where are the black secretaries who are always nudged out of recognition, the older secretaries whose years of experience make them ideal candidates for temporary work, the mothers who take advantage of the flexible working arrangements to suit school hours and term times?

If today's secretary is not satisfied, of course, she is free to further her education. Beaming secretaries who 'kn rd ths msj' lead the way with speedwriting. Then there are word processing skills, which the advertisements would have us all believe were developed for us alone: 'Ever felt that your career had come to a bit of a dead end? That your job as a typist has become little more than a daily drudgery?' asks one advertisement.[2] But there her aspirations must end: no employer will be tempting her with real career prospects – after all, good secretaries are hard to find.

Not only have the secretarial agencies latched on to the changing desires of their employees, the manufacturers of new technology have suddenly realised how important the secretary is in getting them sales. In the newspaper and magazine advertisements secretaries are shown as bright, smart and capable people who can twist their bosses round their fingers. They are in control of the office and derive pleasure from operating the new machines. The message of the advertisers is that these machines will free secretaries.

The slogan from one firm advertising electronic typewriters is 'What every young man has been waiting for' and the small print goes on to explain that they can help solve 'one of those situations every secretary could do without. Working late at the office, some last minute letters to type, while your boyfriend is left out in the cold.'[3] Another promoter of a high-tech coffee machine begs 'secretaries who are sick and tired of making the coffee' and have 'an overwhelming urge to stop being the office slave'[4] to persuade their employers to invest in its new product.

A coffee machine certainly cannot overthrow a system dependent on cheap female labour and VDUs were not made to liberate the secretary. In reality, new technology has stripped some secretaries of their skills and status; they now sit in rows like battery hens doing soul-destroying work, often without regular breaks. That is if they are lucky enough to escape redundancy brought about by high-tech employers. Older secretaries are being pushed out to make way for college leavers who can quickly adapt to the new machinery. Any secretary, in fact, who does not meet agency requirements may find herself out of work. What little autonomy secretaries had is gradually being eroded as their skills are taken over by the latest software such as a recently launched package which corrects spelling.

The media throw out colourful images of working women that purport to reflect their needs, aspirations and desires. Striving to succeed in the face of these stereotypes and the (unattainable) standards they set is a thankless task. Feelings of inadequacy, incompetence, powerlessness are aggravated by the fact that a secretary's skills are rarely recognised and she is forgotten in the decision-making process. Above all secretaries are isolated from one another. False images are dear not just to the media. They are solidly anchored in the minds of women, who constantly find themselves in opposition to one another, always believing themselves to be less confident, capable and successful than others.

Media images justify and reinforce the status quo. During the Second World War, women were mobilised to satisfy the need for production line workers. Photographs depicted the uniformed men and women standing side by side. Propaganda said that women without a role outside the home were dull: 'The accent on cosmetics dropped. Women were encouraged to give up their frilly accessories and nylons for the war effort.'[5] When the war ended, so did the publicity encouraging women to take up new responsibilities. Crèches were closed down and the work done by women once again became invisible.

Forty years on, women are still publicly seen and treated in terms of their relationship to men and the support that they bring to them. A woman's contribution is rarely recognised and, in general, contemporary images do little to change this. One example of a writer who portrays the secretary in a positive light is Zöe Fairbairns. In *Here Today*,[6] her protagonist Antonia is temp of the year. In contrast to the usual stereotypes she is the character upon whom all the action depends and we see her trying against all the odds to balance her work and home life. Moving away from fiction, though, many secretaries are questioning their status in the office and the way in which this is reflected in the media. They are beginning to learn how to use their power and are recognising the value of joining together to improve their working conditions. After all, if secretaries were to down tools tomorrow in common protest, the office world would suddenly come to a standstill.

Sylvia, Marion and Carrie, TYPECASTE

Notes

1 *Advertisement run by Kelly Girl in Ms London, 1985.*

2 Advertisement run by Brook Street in *Ms London*, 1985.
3 Advertisement run by Canon in *Civil*, 1984.
4 Advertisement run by Café-Bar International (UK) in *Ms London*, 1985.
5 R. Morgan, *Sisterhood is Global*, Penguin Books 1985.
6 Zoë Fairbairns, *Here Today*, Methuen 1985.

We're no angels – images of nurses

Films, novels, newspapers, documentaries, soap operas, cartoons, recruitment advertising and even get-well cards all bombard us with images of the nurse. And despite the variety of sources, and the many different kinds of nurses and nursing work, these images are remarkably consistent.

Angels, battle-axes and sex symbols are the three groups into which most of the images fall. Angels appear so often that in Fleet Street the word is used synonymously with nurses. Innocent, unselfish, utterly dedicated to caring for the sick, they always put service before self; everyone agrees that they have been exploited and should be protected, but no one suggests that they should take their destiny into their own hands. Their supposedly submissive nature can perhaps be traced back to one of nursing's roots, the religious orders which provided much of the early institutionalised care. Even the title 'sister' harks back to the convent.

Today, the vocational qualities vested in the angel figure are often emphasised to nursing students as their suggested professional goal. Dedication and service to others are put alongside patience, compliance, and a refusal to be ruffled or to show feelings of anger or hurt. The 'good nurse' does not complain but accepts with grace and composure everything thrown at her (or him), and self-sacrifice is seen as a virtue.

The angel label is also an easy way for the public to show its gratitude for the work nurses do. Many patients are genuinely grateful and admiring: 'I wouldn't do your job for a million pounds.' Governments, too, use the same kind of language. Many nurses like this image of themselves, and fail to see that it has become a substitute for positive action to improve their pay and conditions. Moreover, from constant repetition the praise grows stale and the virtues it is supposed to commend ultimately devalued. If all nurses are angels simply because they are nurses, not because they do the job especially well, it's an empty compliment.

Another problem with the media view of angels is that they tend, unless rescued by marriage, to age into battle-axes (ageist, as well as sexist!). The dedication which is depicted so charmingly in the soft young nurse turns into fanaticism in the middle-aged spinster, shown in the image of the fierce ward sister who insists on having the beds in a straight line and makes the junior nurses cry. Like the angel images, these dragons are a nurse version of a stereotype often applied to women in general – 'old maids' who, failing to marry and have children as women 'should', turn sour and vent their frustrations in petty tyranny. These sisters and matrons are never shown organising the ward work or using their clinical skills; instead, they sweep through the ward while everyone stands to attention, like the late Hattie Jacques in *Carry On Doctor*, or become evil manipulators like Big Nurse in Kesey's *One Flew Over the Cuckoo's Nest*, who gets her revenge on men by terrorising her patients.

The angel and the dragon are old favourites, but in the last twenty years they have been joined by a third stereotype which has become the most popular of all – the nurse as sex symbol. Barbara Windsor in the *Carry On* films is perhaps the best known (and her sexy nurse is interchangeable with all the other characters she portrays), but there are many other examples of the feather-brained female who wears black stockings and whose main interest is flirting with the houseman. Newspapers love pin-ups of nurses in bikinis, captioned 'What the doctor ordered . . . ', and the busty nurse is a favourite subject of seaside joke postcards, get-well cards and even trade union Christmas cards.

Men suffer from this stereotyping too. The lack of images of men in nursing in the media – although the TV series *Angels* has tried to redress the balance and has had a number of male nurse characters – means people are often surprised to find men working as nurses. A large number of them work in psychiatry and mental handicap, which are rarely depicted, but there are also many men in general nursing, with one male to every five female registered nurses. The failure of the images to reflect reality, combined with the belief that nursing is women's work, results in the idea – shared by many female nurses – that there is something funny and effeminate about men who choose to do nursing.

These images are all a distortion of reality. Not only do they fail to reflect the daily concerns and problems of the people who nurse, but they belittle nurses by describing them in stereotyped ways. They tell only part of the story, remaining silent about the fact that many nurses are male; that much nursing takes place outside hospital surgical wards and casualty departments; that many nurses are West Indian, Asian or black British citizens; and that nursing is more than passing scalpels to the doctor, taking temperatures and wiping bottoms.

Most of all, the images sanitise nursing and deny the real hardship and stress of the work. Dealing with the physical and mental needs of numerous patients on a single shift, at a time when most wards are understaffed and the length of stay in hospital is going down, is physically and mentally shattering for the nurse. At the best of times it is a demanding job, and in current circumstances the nurse's ability to cope with those demands is eroded by her knowledge that she cannot do the job as well as she would like.

The myths also give a false impression of what health care is all about. The stereotype nurse is likely to work in a hospital ward caring for surgical patients or others with diagnosed diseases from which they will soon recover, but the National Health Service actually deals with many other problems. Over half the NHS beds are occupied by people with long-term problems caused by old age, mental or physical handicap or mental illness. In romantic novels and comedy films, however, doctors cure diseases, nurses clear up the mess and hold the patient's hand, the patient goes home well, and nurse and doctor celebrate by getting married.

It is easy to poke fun at Mills & Boon's clichéd hospital settings, where a throbbing pulse usually means a different kind of fever! Even the titles are suggestive: *A Bride for the Surgeon* by Hazel Fisher, *Over the Green Mask* by Lisa Cooper, *Tender Loving Care* by Kerry Mitchell. But with two new titles and one reprint appearing every month, and translations published in France, Holland, Germany and Brazil, the company can afford to ignore what it has described as 'the snigger factor'.

The sales of these low-priced, readily available paperbacks run into millions, devoured by an almost exclusively female readership including many nurses, the company claims. Some are written by qualified nurses and all are checked by technical advisers to get the clinical details right. 'The main storyline is always a love story between a tender young nurse and an older, experienced, usually haughty doctor,' says Mills and Boon. Invariably there is a happy ending.

Nurses themselves may well dismiss such stuff as lightweight trivia or harmless escapism. Yet a survey of new nursing recruits and of patients might reveal expectations that hospital life bore more of a resemblance to the world of doctor–nurse romances than professional pride would care to acknowledge. Nor can those of us who don't read hospital romances assume we are unaffected by their stereotyped images of nurses and nursing. 'Pretty staff nurse Anna Foster' reappears with alarming regularity in TV serials, films, comedy, the gutter press, get-well cards, seaside postcards, and even in recruitment literature for the Department of Health and Social Security.

Hospitals are, of course, obvious settings for real-life and fictional drama. Soap operas and documentaries alike play on our fear of death and disease and arouse a ghoulish fascination, like watching horror films through parted fingers. The fixed backdrop of casualty department or surgical ward in a television drama series allows for the regular portrayal of stock nurse/doctor characters, though not of the ancillary workers, whose rare appearance is likely to be 'comic' or 'earthy'. A steady stream of patients provides the all-human-life-is-there drama (though not the trickier narrative of learning to speak after a stroke, or mastering a knife and fork if you are severely mentally handicapped).

In reality the doctor often does not know what the disease is, or may be unable to do more than alleviate the symptoms. Medicine can do little about the factors which cause so much illness today – such as bad housing, unbalanced diets, unsafe conditions at work, accidents, addictions, or stress. A hospital stay for many people, like the 'revolving door' patients in psychiatric hospitals, does not produce cures, but only patches up the damage sufficiently to enable the ill person to go home – and face the same risks all over again.

Several groups of nurses have been concerned to assert their identity and to rectify the generally unbalanced view of health care and nursing. In particular, those who work outside hospitals – in health centres, general practice surgeries, schools, and factories – are beginning to join midwives in the struggle to gain recognition of the enormous diversity of nursing work, and to ensure they get a fair share of the resources for training and care.

To conclude, there is a huge gap between the ideas about who nurses are, what they do and where they do it, and the reality. Unfortunately that gulf, maintained by media misinformation and prejudice as well as various power structures, often yawns inside the nursing profession, especially at the top levels. There is a crying need to close the gap – so discussion can at least start from a realistic base, in place of fantasy, wishful thinking, prejudice or self-interest.

Jane Salvage

Further reading

C. Davies, ed., *Rewriting Nursing History*, Croom Helm, 1980.
L. Doyal, *et al.*, *Migrant Workers in the NHS – report of a preliminary survey*, Department of Sociology, Polytechnic of North London, 1980.
C. Hicks, 'Racism in nursing', in *Nursing Times*, 78(18), 743–48; and 78(19), 1982.
J. Muff, ed. *Socialization, Sexism and Stereotyping: women's issues in nursing*, C.V. Mosby, 1982.
J. Salvage, *The Politics of Nursing*, Heinemann, 1985.
For Radical Nurses Group Newsletter, write to: 20, Melrose Road, Sheffield 3, South Yorkshire.

Conclusion: what are we doing about it?

Introduction

The enormity of the effects of media sexism and of the task of eliminating it cannot be underestimated. Disregard and contempt for women are (after all) not all that inspire the media: powerful class and race interests are at stake. The situation of women cannot be divorced from patriarchal capitalism and white imperialism, since the system depends on women and black people to prop it up.

Media sexism is an issue which has been neglected by the traditional left, uncomfortable with notions of censorship, and reluctant to think through alternatives. Increasingly, however, a commitment to equal opportunities policies is becoming apparent; applied to the media, many changes become possible.

The 'moral majority' have of course long been concerned with sex and violence issues. Their consideration of the portrayal of women is always limited by being seen within the context of 'decency' and 'Victorian values'. This does have something to do with respect for women – but for women who behave in an 'appropriate' manner. There is no understanding that abuse of women will not disappear unless the sexist basis of society is eradicated, and that such abuse arises from precisely the kind of ideology they espouse: it is the other side of the Victorian coin.

Feminists have not wished to ally themselves with the moral right, and many have also been uncomfortable with the notion of censorship, since it can so easily be used against them (especially lesbians) and other unacceptable groups. How can women ensure that legislation will work in their interests when it is not women who make or enforce the law? Feminist controversy over censorship of pornography has raged bitterly in the United States, focusing especially on the ordinances drawn up by Catherine Mackinnon and Andrea Dworkin. In this country too there are strongly felt divisions within the women's movement, which there is not space to deal with thoroughly here.

For many women (including those who do not label themselves feminists) Clare Short's unsuccessful Bill to ban Page 3 pictures in newspapers provided an opportunity to express their dislike of such material. Questionnaires such as those run in 1986 by Woman *and* Just Seventeen *further demonstrated the extent and depth of these feelings.*

It is sometimes forgotten that campaigning for legislation in this area does not necessarily mean banning material. After all, the major form of censorship which already exists in this country is the silencing of the voices of women and all oppressed minorities. Some forms of legislation could act to overturn this unofficial censorship by making the media more accountable, accessible, democratic and diverse. In fact, until we have media reform legislation, it is unlikely that the position of women and women's images within the media will change very radically.

Unfortunately, perhaps, most feminist campaigning has to date taken place outside the legislative arena. Established women's groups, one-off campaigns like that against Sunday Sport, *and individual women attempt both to influence image-makers and to raise the consciousness of other women so that they are no longer passive consumers of media sexism (though it is doubtful that women ever have been merely passive consumers). Still other women are more concerned with the struggle to become image-makers themselves, in the knowledge that it is only when we control the production of images that we will be represented more diversely and fairly.*

But women wishing to challenge media sexism and to work for more positive portrayal face a number of problems. The media themselves can appear monolithic and faceless, and changing them seems a daunting prospect. Most women have little understanding of how they work, and how we can make interventions that will be effective. It is very important that women 'know their enemy'; the bibliography lists many informative books on the subject (see page 227).

Other problems arise out of the position of women in society: lack of resources, competing demands on our time and energy (maybe Ralph Nader didn't have to mind the children or cook the supper!), and lack of access to decision-making processes. Black and working-class women are particularly disadvantaged in these respects. Lesbians are liable to be ridiculed and abused for their efforts, and women with disabilities patronised. One way of getting support and of combining resources is of course to join a women's group.

There is also a danger that the media will report protests in such a way as to belittle women even further. When Women's Media Action Group wrote in a report about the offensiveness of a motoring magazine, the magazine's next issue featured a semi-clad woman on the front cover with the caption 'This [magazine] degrades women – official'. The entire issue was devoted to provocation, insult and misogyny.

One of the most pernicious difficulties we face as women is in believing in our own power and acting on it: in really knowing that we can change things and being determined to do it. The reason we don't fully believe in our power is that we have internalised society's lowly view of our gender. It doesn't help that when we do protest at our oppression – in this instance media sexism – we get told we are butch, humourless, strident, ugly, jealous, puritan, castrating, hysterical or the lunatic fringe. Not surprisingly many women do not wish to be publicly associated with 'women's lib'. To do so is to risk these insults. So many keep quiet. If we do muster up courage to object, we are put on the defensive – not the most powerful position from which to argue.

Within our women's groups, we tend to spend little time in actually thinking about how we want the media to be, about overall strategies, the 'larger picture'. We often get lost in minutiae, and attending to business matters; we expend too much energy making pin-pricks in the side of the media edifice instead of thinking out the more radical structural reforms that are necessary. Sometimes we pay too much attention to inter- or intra-group relationships – of course we need to work out our personal politics and engage in debate, but prolonged and sometimes acrimonious navel-gazing has limited effectiveness in changing the world. The proper targets for our energy are the media magnates who are making their fortunes at our expense.

We need to think big, think powerful, develop strategies and a coherent policy, and promote a concerted campaign to tackle the problem. We must constantly evaluate and re-evaluate priorities of energy, time and resources. We must weigh up whether the likely effect deserves the effort, and discover how to get the maximum effect with the minimum exertion. (After all, we deserve time to enjoy ourselves and our own creativity as well!)

We need to create alliances with as many other progressive groupings as possible, both grass-roots and established, and to attack on all fronts. These groups will keep us informed about other pertinent issues and give a broader perspective – for example, an anti-racist perspective if the group is predominantly white.

It is crucially important that we change the nature of the media with regard to women – all women. We need to recognise the complexity and size of the task ahead, but also the strength and capacity of women as instruments of change. There is no reason, given our knowledge, resourcefulness, inherent strength and sense of righteousness, why we should not build an effective and powerful mass movement against media sexism.

The present trend in the media is for more concentration of ownership, more support for established interests, less opportunity for criticism and access. On the positive side however the organisations and initiatives detailed in this chapter have already created an excellent base for a mass movement. There is an increasing number of male allies. There is already a large number of women with experience in protesting, and many more who are aware of and concerned about the issue. There is an increasing number of feminists employed in the media, greater media union activity, and a whole new generation of trainee journalists and technicians. There is certainly reason for optimism.

Campaign information

This section gives information about how women can join the campaign against media sexism, and about different ways of protesting.

How to complain

Complaining about sexist and offensive material is always worth-while, though as mentioned in the introduction to this chapter it pays to judge the appropriate amount of effort in relation to the outcome. An individual woman's complaint, though it can often feel like a lone and futile battle with a megalithic structure, can be seen as an empowering act and an act of resistance.

These individual protests are important, but well-organised mass protest is likely to be more effective. Every woman is capable of organising a group protest, even on a limited scale.

The rest of this section lists ways in which, and channels through which, protest can be made by both individuals and groups.

Letter-writing

This is a cheap and relatively easy way to complain. Remember to record exact details of where and when the offending item or pro-gramme appeared, and keep a copy. It will be useful if the corres-pondence develops. As a general rule letters should be succinct and firm but civil. Lengthy lectures about patriarchal relations abounding with feminist jargon will probably cause the reader to switch off – and though it may relieve your feelings, abuse will probably achieve little else!

If complaining about advertisements, write to both the manufac-turer and the editor (if printed media) or the Independent Broad-casting Authority (if broadcast media). Stress that you will be encouraging others to boycott the product (though this may not seem appropriate if the advertisement is for say, a Rolls Royce!).

The Advertising Standards Authority is the industry's own watchdog. It has a Code of Advertising Practice (CAP) and con-siders around 100 complaints a month. The results of these are published in their monthly reports. On average two complaints per month refer to sexism, but few of these are upheld (though some-times the advertisement is 'deprecated'). They are more likely to uphold a complaint if it contains violence towards women. Com-plaints against sexism are brought under the section below.

Decency
Advertisements should contain nothing which, because of is

failure to respect the standards of decency and propriety that are generally accepted in the United Kingdom, is likely to cause either grave or widespread offence.

Some advertisements, which do not conflict with the preceding sub-paragraph, may nonetheless be found distasteful because they reflect or give expression to attitudes or opinions about which society is divided. Where this is the case, advertisers are urged to consider the effect any apparent disregard of such sensitivities may have upon their reputation and that of their product; and upon the acceptability, and hence usefulness, of advertising generally.

The fact that a product may be found offensive by some people is not, in itself, a sufficient basis under the Code for objecting to an advertisement for it. Advertisers are urged, however, to avoid unnecessary offence when they advertise any product which may reasonably be expected to be found objectionable by a significant number of those who are likely to see their advertisement.

The problem is that feminist objections have little to do with 'decency', and in any case theirs is seen as a minority viewpoint. If an advertisement appears in a publication which the ASA assumes has a predominantly male readership, they consider it will not cause widespread offence – they are not concerned with the effect of these advertisements on men's attitudes to women. Like the media generally, they say advertisements merely reflect attitudes and therefore that is what they are concerned with. They are not in business to attempt to change them. But their record on tobacco and alcohol advertising belies this.

Even if a complaint is upheld and the advertiser is asked to withdraw the advertisement, it has probably already done its damage. The ASA has no powers of restraint over advertisers who repeatedly offend. Sometimes however the publisher apologises and promises greater circumspection in the future.

It can be argued that advertising is too influential to be monitored by an internal body with no teeth, and that it should be replaced by an independent statutory body representative of and accountable to the public and with effective powers of sanction.

Advertisements on radio and television are the responsibility of the IBA, which has its own Code of Advertising Standards and Practice, modelled on the ASA code, and with the same limitations (though standards for broadcast advertisements tend to be much stricter).

Phoning

Complaints to radio and TV stations should be made straight away. All calls should be logged – make sure this is done. These calls *are* generally taken seriously, especially if there are lots of them, so it is worth doing. However there is little point in haranguing the person who answers the phone.

Right of reply

A right of reply should be requested if an article or news story is distorted or prejudicial; your reply should be given equal space and equal prominence to the original and should not appear alongside critical editorial comment. Getting a right of reply requires persistence and forcefulness; it is even more difficult to achieve in broadcast media. The Campaign for Press and Broadcasting Freedom's Right-of-Reply Unit may be able to help.

Media trades unions support the principle of right of reply, and may be able to assist; in any case it is worth informing them of your protest.

Media trades unions

The National Union of Journalists (NUJ) states in its Code of Conduct: 'A journalist shall neither originate nor process material which encourages discrimination on grounds of race, colour, creed, gender or sexual orientation . . . ' (Clause 10); it also has an equality officer, an equality council, a lesbian and gay group and a race relations working party. The union has done much good work in raising the consciousness of journalists on these issues. The other print unions are the **National Graphical Association (NGA)** and the **Society of Graphical and Allied Trades (SOGAT)** which are male-dominated and not noted for their enthusiasm for feminism, though both do have women's groups.

The broadcasting unions are the **Broadcasting and Entertainment Trade Alliance (BETA)**, which is principally for BBC workers, and has an equality officer, and the **Association of**

Cinematographic, Television and Allied Technicians (ACTT), which has codes of practice on sexism and racism, an equality officer and council, a women's section, a lesbian and gay group, a black group and a disability group.

Members of the public can bring complaints under the union codes of conduct. Contact the relevant union head office to find out how to do it. One woman who did this was Annie Bachini. She complained to the NUJ about a *Sun* article in 1983, headlined 'What's the sexiest bit of a woman?' It was accompanied by a photograph of a woman in a bikini whose body had been divided up like a carcase of meat, with insulting comments beside each part of the body. The journalist was found guilty by the union and reprimanded, though the reprimand was withdrawn after appeal. However, Annie Bachini herself felt empowered as a working-class woman by the experience, and a great deal of debate was raised by her action.

But the ineffectiveness of the NUJ procedure as a whole was illustrated when, after the original decision, Bernard Levin wrote an article in *The Times* attacking the NUJ and Annie Bachini herself. A complaint was then taken out by another woman against Bernard Levin, and he was duly reprimanded. But was he chastened? He thereupon wrote two further articles attacking the NUJ and both women.

In 1986 the NUJ set up an Ethics Council which aims to simplify the NUJ complaints procedure. However, since unions are (understandably) reluctant to be seen as 'spying' on their own members and imposing severe sanctions, the role of the Ethics Council is seen in an educational/persuasive capacity rather than as a watchdog.

Advisory groups

Local Advisory Councils of most BBC local radio stations and **Local Radio Committees** of commercial radio stations in theory represent the views and complaints of the public to station management. You can even be elected on to them – or you can apply to address their meetings. In practice their views differ little from the bodies they are supervising; after all, they are appointed (and dismissed) by those bodies. But it is still worth approaching them.

The Broadcasting Complaints Commission

The Commission adjudicates on complaints relating to all material broadcast by both the BBC and the IBA including advertising. It only considers complaints from the person directly affected by unjust or unfair treatment, or who has suffered an unwarranted infringement of their privacy. If a complaint is upheld, the station may publish a summary of the complaint and the result. However, in 1985-6 it dealt with only 208 cases. Of these, 47 fell within its jurisdiction. Twenty cases were adjudicated upon; thirteen complaints were upheld.

Campaign for Press and Broadcasting Freedom (9 Poland Street, London W1V 3DG, 01-437 2795), is the only organisation which lobbies on a broad front for media reform. It is a non-party (though left-inclined) campaign tackling the issues of media ownership, structure and control, and all forms of bias and distortion. It operates a right of reply unit to assist those who have been badly used by the media, and to promote right of reply policies throughout the media. Membership includes many media workers, media and other unions, political groups, campaigning organisations and individuals. They publish a bi-monthly journal *Free Press*, with supplements on specific topics, and a number of books and pamphlets. They promote their codes on sexism and racism in the media, and there are separate groups within the Campaign for women, black people, lesbians and gay men and people with disabilities. These can be very good places to learn about the working of the media, to become integrated into the overall work of the Campaign, and to develop wider contacts.

The *TV Users Group* and the *Campaign against Racism in the Media* are two other groups which have become incorporated into the CPBF.

The Obscene Publications Act

This Act is administered by the Department of Public Prosecutions. Cases brought under it are judged by the 'tendency to deprave and corrupt' ordinary citizens. It is a lengthy procedure, and is informed by notions of 'decency' rather than concepts of sexism. An attempt in 1986 to get the Act extended to cover broadcasting (the Churchill Bill) was defeated.

Libel laws

If you feel you yourself or your group have suffered severe misrepresentation, these laws are not much use. It is extremely time-consuming and expensive to bring a case, and legal aid is not available for libel cases.

The Press Council

The Council is an internal 'watchdog' which looks after the interests of its own, rather than those of the public. It upholds around 4 per cent of complaints and has no effective sanctions. It has little interest in sexism (though some in 'decency'). The NUJ and the CPBF both discourage people from using it, since this lends it credibility.

Feedback

All feedback channels can be utilised: Channel 4's *Right of Reply*; BBC's *Points of View*; phone-in programmes. Given the general antipathy of many phone-in presenters to feminism you should be well prepared if you intend to use them. It is a good idea, when asked what you want to say on air, not to give too much away. Letters to the *Radio Times*, *TV Times*, *The Listener* and Radio 4's *Feedback* can also be effective.

Direct action

This can sometimes be effective – and satisfying! Graffiti on walls and advertisements, public meetings, pickets, sit-ins, petitions. Three action examples follow, but beware of possible legal consequences!

1 The British Telecom protest

With the privatising of British Telecom the feared decline in standards for the sake of profit actually happened: the introduction of 'Petline', offering pornography by phone. Women in Telecom first took up the cause, writing letters of complaint, circulating a monthly newsletter, and securing support from the unions to which their members belonged. At this point, Women against Violence against Women (WAVAW) became aware of 'Petline', and organised pickets, leaflets and petitions. This public action in turn attracted the attention of the *Daily Mirror*, which ran the story for three days, adding to the growing protest against the service.

Women in Telecom, as well as supporting the WAVAW picket, organised one of their own, with union support. They have also put motions forward at their union conferences, though the male members of the union are not entirely sympathetic. As a result of all the protesting, the management at Telecom have become very sensitive about the issue, and although they plan to extend the service to cities other than London, they have toned down the nature of the phone calls; still sexist but relatively innocuous.

Women in Telecom and WAVAW are aware that the decrease in pornographic content of the 'Petline' phone service make it more difficult to campaign against. If the campaign is not sustained the service will revert to its former state, and more lines will appear. Constant vigilance is needed.

2 The Lewisham porn protest
In 1982 a 'private shop' opened in the main street of Lewisham. A group of local women wanted to draw attention to its function as an outlet for pornography, and to demonstrate their anger. One night they glued the locks, wrote graffiti and threw red paint on the shop front. They were arrested and charged with criminal damage.

In the time leading up to the court case there was picketing and petitioning every Saturday outside the shop, and men going into it were challenged. Some local Communist Party men even organised an all-male picket in protest. The court case had been well publicised and was taken up by both local and national newspapers; the local press was particularly good. The women gave interviews on Radio London and LBC.

The women encountered a sympathetic (female) magistrate who gave them a conditional discharge and refused to grant costs to the sex shop.

The shop continued, albeit under a new name and more discreetly. However, the action was a success in terms of the public support that the women received, the raising of the issue of pornography (including amongst left circles locally), and the fact that the local council, alerted by the women's action, imposed a large licence fee on the shop.

3 The Glasgow 'Page 3' protest

The media views women's bodies as sex objects, offered for the price of a daily newspaper. The most obvious example of this is the notorious 'Page 3' pin-up picture of a half-naked – or almost naked – young woman. The management of the *Sun* and the *Daily Star* appear to believe that their readership would fall away on the spot should it be deprived of its daily dose of soft porn.

The Scottish *Daily Record* remains convinced that manhood must be serviced in this way. Women from Glasgow Women's Pornography Action Group wrote to the editor, and asked for an interview with him. The letter was unanswered and requests for an interview refused. So forty-three women occupied the paper's offices. Two national (Scottish) newspapers, the *Glasgow Herald* and the *Scotsman*, BBC radio and BBC evening TV news covered the story.

Eventually the women did meet the editor. In an article in *Outwrite* (issue 16) he is quoted as saying that Page 3 was 'the easiest thing to put in the paper' and that he was not going to remove this 'saucy feature'.

The feelings of the women were expressed in a statement they had wanted to make to the paper's readers, but the editor refused to print it.

At the time it seemed that the protest had failed. However, recently the continued representations of women's groups to the editor and management of the *Daily Record* have had some effect. The *Record* will not drop its pin-up photographs, but it *has* undertaken not to print reports of sexual assault or rape next to them. A small, but significant, step forward for women.

Putting media sexism on the agenda

Whatever organisation you belong to (trade union, local constituency party, National Childbirth Trust) or wherever you work, you can make sure that the media are the subject of debate. This heightens people's awareness of its shortcomings and will stimulate lobbying from all quarters. Discussion of media sexism can be initiated from whichever approach is most relevant to your group (e.g.

portrayal of women workers, children's television). The group could invite a speaker from a women's media organisation.

Encourage the group to write letters of complaint or take other appropriate action. Suggest that the group affiliates to an organisation such as the Campaign for Press and Broadcasting Freedom. If you belong to a trade union, remind them of the motion passed at the 1982 Congress. Make links with Equality Committees of the media unions. Try to get a code of conduct on sexism adopted, to apply to your organisation's publications.

If you belong to a women's group, raise media sexism as a topic for discussion. Organise specific projects: monitoring, letter-writing, petitions, direct action. Seek media attention for all your activities, developing your media skills. All information about feminist activity counteracts the usual distorted images. For a very useful guide to getting media coverage, see *Get It On* by Jane Drinkwater (Pluto Press, 1984). The London Media Project (237 Pentonville Rd, London N1) advise on this too and hold workshops. In Scotland the Scottish Council for Community and Voluntary Organisations (SCCVO, 19 Claremont Crescent, Edinburgh EH7, 031-556 3882) has produced an excellent guide called 'Getting into Print'. This gives hints on how to prepare material for print media, and where to place it.

Edinburgh Women in Media offer training seminars to women's groups from time to time (see page 217). The aim is to demystify media processes, and to help women's groups give – and get – the best from the media in terms of publicising their activities.

Women's initiatives to counter media sexism and promote positive images of women

The following is a selection of women's groups which campaign against media sexism and/or for better employment opportunities for women in the media.

WITCH
Women's Independent Cinema House is a grass-roots alternative media network in Liverpool, formed five years ago. Since then

they have established an alternative film screening, produced films by, for and about women, and run workshops for women in video, photography and animation. WITCH provides Merseyside women with a foot in the mainstream media door. As they say 'It enables the media to be seen as something relevant to you. You become less of a (passive) consumer. It heightens your own aware-ness. You discover your own attitudes to sexism and racism.' Funding was originally derived from Merseyside County Council, c/o The Women's Centre, 7 Upper Parliament Street, Liverpool 8.

Women's Airwaves
is a feminist collective which produces radio programmes addressing subjects and issues of concern to women, from a feminist perspective. They aim to make radio more accessible to women by increasing participation in programme-making and negotiating for the broad-casting of their programmes to the mass audiences of local and national radio. They train new members in the techniques of radio production; any woman interested in radio can join the group and/ or take one of their training courses. 12 Praed Mews, London WC2 1QY, 01-402 7651.

Women in Entertainment
is a London-based national organisation committed to creating better opportunities for women of all races and cultures in all areas of arts and entertainment, in the belief that the development of women's culture must play a crucial part in changing the position of women in society. From 1979 when it started, its activities have included organising festi-vals (for example Women Live 1982), running workshops for both members and women in community groups, organising conferences and members' meetings, circulating a newsletter, campaigning and running an information and resource centre. Women working in – or just interested in – all branches of arts and entertainment are welcome to join. 7 Thorpe Close, London W10 5XL, 01-969 2292.

Women's Film, Television and Video Network
was set up by and for women to deal with the specific problems of gaining access to jobs, training, retraining and expression within those communication media. They organise familiarisation/

training sessions, focusing on particular aspects of working in the media, both mainstream and independent. They have published a directory of women in film, TV and video, designed for educational institutions, production companies, TV companies and cultural pressure groups, as well as for women with similar or complementary skills to make contact with one another. This reveals the large number of women working in these industries and encourages their employment. Though London-based, it has an active regional network. 79 Wardour Street, London W1, 01-434 2076.

Women in Media
was formed by women who work in journalism, education, publishing, broadcasting, film, theatre, advertising and public relations, who believe in the women's movement and want to use their skills to work for an improved situation for all women. Their aims are to pressure for the abolition of discriminatory laws concerning women; to make both men and women aware of the distorted images of the sexes presented by the media; to break down discrimination by examining conditions of women's work and promotion opportunities, providing facts to influence change. c/o The Fawcett Society, 46 Harleyford Road, London SE11 5AY, 01-587 1287.

Women in Media (Edinburgh)
holds regular monthly meetings, offers training seminars on how to approach the media. It mounts campaigns, for example, for Scottish Divorce Law Reform, and against sexism in education. It helps other women's groups with their campaigns. Members give talks to local groups, schools, adult education courses (Women's Studies, Wider Opportunities for Women, etc.) on media sexism. It contributed to the Scottish Plan of Action for the UN Decade for Women. The group sponsored seminar leading to the EOC project, *Women and the UK media 1981–3* (report 'The Mirror Cracked', from EOC, Overseas House, Quay Street, Manchester). The group is open to anyone working in, or interested in, the media. Contact 031-332 9672.

Women's Media Action Group
was formed in 1978 to oppose sexism in the media and work for positive images. They produce a bi-monthly newsletter and

co-ordinate the national Women's Monitoring Network, which
has so far produced six reports on specific issues. They have held
two conferences in London, run courses, disseminated
information and given talks, with a slide-show on advertising, all
over the country. They have consistently pressured the
Advertising Standards Authority to change their code of practice,
and organised a petition against 'Pretty Polly' advertisements.
Members have appeared on radio and television, and provided
speakers at events. Media students frequently apply to the group
for information and encouragement. c/o A Woman's Place,
Hungerford House, Victoria Embankment, London WC2.

Women's Groups of the Campaign for Press and Broadcasting Freedom

The London Women's Group is a semi-autonomous group within
the Campaign, with representation on the National Council. They
have regular meetings on specific topics with invited speakers, and
are involved in a number of campaigns, such as co-ordinating a
policy on censorship/legislation, advocating greater participation
of women in community radio, promoting their code of conduct on
media sexism in the media unions and other organisations. They
have developed links with many organisations, and regularly
provide information; they publish pamphlets, hold conferences
and public meetings, and provide speakers. 9 Poland Street,
London W1V 3DG, 01-437 2795.

The Manchester Women's Group provides a focus for women in
the north of England. They originally came together in order to
undertake a monitoring project on the Manchester *Evening News*,
which achieved wide publicity among women's groups locally.
c/o NWCPBF, 136 Corn Exchange, Hanging Ditch, Manchester
M4 3BN, 061-832 6991.

Women in Publishing

is dedicated to improving the status of women working in publishing
and related trades. With over 400 members, they function as a network and support system; provide a forum for discussion and
exchange of information through monthly meetings and newsletter;
and assist in training and career development with an annual

conference and a series of training workshops. Contact Lisa Tuttle, 1 Ortygia House, 6 Lower Rd, Harrow, Mx HA2 0DA, 01-864 1957.

Women's Media Resource Project
exists to provide greater access to media skills for women. In the basement of the Rio Cinema (107 Kingsland High Street, London E8) they have women-only showings of women's videos; they also have a women-only sound studio, offering recording facilities as well as training courses in sound engineering. Unit A12, Metropolitan Workshops, Enfield Rd, London N1 5AZ, 01-254 6536.

Examples of other kinds of initiatives

Black Women and Representation
'Progressive meanings can only come out of a society with progressive values . . . Until then we will continue to look at media images without fully seeing . . . Without fully understanding' (BWAR statement). Media images have only recently been made *with* Black women; what is missing are images and messages made *by* Black women. It is this very important 'by' element that Black women film, television and video makers are trying to address in the ever-increasing work which is emerging from the Black independent sector. In addition to this BWAR, along with other Black women, realised it was important not to produce in a vacuum. Consequently various events such as the 'Black Women in the Media' conference (1984) and BWAR seminars, screenings and practical workshops have been held all over London. Unit 5, Cockpit Yard, Northington Street, London WC1, 01-831 0024.

Letterbox Library
'Alternative', including feminist, publishing for adults is well-established, but there are still relatively few books for children that do not present characters in a sexually stereotyped way, and that are not based on a white, middle-class heterosexual view of the world. Such books of this kind as do exist are not readily identifiable, and generally unavailable outside London.

In order to cater for the need for non-sexist, non-racist children's books, we decided to form a co-operatively-run bookclub. With support from other women such as the Women's Press Bookclub, we formed an advisory group, underwent a short TOPS business course, and visited publishers – few of whom believed there was a significant market for the kinds of books we wanted to sell. With initial funding from the Greater London Enterprise Board, we had our first 40,000 catalogues printed in October 1983, and mailed them out in *Spare Rib* and other outlets. The response was immediate and overwhelming: letters of support came from parents, grandparents, teachers and librarians – some from as far away as Australia and Zimbabwe. Largely due to the enthusiasm of existing members, two years later we had 3,000 members.

We produce quarterly catalogues with about 25 titles for children of all ages, selling hardbacks at discounts and a range of paperbacks. All books are tested on adults and children, and in the classroom, and a newsletter and displays at schools, festivals etc., help keep us in touch with needs. Importantly for us, we are just able to fit work around school hours, with the help of a friendly local computer firm.

By writing to authors and illustrators whose books we sell we hope to give them encouragement in what they are doing; some respond enthusiastically, and several have joined Letterbox Library. Educating publishers however is proving a long and difficult process. A few have produced lists of their non-sexist or multi-cultural books, but a substantial number still think that to have a girl as the central character or a black face among the white ones is all that it takes. Finding books which fit our criteria is not significantly easier than when we started. Community publishers such as Centreprise and Peckham Publishing Project in London have produced anti-sexist, non-racist working-class books for children, and Sheba feminist publishers brought out some excellent titles, but publishing as a whole has yet to realise that few of us live in affluent white nuclear families, and that for all of us, good non-sexist, multi-cultural books are an essential part of growing up equal.

Sue and Gillian, Children's Books Co-operative

National Feminist Film and Video Festival

The first festival, organised by the South Wales Women's Film Group and funded by the local arts authority, took place in Cardiff in Spring 1983. It was the first conference to draw together women in commercial and independent sectors, women behind the camera and in front, and practical and theoretical issues. That such an event was long overdue was indicated by the numbers of women attending and the liveliness of debate.

The second conference, on the theme of class, was held in November 1984 – after a long series of planning meetings. The major funder this time was Channel 4. The organisers, while providing a structure, tried to keep the conference as fluid as possible. This was felt to be an important departure from many other events and reflected, hopefully, the plurality of concerns and interests of women in the broadening area of film and video. Once again there was capacity attendance.

Expense, time and uncertain funding mean that it is difficult to know whether the conference can be established as an annual event. Consistent support is clearly needed. But a beginning has certainly been made in finding our confidence and our voices.

Glynis Powell, co-organiser, second conference

GLC Spot Sexist Ads Campaign

In response to many complaints by women about advertising on London Transport – including posters for films depicting violence against women – the GLC Women's Committee spent several months pressuring the LT executive to change their code of practice governing acceptance of advertising. These meetings included a slide show of particularly offensive advertisements, for the board. Finally they did agree to amend the code, although in a weaker form than that suggested by the Women's Committee. Two new conditions were also added: 'Advertising content should not depict, refer to, or imply violence specifically against women', and 'Advertising which seeks to depict women as sex objects is unacceptable.'

After that, the GLC lost control of LT; it became the government-controlled London Regional Transport. However the number of sexist advertisements did drop significantly at first; although some crept back, they did not reach their former level of brutality. The Women's Committee, at the beginning of 1985, launched their Spot Sexist Ads coupon booklets, encouraging women to send in detachable postcards registering their complaints about any advertisements they found offensive. Around 100 complaints per month were received; one of the final actions of the Women's Committee before abolition was to mount a large exhibition about sexist advertising, including in it examples of the complaint postcards.

GLC Ethnic Minorities Unit

From summer 1982 until abolition in 1986 the Greater London Council Ethnic Minorities Unit established an infrastructure of black arts in London. Workshops, training programmes, exhibitions, and promotion schemes were set up for film and video, visual arts and dance; special attention was paid to the needs of black women, and a number of women's projects were funded. (These included the Asian women's film company Film Lok, Heiny Srour's film *Leila and the Wolves* – jointly with Channel 4 – and Retake's film *Majdhar* about Asian women's lives.) Black and Third World film programmes were organised, and the unit participated in the organisation of a major film and video forum at the End of Decade Conference in Nairobi, where there were collected together for the first time 150 films and 200 videos by black and Third World women. Since the abolition of the GLC there have inevitably been casualties, but the infrastructure has been firmly established. This has empowered people to organise and to demand their right to resources. Art has been brought into the political arena, as a platform for social change, and black women will continue to benefit greatly from this.

From an interview with Perminder Vir, Race Relations Adviser,
Ethnic Minorities Unit, GLC

In From the Cold

In From the Cold is the magazine of the Liberation Network for People with Disabilities. It contains alternative images of women with disabilities, showing them in charge of their own lives in a way seldom done by the mainstream media. *In From the Cold*, Townsend House, Green Lane, Marshfield, Chippenham, Wilts.

Biographical Notes on Contributors

Carola Addington: 'After my first visit to Greenham in December 1982, I subsequently stayed – to discover that my experiences there rarely related to the same events as reported by the media. The full implications of the "Power of the Press" had never been so deeply impressed on me till then.'

Liz Allen: worked for four years as the Women's Officer for the Electrical, Electronic, Telecommunications and Plumbing Union (EETPU). She is now working for the National Association of Teachers in Further and Higher Education (NATFHE).

Amanda Amos: has worked in medical research and health education and is currently Lecturer in Health Education at the Department of Community Medicine, Edinburgh University. Her interest in women's health developed through her involvement in the Scottish Women's Health Fair in 1983.

Jane Apsey: has been involved in the Women's Media Action Group, the Women's Monitoring Network, and the anorexia helpline ABNA. She is a social work assistant.

Charlotte Brunsdon teaches in the Joint School of Film and Literature at Warwick University.

Beverley Bryan, Stella Dadzie and Suzanne Scafe: are all involved in education, and are active in Black and women's politics. Beverley and Suzanne, both born in Jamaica, are long-standing members of the Brixton Black Women's Group; Stella, whose mother is English and whose father is Ghanaian, is a founder member of OWAAD (Organisation of Women of African and Asian descent).

Cambridge Rape Crisis Centre: is a voluntary collective which was set up in 1982, by women for women: It operates a twice-weekly phoneline for women who have been raped or sexually assaulted, and promotes visits and talks in the area to improve understanding of sexual violence.

Norma Cohen: taught movement and dance before becoming an actress and freelance journalist. A Liverpudlian, she lives in Hackney with her seven-year-old daughter.

Gill Cox: is Problem Page Editor of *Woman's Realm*, co-author of *Making the Most of Yourself* and a regular broadcaster on social and health topics. Her interest in the slimming industry comes from years of personal battling with the subject.

Liz Curtis: works with Information on Ireland, a voluntary London-based publishing group. She is the author of *Ireland: the Propaganda War* (Pluto Press 1984), a study of British media coverage of the current conflict.

Sheila Dillon: writes and broadcasts on food and agricultural policy in Britain and the USA. She is a contributing editor to *Food Monitor*, a US magazine which campaigns for a radical change in food and agricultural policies in both North and South.

Sheryl Garratt: started writing about music for a Birmingham fanzine, moved on to NME and then became Music Editor at *City Limits* magazine in London. She is now a freelance journalist and is also co-author with Sue Steward of a book on women working in the pop industry, *Signed, Sealed & Delivered* (Pluto Press 1984).

Veronica Groocock: is a freelance writer who has contributed to *Radio Times*, *Sunday Times Magazine*, *Observer*, *New Statesman*, *SHE* and *Living*.

Sue Hancock and Kirsten Hearn: Sue is a blind mother, ex-teacher and qualified counsellor involved in disability politics. She currently works as staff welfare officer at ILEA. Kirsten is a blind lesbian feminist, artist, writer and disability activist. She currently works for the Haringey Lesbian and Gay Unit.

Bobbie Jacobson: is Research Fellow in Health Promotion, London School of Hygiene and Tropical Medicine and author of *Beating the Ladykillers – Women and Smoking* (Pluto Press, 1981). She was previously deputy director of Action on Smoking and Health, before qualifying in medicine.

Sheila Jeffreys: is a lesbian and a revolutionary feminist who has been active for many years in women's liberation campaigns against male violence. Her book, *The Spinster and her Enemies*, was published by Pandora, 1986.

Anne Karpf: is a freelance journalist and critic, contributing regularly to the *Guardian*, the *Observer*, *New Statesman* and *Cosmopolitan*. Her book on *Health, Medicine and the Media* is published by Routledge & Kegan Paul, 1987.

Preethi Manuel: is a Media Resources Officer with the Inner London Education Authority. She has lectured in television production and taught media studies at secondary school and in Further Education.

Micheline Mason: is a founder member of the Liberation Network of People with Disabilities (having had a disability since birth). She is a mother, an artist, a writer and a teacher of re-evaluation co-counselling.

Older Feminists Network: was formed in the early 1980s and gives older women opportunities to explore together their feminism, to share their experiences and to support each other. OFN is involved in peace work, writing and campaigning. Members meet in London and regionally. For info contact OFN c/o A Woman's Place, Hungerford House, Victoria Embankment, London WC2.

Chinyelu Onwurah: was born in Newcastle upon Tyne of Nigerian and Irish descent. She is now studying for a degree in Electrical Engineering whilst working as a freelance journalist.

Jennifer Peck is an Australian living in London. She was co-author of *Sexual violence: the reality for women*, (The Women's Press, 1984), for the London Rape Crisis Centre, and is a committed 'writer for women'.

Jane Salvage: is a registered general nurse who works as a free-lance writer and lecturer on nursing and health care. She is a member of the Radical Nurses Group, which offers personal support to nurses as well as tackling sexism and racism in the NHS.

Jennifer Simon: is a journalist who, as Women's Editor of the Aberdeen *Evening Express*, introduced a strong feminist slant to its women's pages. A former member of the NUJ's Equality Council, she joined the GLC to be press officer to the first local government Women's Committee in the UK. She is now chief press officer for Islington Council.

Jo Spence: is an educational photographer and writer. She has also written several books on photography and is currently working on a series of educational programmes on 'the family album' for Channel 4 television.

Typecaste was set up in 1984 by a group of women who work as secretaries. They work to change attitudes towards secretaries and to gain recognition for the work that women do in offices. They meet regularly and can be contacted at: City Centre, Sophia House, 32/5 Featherstone Street, London EC1.

Paddy Stamp: worked for London Women and Manual Trades from 1983 to 1985. She currently works in the Women's Rights unit of the National Council for Civil Liberties on women's employment and training issues. She is co-author with Sadie Robarts of *Positive Action: Changing the Workplace for Women* (NCCL 1986).

Select Bibliography

Baehr, Helen (ed.), *Women and Media*, Pergamon 1978.
  * Collection of essays by women about imagery and working in the media.
Baehr, Helen, and Ryan, Michele, *Shut Up and Listen! Women and Local Radio: a View from the Inside*, Comedia 1984.
  * Experimental women's programming at Cardiff Community Radio.
Barker, Martin, *The Video Nasties: Freedom and Censorship in the Media*, Pluto 1984.
  * Lucid rebuttal of pro-censorship arguments, plus detailed history of the Video Recordings Act; but without a feminist perspective.
Berger, John, *Ways of Seeing*, BBC/Pelican 1972.
  * Classic description of Woman as Object Viewed.
Cadman, Eileen *et al.*, *Rolling Our Own: Women as Printers, Publishers and Distributors*, Comedia 1981.
Campaign for Press and Broadcasting Freedom, *The Press, Radio and Television. An Introduction to the Media*, Comedia 1983.
  * Good basic introduction to how the media work.
——, *Right of Reply Pack*, CPBF 1986.
  * How to secure a right of reply, with case studies.
Campaign against Racism in the Media, *It Ain't Half Racist, Mum: Fighting Racism in the Media*, Comedia 1982.
  * Collection of articles to accompany video of the same name.
Curran, James *et al.* (eds), *Bending Reality: the State of the Media*, Pluto/CPBF 1986.
  * Thorough account, including chapters on media sexism.
Curran, James, and Seaton, Jean, *Power Without Responsibility. The Press and Broadcasting in Britain* (2nd edn), Methuen 1985.

* Important, detailed history from left viewpoint, but doesn't mention women.

Curtis, Liz, *Nothing but the Same Old Story. The Roots of Anti-Irish Racism*, Information on Ireland 1984.

* The origins and functions of anti-Irish stereotyping.

Davies, K., 'The Mirror Cracked: Women and the UK Media', Report to EOC, 1983.

Davis, Howard, and Walton, Paul, *Language, Image, Media*, Blackwell 1983.

Dickey, Julienne and CPBF Women's Group, *Women in Focus; Guidelines for Eliminating Media Sexism*, CPBF 1985.

* Illustrated 44-page guide with campaigning ideas.

Downing, John, *The Media Machine*, Pluto 1980.

* Readable Marxist analysis, taking sexism, racism, etc., into account.

Drinkwater, Jane, *Get It On Radio and TV: A Practical Guide to Getting Airtime*, Pluto/London Media Project 1984.

Dworkin, Andrea, *Pornography: Men Possessing Women*, The Women's Press, 1981.

* Hard-hitting analysis.

Dyer, Gillian, *Advertising as Communication*, Methuen 1982.

* Rationale behind advertising messages.

Ferguson, Marjorie, *Forever Feminine: Women's Magazines and the Cult of Femininity*, Heinemann 1983.

* Historical account, descriptive rather than analytical.

Gallagher, Margaret, *Unequal Opportunities. The Case of Women and the Media*, UNESCO 1981.

* Contains a wealth of material about the position of women in the media in many different countries.

Glasgow University Media Group, *Bad News*, Routledge & Kegan Paul, 1976.

——, *More Bad News*, Routledge & Kegan Paul 1980.

——, *Really Bad News*, Routledge & Kegan Paul 1983.

——, *War and Peace News*, Routledge & Kegan Paul 1986.

* All the above are the result of thorough, detailed research into exactly how news is manipulated to suit the status quo.

Goffman, Erving, *Gender Advertisements*, Macmillan 1976.

* Still valid, lucid account of how women are used in advertising.

Griffin, Susan, *Pornography and Silence*, The Women's Press, 1981.
* Pornography and its effect on American culture.

Hobson, Dorothy, *'Crossroads': The Drama of a Soap Opera*, Methuen 1982.

Hood, Stuart, *On Television*, (2nd edn) Pluto 1983.
* Highly readable critique of the working of television and how it constructs the world for us.

Isis International, *Women and Media: Analysis, Alternatives and Action*, Isis 1984.
* Produced by the Pacific and Asian Women's Forum; criticisms of the media in those countries, and initiatives for change.

Kaplan, E. Ann, *Women and Film: Both Sides of the Camera*, Methuen 1983.

Key, Wilson Bryan, *Subliminal Seduction*, Signet (NY) 1974.
——, *Media Sexploitation*, Signet 1976.
* Both the above reveal the tricks of the image-makers in the States (and maybe here?).

London Radio Workshop, *Nothing Local About It. London's Local Radio* (new edn.), Comedia 1983.
* Contains input from women's radio groups.

King, Josephine, and Stott, Mary, *Is This Your Life? Images of Women in the Media*, Virago 1977.

Kuhn, Annette, *Women's Pictures: Feminism and Cinema*, Routledge & Kegan Paul 1982.

MacShane, Denis, *Using the media: How to Deal with the Press, Radio and Television* (2nd edn.), Pluto 1983.
* Originally written for trade unionists.

Masterman, Len, *Teaching the Media*, Comedia 1986.
* Invaluable, thorough text for teaching media studies.

Mattelart, Michele, *Women, Media, Crisis: Femininity and Disorder*, Comedia 1986.
* Rather esoteric case studies.

Miller, Casey, and Swift, Kate, *Handbook of Non-sexist Writing for Writers, Editors and Speakers* (revised British edn), The Women's Press 1981.

Myers, Kathy, *Understains. The Sense and Seduction of Advertising*, Comedia 1986.
* Controversial work on semiology and effects of advertising, questioning feminist assumptions.

Robarts, Sadie, 'Report on Thames Television Project', NCCL 1982.

Root, Jane, *Open the Box*, Comedia 1986.
   * Written to accompany the television series; interesting analysis of television, incorporating a critique of 'effects' theories.

Spender, Dale, *Man Made Language*, Routledge & Kegan Paul 1980.
   * Classic work on the subject of gender bias in language and its ramifications.

Spender, Lynne, *Intruders on the Rights of Men. Women's Unpublished Heritage*, Pandora 1983.
   * Critique of the 'gentlemen's network' of publishing.

Steward, Sue and Garratt, Sheryl, *Signed Sealed and Delivered*, Pluto 1984.

TUC, *Images of Inequality: The Portrayal of Women in the Media and Advertising*, TUC 1984.
   * Attractively produced basic guide.

Tuchman, Gaye *et al.* (eds), *Hearth and Home. Images of Women in the Mass Media*, Oxford University Press (NY) 1978.
   * Interesting though somewhat dated American case studies.

Williamson, Judith, *Decoding Advertisements: Ideology and Meaning in Advertising*, Marion Boyars (reprinted) 1983.

Women's Monitoring Network, Six Reports of monitoring exercises:
   1 *Women as Sex Objects*.
   2 *Violence against Women*.
   3 *Sex Stereotyping of Women*.
   4 *Sugar and Spice: Stereotyping of Children*.
   5 *Women and Ageing*.
   6 *Women and Food*.
   * Illustrated surveys of material sent in by women from all over the UK. Available from Women's Monitoring Network, c/o A Woman's Place, Hungerford House, Victoria Embankment, London WC2.